CONRAD AIKEN'S PHILOSOPHY OF CONSCIOUSNESS

CONRAD AIKEN'S PHILOSOPHY OF CONSCIOUSNESS

Ian Kluge

Copyright © 2009 by Ian Kluge.

Cover art by Wanda Kluge

ISBN:	Hardcover	978-1-4363-1994-2
	Softcover	978-1-4363-1993-5

All rights reserved. No part of this book may be reproduced or transmitted in any form or by any means, electronic or mechanical, including photocopying, recording, or by any information storage and retrieval system, without permission in writing from the copyright owner.

This book was printed in the United States of America.

To order additional copies of this book, contact:
Xlibris Corporation
1-888-795-4274
www.Xlibris.com
Orders@Xlibris.com

Contents

Preface 7

Introduction: Philosophical Background 9

Chapter One: An Overview of Aiken's Long Poems 17

Chapter Two: The Meditative Stance 24

Chapter Three: The Quest for Identity 32

Chapter Four: Issues in the Pursuit of Identity and Consciousness 48

Chapter Five: Further Issues in the Pursuit of Identity and Consciousness 77

Chapter Six: The First Stage of Consciousness: Divisive Consciousness 91

Chapter Seven: The Second Stage of Consciousness: Narcissistic Consciousness 111

Chapter Eight: The Third Stage of Consciousness: Synoptic Consciousness 129

Chapter Nine: The Evolution of Consciousness. 151

Chapter Ten: Summary and Conclusion 186

Select Bibliography 193

PREFACE

Any account of Conrad Aiken's theory of consciousness faces three challenges, each more difficult than the last. The first, and least, is the sheer volume of Aiken's poetical work: over one thousand pages of mostly long poems in the final edition of the *Collected Poems*.[1] None of these long poems is simple insofar as they contain an initially bewildering mixture of relatively simple narrative, often fantastic reverie and complex philosophical reflection.

The last of these leads to the second problem, namely, the complexity of philosophical content. Already in the 1930's, that is, quite early in Aiken's career, Houston Peterson's *The Melody of Chaos*[2] recognised that the poet's work synthesised ideas from a wide variety of philosophers, most notably Hume, Kant, Hegel and Schopenhauer. To synthesise ideas from such important and seemingly conflicting philosophers into a generally coherent and distinctive whole is itself no small achievement, and possibly—had Aiken expressed himself more abstractly as philosopher – would have made him an important thinker of the twentieth century. Of course, the enjoyment and appreciation of Aiken's stunningly beautiful poetry requires no great philosophical knowledge but to fully understand what is actually happening in his poems does, in fact, require some background in the field. This, and the sophistication of Aiken's synthesis is probably one of the key reasons why Aiken's work has never attained the fame one would expect for an author of such obvious talent. Some readers are able to appreciate the poetry simply for itself, but many, and most especially academic critics, are put off by the fact that while they recognise the talent and beauty of the work, they cannot quite make out what is actually going on. They know something is happening, but are mystified by what.

As if the second challenge were not enough, readers and scholars face a third test: Aiken's method of writing and developing his ideas. The problem is that Aiken's theory of consciousness was already present—at least in outline—at the very outset of his career. After the false start of *Earth Triumphant*, his first volume of poems, he went, via *Turns and Movies* to *The Charnel Rose* and *The Jig of Forslin;* in these latter two works, we already observe the main elements of his philosophy of consciousness: the vision of life as a performance; the pursuit of love and perfection; the Heraclitean universe; the

---

[1] Conrad Aiken, *Collected Poems*. New York: Oxford University Press, 1970.
[2] Houston Peterson, The *Melody of Chaos*. Toronto: Longman's, Green and Co., 1931.

evolution of consciousness through various phases; the mixture or inter-penetration of all things and the role of introspection in the evolution of consciousness. Like Athena from the head of Zeus, Aiken's theory of consciousness sprang, almost fully formed, from the head of its creator. What he did over the next half century was to develop these themes and related sub-themes in long poems of various types written in various styles and structures.

What all this means for readers and scholars is simple: we cannot expect to find a straightforward developmental structure in either the individual poems or in his poetical canon as a whole. In effect, his whole *Collected Poems* should be considered as a vast symphonic poem in which particular poems are parts or movements. Earlier poems will foreshadow later themes, later poems will echo and further develop earlier themes, themes will be re-stated using different images or variations of earlier images and, now and again, new themes will be introduced. There will be, as Aiken says in the *Appendix*, "echoes, [and] contrapuntal effects" (*Collected Poems*,1027), contrasts and juxtapositions, evocations and resonances. The result is that a detailed study of Aiken's theory of consciousness as developed by his symphonic method both in particular poems and throughout the entire poetical canon itself, makes any straightforward, linear explication of his ideas impossible. A single aspect—say, the role of imaginary selves in the evolution of consciousness—may be partly developed in *The Jig of Forslin* and *The Pilgrimage of Festus*, then receive further development in *Preludes for Memnon, Time in the Rock* and *A Letter from Li Po*. However, there is no necessary or logical order about where different philosophical details are developed. Consequently, any systematic explication of this theme, any presentation that aims at giving a whole picture of it must inevitably draw on all these works, and not necessarily in their proper historical sequence because different aspects were developed at different times.

Consequently this explication of Aiken's theory of consciousness becomes 'symphonic,' turning to different poems in no particular historical order to explicate Aiken's philosophy as clearly and completely as possible in a work of reasonable length. Those who are interested in the developmental history of Aiken's ideas will, of course, find this unsatisfactory, but those who are interested in knowing what Aiken's theory of consciousness looks like when presented as a finished production, will be correspondingly pleased. The latter approach simply treats the entire *Collected Poems* as a single work with many parts. This procedure is justified by the fact, to be discussed in detail later, that unlike the careers of most other poets, Aiken's career is not marked by any great leaps and shifts in interests and methods. As he makes clear in a late interview (see below), Aiken was never interested in anything except writing philosophical poems about the evolution of consciousness. Thus his work has an intentional unity that few other poets can boast. In common parlance, Aiken basically had it "all together" when he started.

INTRODUCTION

Philosophical Background

In his essay "*The Transcendentalist*", Ralph Waldo Emerson tells us that what "is popularly called Transcendentalism among us, is Idealism; Idealism as it appears in 1842." According to *The Oxford Companion to American Literature,* both the name and the main ideas were inspired by Kant's *Critique of Practical Reason* in which he defines transcendental knowledge as knowledge not concerned with particular objects but with our *a priori* knowledge of objects insofar as this is possible. The intellectual heritage of American Transcendentalism includes a large number of nineteenth century German philosophers and poets at first and second hand (through Wordsworth, Coleridge and Carlyle) as well as an eclectic mixture of sources raging from the *Upanishads* and Sufism to the works of Swedenborg. *The Oxford Companion to American Literature* informs us that Transcendentalism is

> ... the belief [that has] as its fundamental base a monism holding to the unity of the world and the immanence of God in the world. Because of this indwelling of divinity, everything in the world is a macrocosm containing within itself all the laws and meaning of existence. Likewise the soul of each individual is identified with the soul of the world and latently contains all that the world contains. Man may fulfill his divine potentialities either through a rapt mystical state, in which the divine is infused into the human, or through coming into contact with truth, beauty, and goodness embodied in nature and originating in the Over-Soul. Thus occurs the doctrine of the correspondence between the tangible world and the human mind, and the identity of moral and physical laws. Through belief in the divine authority of the soul's intuitions, and impulses, based on the identification of the individual soul with God, there develops the doctrine of self-reliance and individualism the disregard of external authority, tradition and logical demonstration, and the absolute optimism of the movement.
>
> (*The Oxford Companion to American Literature,* 4th edition, 859)

As this study will demonstrate, there are at least five major points of agreement between Conrad Aiken's philosophy of consciousness and American Transcendentalism: (1) all things are inherently divine; (2) everything is a microcosm; (3) the personal soul is the world soul; (4) we need to rely on ourselves and (5) we should maintain an optimistic outlook on existence.

A few comments are in order. In Transcendentalism, all things are divine insofar as they participate in the creative cosmic process. The personal soul or Self and the world are, in essence, identical insofar as they are the same kind of process. As a part of this cosmic process, indeed, as a microcosmic version of it, the Self must take responsibility for its own development to higher levels of consciousness. This microcosm may be considered 'divine' because it includes the totality of everything there is; in Aiken's view, there is no God metaphysically beyond the process that makes up the universe. Because the universe is an unending process in which everything is destined to change, no situation or condition is ever permanently negative; for this reason, there is always ground for optimism.

The 'rejection' of history also seems to be a part of Aiken's philosophy. In his article "*Conrad Aiken: From Savannah to Emerson*" (*The Southern Review*, XI, #2, Spring, 1975), Malcolm Cowley defines history as "an irreversible process, a causally linked series of events in which the masses as well as 'representative men' play their part" (ibid., 252). He then cites Wilder's concept of history as a "tapestry or carpet in which various patterns are repeated at intervals" (*The Southern Review*, XI, #2, Spring, 1975, 253). Although he does not explicitly say so, Cowley apparently intends us to accept Wilder's concept as a 'properly' Transcendentalist view of history. If Wilder's concept is correct, then Aiken's view of history is clearly 'transcendental.' This is most clearly seen *The Kid*, a poem that is highly repetitious insofar as it is cyclical. It shows an actual, this is, historical advance to the farthest limits of a frontier followed by a return to the starting point in order to begin the entire process again at a higher level of consciousness.

The agreement between Aiken's thought and many of the principles of Transcendentalism lead naturally to speculations regarding the possibility of Emerson's influence. To make definitive claims on this particular matter is beyond the scope of this work which is not a formal study of influences on Aiken's thought. Nevertheless, it is impossible to avoiding noticing, in addition to those similarities already noted, further agreements between Emerson and Aiken. In *The Over-Soul* for example, Emerson writes,

> If we consider what happens in conversation, in reveries, in remorse, in times of passion, in surprises, in the instructions of dreams wherein we often see ourselves in masquerade—the droll disguises only magnifying and enhancing a real element, and forcing it on our distinct notice—we shall catch many hints that will broaden and lighten into knowledge of the secret of nature. All goes to show that the soul in man is not an organ, but animates and exercises all the organs . . . [it is] a light . . . From within or from behind, a light shines through us upon things and makes us aware that we are nothing, but the light is all.

CONRAD AIKEN'S PHILOSOPHY OF CONSCIOUSNESS

The essential message seems to be that in its activities, in imaginative dreams such as those found in *Festus* and *Forslin* or in 'conversation' such as in *Memnon* and in *Time*, the Self gains knowledge not only of itself but also of nature. The Self learns that the 'soul' or identity really is a process manifesting itself at a particular location or in a particular entity. The similarity between Aiken's and Emerson's thought is fairly clear, at least on this point.

Both also believe that "the only sin is limitation" (Emerson, "*Circles*"); that the "universe is fluid and volatile" (ibid.); that the soul is "progressive" (Emerson, "*Art*"); that "incessant growth" (Emerson, "*Character*") is a sign of life; and that "there is throughout nature something mocking, something that leads us on and on, but arrives nowhere (Emerson, "*Nature*"). On the latter point one may recall that for Aiken the evolution of consciousness is an "endless voyage" (*Time*, XXXVII, 701).

Emerson's remark presents this study with a challenge which can be formulated in the following manner: if Aiken's philosophy of consciousness resembles American Transcendentalism does it resemble any of the European idealist philosophies contemporary with the Concord School? Or, to phrase it differently: can Aiken's philosophy be said to resemble important expressions of idealist thought?

The answer is that, in the first place, Aiken's philosophy of consciousness—as we shall have ample occasion to demonstrate throughout this study—is remarkably similar to the philosophy of Kant. Indeed, without a basic knowledge of Kant's theory of perception, a philosophical understanding of Aiken's philosophy of consciousness is impossible. According to Kant, we do not actually perceive the world as it is in itself. All data coming from the external world is processed, that is, shaped by what Kant called the 'categories' which are in the mind. These categories, in the process of forming the in-coming data, add such features as time, space and causality. Because we are locked into our perceptions, we have no way of actually knowing whether or not the original data has any of these characteristics. We are enclosed in a world of our own perceptions. Kant referred to the world *before* our minds process the data as the *noumenon* and the images we perceive afterwards as the *phenomenon*. The two worlds are completely disjunctive and we cannot make any logical inferences from the phenomenal world to the noumenal world of "things-in-themselves;" the latter remains forever unknowable.

Kant's position has two decisive implications for Aiken's philosophy. First, Kant made theology (and metaphysics) untenable. As already noted, we cannot know what reality is 'really' like underneath the phenomenal appearances. Consequently, even God is simply a mental construct, an idea, like all others and has no special status. Indeed, Aiken's concept of God is much like Ludwig Schleiermacher's who held that 'God' is merely a magnification and projection of our own best human qualities. Although we continuously seek to emulate these, we must not deceive ourselves that such a being actually exists outside of the phenomenal world we create for ourselves. As this study will show, in Aiken's philosophy, God functions exactly as such an ideal that draws us ever onward in the evolution of consciousness. Another way of saying all this is that in

Aiken, as well as Kant, psychology, the study of how the mind processes data, becomes merged with metaphysics, the study of the nature of reality per se. We can only know our own constructs, and not reality as such—if there is such a reality to know.

The second consequence of Kant's philosophy is a potentially mind-numbing sense of entrapment: if we know nothing but our own ideas, then we are all caught within a self-made 'bubble' that prevents us from ever knowing anything or anyone else. In fact, we cannot even be sure that an external world exists for us to know. The belief that the external world does not exist or, at least, is utterly unknowable is called 'solipsism', an idea that seems to have haunted Aiken especially during the early years of his career until he finally adopted the solution proposed by the German philosopher Arthur Schopenhauer. According to Schopenhauer, all things were made of Will or were manifestations of a single cosmic Will. While Schopenhauer accepted Kant's logic about perception—the noumenal, the external "thing-in-itself" is forever beyond us—he rejected it in relationship to experience. Perception takes us outward but by turning inward into ourselves and experiencing our own subjectivity, we can know the Will as it appears within us, and, thereby, as it appears in other things. Through our own inward experience, we are able to know the noumenal "thing-in-itself" because we can know ourselves as the very process of Will that makes up all things. There is, so to speak, a 'tunnel' through ourselves to the noumenal realm of "things-in-themselves". Aiken also accepted Schopenhauer's belief that music was the closest analogue to the Will because music was pure creativity for its own sake. Later in this study, we shall have occasion to expound these ideas in greater depth in the context of particular passages.

Aiken's philosophy of consciousness also bears a striking resemblance to the philosophy of Hegel, perhaps the greatest European philosopher in the idealist tradition. There are three ideas that Aiken seems to have borrowed from Hegel. The first is that consciousness is always 'self-consciousness' and that it begins with an assertion of 'I' defined in contrast to everything else or 'not-I'. Until that assertion happens and 'divides' reality into two, the individual is not aware of himself as an entity distinct from the rest of reality. The second is that reality as a whole and all of its parts are interminable processes. Finally, Aiken accepted Hegel's characterisation of this process as essentially 'ideational', that is, concerned with thoughts and ideas. Whether or not he agreed with Hegel that matter is only the outer manifestation of thought is difficult to determine, but, as we shall see in considerable detail, his ideas match Hegel's to a significant extent. In Hegel's philosophy, the Absolute, thinks itself and in so doing, objectifies itself as other beings just as Aiken's dreamers projects themselves as various characters or 'dream egos' during their reveries. (The speakers in *Preludes for Memnon* and *Time in the Rock* may be said to objectify themselves through speech, or, 'speak themselves'; the situation is structurally the same.) For Hegel, one of the Absolute's objectifications is humankind through whose consciousness developing in the process of history the Absolute becomes conscious of itself as Spirit. Similarly, by means of the character and monodramas, Aiken's dreamers become conscious of themselves as and endless process of thoughts and feelings. The process which the Self discovers to be its own fundamental identity is, in essence, identical to the cosmic process. One must recall that Hegel's Absolute also recognises itself as the cosmic process, or, as Spirit; "the Absolute knows itself as the Totality, as the whole process of its becoming . . ." (Copleston, 209). Moreover, just as the identity of Aiken's dreamer *is* the process by which it seeks identity, so the Absolute "*is* its self-manifestation" (Copleston, 206). In both cases, true self-knowledge is the aim. The historical drama put on by the Absolute and the dreams and soliloquies of Aiken's dreamers are mainly techniques of attaining this kind of self-knowledge.

In *The Phenomenology Of Spirit*, Hegel posits three main stages in the development of consciousness. These too, remarkably enough, have their approximately corresponding stages in Aiken's philosophy. The first of Hegel's phases is that in which the Absolute, the subject, recognises its own existence, or sense of 'I', as distinct, and thereby, in opposition to the external 'other' or object. The world is divided into me/not-me. This is exactly the situation in the 'divisive consciousness' in Aiken's work. By asserting its existence, the Self splits itself from the world in which it seems a stranger. It is alienated, and does not see that its own basic identity as process is also the identity of the objects before it. These objects are the phenomenal world.

Hegel's second phase of consciousness is self-consciousness but an expanded self-consciousness in which consciousness discovers itself as the reality from which the phenomenal world originates. The complexity of this phase of consciousness in Hegel's philosophy far outstrips the complexity of Aiken's thought on this issue; at this point the similarities between the two philosophies are not as close as before. Nonetheless, the two phases are not entirely beyond comparison. In Aiken's second stage, 'narcissistic consciousness', symbolised by the man looking into the mirror, the Self also faces itself as object just as in Hegel's view, consciousness recognises itself as source of reality. In both cases, the former subject/object dichotomy, in its special form a me/not-me division is overcome. Both subject and object a*re* represented.

According to Hegel, the third stage of consciousness is Reason at which point a particular, limited Self or self-consciousness sees that it is identical with the phenomenal world insofar as the phenomenal world is a process. The two are identical in nature and the particular Self is merely a moment in the life of the Absolute spirit. Turning to Aiken's 'synoptic consciousness', one finds that the Self at this stage also becomes aware of itself as the cosmic process. The similarity to Hegel's doctrine is apparent. Although there are, of course, differences between the philosophies of Hegel and Aiken, the similarities examined here are too striking to be overlooked.

There is at least one more general similarity between Hegel and Aiken. According to Hegel, (though he did not use this precise terminology) the dialectic or world process of the Absolute proceeds on the basis of the contradiction between the 'thesis' and the 'anti-thesis.' By means of negation, the difference between the two is 'dissolved', sublimated into a higher, more inclusive 'synthesis.' Naturally, the details of this process as expounded by Hegel involve enormous complexities not reflected in Aiken's work. Nevertheless, a general form of the negating activity seems to be present in Aiken's writing. We find such a dissolution when both the Self—the thesis—and the vague, imaginary, superior God—the anti-thesis—in which the Self is subsumed, *together* become part of an enriched chaos. From this chaos, enriched by contributions from the past, the growth process starts again. As in Hegel's philosophy, the synthesis is only the first step in a renewed progress of 'thesis' and 'anti-thesis.' Pressing farther, one may ask whether the same progress does not occur in Aiken's portrayal of the activity of self-carving? The Self as subject or thesis turns its imaginative powers on itself according to some ideal or anti-thesis. Both the present Self and the ideal are dissolved in the emergence of a new, more inclusive Self or synthesis. It is possible to extend this similarity with Hegel as far as Aiken's theory of creative murder.

With Hegel, Aiken believes that the changes in human consciousness are progressive or evolutionary, that the process of developing consciousness is accumulative in which ever more inclusive forms of consciousness replace narrower, less inclusive ones. The evolution of consciousness is, therefore, a process of expansion.

Readers will have noticed that Hegel's and Schopenhauer's ideas bear a remarkable affinity to the traditional doctrine of the microcosm and macrocosm. The belief that the processes occurring within the cosmos and within the individual are one and the same has radical consequences for epistemology, suggesting, among other things that subjectivity, turning inward, can provide us with true knowledge about the external universe. The notion that scientific truth may be sought by personal and subjective means directly challenges the prevailing belief that impersonal, objective knowledge is the only way to learn about the cosmos. Why does Aiken, a firm believer in science and the scientific method, open the way for radical subjectivity when doing so gives at least the appearance of legitimising all kinds of crankery? He does so precisely because he believes in the power of science. If science is to be comprehensive and provide a complete explanation of the world, and if, in the last analysis, all such explanations must harmonise in some way, then even the crankiest notions must be part of that explanation. Cranky as some ideas may be, they are nonetheless parts of the universe; they are among the data to be explained, and, in some cases, as, for example, in understanding somebody's motivations, part of the explanation. They are stubborn facts that cannot simply be swept aside. Excluding them makes any scientific theory incomplete.

There are, however, two other philosophers whose teachings re-enforced some of Hegel's ideas. The first of is Heraclitus, a Greek philosopher, who was the first to promulgate that everything is perpetual change or process. He is famous for comparing the universe to a fire, that is, in perpetual flux, and stating that "No man can step into the same river twice". The reason, of course, is that the river and the man have changed in the interval between the two forays into the water. For this reason, this study will often refer to cosmos as being 'Heraclitean'.

The other philosopher whose ideas we must take into account is John Locke, who, according to Houston Peterson's *The Melody of Chaos*, also had a decisive influence on Aiken. It is not hard to see how. According to Locke, all consciousness is, in effect, self-consciousness. He writes, that consciousness is "the perception of what passes in a man's own mind" (Locke, *Essay Concerning Human Understanding* Bk II, Chp. 1, Section 19). Certainly exploration and expression "of what passes in a man's own mind" (ibid.) pre-occupies the majority of Aiken's protagonists and narrators through the majority of the poems. In other words, for Aiken the primary meaning of 'consciousness' is 'self-consciousness'.

CHAPTER ONE

An Overview of Aiken's Long Poems

The poetic canon of Conrad Aiken is informed by his life-long dedication to the understanding and exploration of three distinct but related themes: consciousness, the evolution of consciousness and identity. As even his earliest writings demonstrate, this immense poetic and philosophic project occupied him from the very outset of his career. As early as 1917, in an essay entitled "*The Mechanism of Poetic Inspiration*", Aiken writes that mediocre poets, as opposed to superior ones, "do not extend the field of our consciousness in any new direction" (*Collected Criticism*, 40). This statement clearly implies not only that poetry and consciousness are inextricably linked but also that the task of poetry is to extend, expand, or evolve consciousness into hitherto unattained and unexplored areas of human thought. A poet, in other words, is an explorer who invites readers on a voyage of discovery and self-discovery into the mind. Interviewed by Richard Wilbur near the end of his life, Aiken—in a display of remarkable intellectual consistency—still maintained this evolutionary vision:

> Of course I do believe in the evolution of consciousness as the only thing we can embark on, or in fact, will-nilly, are embarked on . . .
> (*The Paris Review*, Vol. 11, No. 42, Winter-Spring, 1968,110)

The prefaces Aiken wrote for his verse symphonies (later collected as *The Divine Pilgrim*) also reveal the importance of consciousness and related themes in his first major poetic works. The earliest of these prefaces, written in 1916 for *The Jig of Forslin* informs readers that the "central theme" (*Collected Poems*, 1018)

> is the process of vicarious wish fulfilment by which civilised man enriches his circumscribed life and obtains emotional balance. It is an exploration of his emotional and mental hinterland, his fairyland of impossible illusions and dreams . . .
> (*Collected Poems*, 1018)

This remarkable preface does several things. First, it clearly focuses attention on the inner, mental and emotional life of the protagonist instead of on outward events. Indeed, from the poem itself, readers cannot know whether or not any external events ever actually take place. As well, this preface points out that dreaming, imagining, and "vicarious wish fulfilment" (ibid.) are among the methods by which the extension or evolution of consciousness may be achieved. The process of imagining himself in various adventures increases the protagonist's self-knowledge as he learns more about the various facets of his character. Such self-knowledge, of course, not only creates increased awareness or consciousness of one's self, but is also an integral part of discovering one's own identity. The preface to *The Jig of Forslin* (1916) also makes it clear that imaginative activities, in other words, the arts, play an integral part of attaining and extending consciousness.

Finally, the preface to *The Jig of Forslin* explains the poetic method by which Aiken plans to pursue these goals. Consciousness is inherently unstable and for this reason "the attempt has been made to release these typical dreams, or vicarious adventures, not discretely, but in flux." (*Collected Poems* 1018). Moods, feelings, images and thoughts all shift as Forslin, the failed juggler, explores his own mind and emotions in a desperate bid to understand where his life has gone wrong and why he feels he is such an absolute failure. The flux of consciousness naturally lends itself to the techniques Aiken employs in this as well as in all of his other major poems: sudden shifts of perspective, mood, thought, imagery, dreams, attitude, action and perception as well as a wide variety of poetic techniques. The preface refers to "harmony and counterpoint" (ibid.), and states that

> [c]acophonies and irregularities have often been deliberately employed as contrast. Free rhythms, and rhymeless verse, have been used, also, to introduce a variety of movement. Mood and movement, in general, have been permitted to fluctuate together . . .
>
> (*Collected Poems*, 1019)

Aiken's next preface, to *The Charnel Rose* (1918), informs readers that "[e]motions, perceptions—the image stream of the mind which we call consciousness—these hold the stage" (*Collected Poems*, 1017). This one statement (the rest of the preface explains the poetic method of the poem) also draws attention to the inner focus of Aiken's poems in addition to the theme of consciousness and the problematic nature of consciousness, which, as an endlessly changing flux or 'stream' of images, feelings, fears and dreams, makes it difficult if not impossible to discover or create a stable identity. Indeed, earlier in this preface, Aiken clearly indicates that in his view, humans, by their very nature, are restless and driven creatures:

> This theme [of *The Charnel Rose*] might be called nympholpesy—nympholepsy in a broad sense as that impulse which sends man from one dream, or ideal, to another, always disillusioned, always creating for adoration some new and subtler fiction.
>
> (*Collected Poems*, 1017)

CONRAD AIKEN'S PHILOSOPHY OF CONSCIOUSNESS

Here, too, the role of creativity, imagination, art or 'fiction' in our inner processes is clearly evident insofar as humans are perpetually "*creating* for adoration some new and subtler *fiction*" (*Collected Poems*, 1017; italics added). The word "adoration" (ibid.) moreover, draws the reader's attention to the religious and/or metaphysical dimensions of this endless search. Man, this passage seems to imply, needs to worship and adore something, even if he must create it himself: if God did not exist, it would be necessary to invent Him. This adoration, this forward movement towards the adored is what drives—or rather draws—the evolution of consciousness forward.

However, a caveat is required: the fact that man has an impulse to adore, to love and to worship, must not be interpreted to mean that a God necessarily exists. Like Pope, who writes, "presume not God to scan / The proper study of mankind is man" (Pope, *An Essay on Man*, Epistle II, line 1), Aiken restricts himself to the empirical facts: humankind has an impulse to adore but this impulse alone does not tell us whether or not the object or adoration really exists. It could be merely "some new and subtler fiction" (*Collected Poems*, 1017). Whether or not the objects of adoration or desire are metaphysically real makes no difference to Aiken, who explores the workings of and issues related to human consciousness solely in the light of this impulse.

In 1919, at the request of Harriet Monroe, Aiken also wrote an appendix to *Senlin: A Biography* (1918), one of the long poems in the collection that became known as *The Divine Pilgrim*. In this appendix, Aiken not only elaborates at length on the poetic method of his verse symphonies, but also takes up the theme of consciousness:

> The theme is the problem of personal identity, the struggle of the individual for an awareness of what it is that constitutes his consciousness; an attempt to place himself, to relate himself to the world of which he feels himself to be at once an observer and an integral part.
>
> (*Collected Poems*, 1029)

The epistemological problem regarding the nature of the knower and the known makes itself apparent here, as it does in the preface to *The Pilgrimage of Festus*. The problem itself is simple to understand though solutions to it lead to devilishly difficult consequences: how can a knower relate to and know himself in a world of which he is a part and in which his increasing knowledge continues to change him and, thereby, since he is a part of the world, change the world itself? There seems to be an infinite regress of changes in which no knowledge is ever stable. But if knowledge is not stable, that is, is not permanently true, how can there be knowledge at all? Is truth no more than 'the flavour of the moment'? And if there cannot be enduring knowledge or self-knowledge, how can there be an identity and "an awareness of what it is that constitutes his consciousness" (*Collected Poems*, 1029)? What are the limitations of human knowledge—indeed, what is knowledge? For almost sixty years, Aiken explored and struggled with these questions, concluding in the end, that the exploration and struggle themselves matter more than any particular answer we might find.

The limitations of human knowledge and impulse to adore also receive mention in Aiken's 1921 preface to *The Pilgrimage of Festus* (1923). Festus, the world weary protagonist looking for new worlds to conquer, discovers that

> the possibility of knowledge itself is limited: that knowledge is perhaps so conditioned by the conditions of the knower that it can have but a relative value . . . [H]e comes, not unhappily, to the conclusion that knowledge is inconclusive. To what, precisely, in the world can one devote one's instinct-to-adore? Beauty is inseparably bound up with ugliness . . . No answer is provided, but Festus finds himself at the end as at the beginning charmed by the prospect of self-exploration.
> (*Collected Poems*, 1023-1024)

This passage brings to attention a number of other issues related to Aiken's three major themes of consciousness, the evolution of consciousness and identity. The first, and most obvious, is a perplexing question in regards to identity. If as Aiken states, knowledge is conditioned by the knower, what will becomes of self-knowledge? Indeed, how can there be self-knowledge? How can the perpetually restless and changing self ever attain any final knowledge of its perpetually restless and changing self? Knowledge, as Festus discovers "is inconclusive" (*Collected Poems*, 1024). That being the case, how can we have—and know—our identity? Is it even possible to answer the question, "Who am I?" with any finality or certainty? The perplexities continue. If we cannot have any final self-knowledge, can we really be conscious since self-knowledge and consciousness seem somehow related? And what does it, then, mean to 'evolve' our consciousness? Does it mean anything more than simply becoming aware of more of our minds? Is it merely a quantitative evolution? And finally, if beauty is "inseparably bound up with ugliness" (*Collected Poems*, 1024), what is the nature of art and poetry in the evolution of consciousness? After all, if the impulse to adore is what moves us onward, what is it precisely that we humans are adoring?

Interestingly enough, almost thirty years later, Aiken wrote another set of prefaces for the poems of *The Divine Pilgrim*. These new prefaces, written in 1948 and 1949, show that Aiken's artistic vision and his basic philosophy of consciousness were, in all fundamental aspects, unchanged. In the 1948 preface to *The House of Dust* (1920), Aiken writes about the nature of consciousness, the evolution of consciousness and the problems of our multiple identities:

> . . . the entire poem is really an elaborate progressive analogy between the city, seen as a multicellular living organism, and the multicellular or multineural nature of human consciousness. Progressive, because as I say the movement is intermittently but steadily from simple to complex, from physiological to psychological; and, in the end, from the relatively simple levels of consciousness to those in which it attempts to see and understand the

> world, or macrocosm, on the one hand, and the consciousness or microcosm, that *sees* the world, on the other. Implicit in it, therefore, is the theory that was to underlie much of the later work—namely,—that in the evolution of man's consciousness, ever-widening and deepening and subtlizing his awareness, and in his dedication of himself to this supreme task man possesses all that he could possibly require in the way of a religious credo: when the half-gods go, the gods arrive: he can, if he only will, become divine.
>
> (*Collected Poems*, 1021)

Aiken adds a post-script to this preface: "The original preface to *The House of Dust* was lost many years ago. The present one however is a fairly accurate summary of it." (*Collected Poems*, 1021). In other words, Aiken was well aware of the intellectual continuity underlying his work.

The 1949 preface to *Senlin: A Biography* (1918) also reveals the conceptual continuity that unifies Aiken's poetic works. This poem, Aiken writes, focuses on the

> fascinating problem of personal identity which perplexes each of us all his life: the basic and possibly unanswerable questions, *who and what am I?*, how is it that I am I, Senlin, and not someone else? . . . [F]or Senlin discovers that he is a whole gallery of personalities, rather than one.
>
> (*Collected Poems*, 1022)

Aiken's last preface, also written in 1949 for "*Changing Mind*" explains how the poem is concerned with issues of identity, in this case, the protagonist's perplexities in "seeing himself resolved into his constituent particles: and this with a purpose, that his increased awareness may be put at the service of mankind." (*Collected Poems*, 1023). This can be achieved by becoming an artist who must "make his experiences articulate for the benefit of others, [who] must be, in the evolving consciousness of man, the servant example . . ." (*Collected Poems*, 1023). The preface not only reveals the theme of artistic creativity as a method for evolving consciousness, but also advances to issues relating to the artist's role and responsibility in the world. Through the self-sacrifice of making his struggles and pains available through his works, the artist helps his readers gain the insights and vicarious experiences they need to become more conscious themselves. Art, in other words, plays a key role in the evolution of human consciousness.

Aiken's other prefaces and notes to such later poems as *The Coming Forth by Day of Osiris Jones* (1931) and *The Kid* (1947), make it clear that his concern with identity and consciousness continued unabated. *The Coming Forth by Day of Osiris Jones*, based on the rituals described in the *Egyptian Book of the Dead*, deals with Jones' memory or consciousness" (*Collected Poems*, 1030) and how Jones is remembered, that is, identified by the objects and people of his life. *The Kid* portrays not only the true, "prototypical American" (*Collected Poems*, 1033) but also the restless spirit inherent in all who are engaged in the evolution of consciousness. He symbolises "those pioneers who sought freedom and privacy in the 'wide open spaces', or the physical conquest of an untamed continent, and those others, early and late, who were to struggle for it in the darker kingdoms of the soul" (*Collected Poems*, 1033). Kin to Tennyson's Ulysses, the Kid cannot stop moving because neither he nor we have any other identity than our movement, our evolution, our passing through and leaving behind places, times and former states of being.

There is, of course, nothing new in asserting the importance of consciousness, identity, art and the evolution of consciousness in Aiken's work. Indeed, this is one subject on which critics agree. Arthur Waterman, for example, states that "all of Aiken's work centres on the term 'consciousness'" (*"The Evolution of Consciousness: Conrad Aiken's Novels and Ushant"*, *Critique: Studies in Modern Fiction*. XV, No. 2. 1973; p 67) while Hoffman maintains that the major portion of Aiken's work strives to "recover consciousness" (*Conrad Aiken*, 19). Jay Martin, whose *Conrad Aiken: A Life of His Art* was only the second book length study of Aiken's work after Houston Peterson's *The Melody of Chaos*, concludes that Aiken's work "has been governed by his continuing conception of his function as a poet." (*Conrad Aiken: A Life of His Art*, 203). The meaning of this claim becomes clear on recalling Aiken's belief that the poet's task is to make himself "as conscious as possible" (*Ushant*, 246), to be "conscious of his own workings, the workings of his psyche" (ibid.) and to reveal these discoveries in art for the benefit of mankind as suggested in the 'Note' to "*Changing Mind*" (*Collected Poems*,1025). Martin's statement clearly implies that Aiken's writing cannot be understood without taking his philosophy of consciousness into account.

One critic in particular, Stephen Tabachnick, recognises the importance of the continuity of philosophical thought throughout Aiken's work:

> The Aiken critic must be attuned to a *poetry of philosophical inquiry*, rather than to a poetry dependent on the New Critical love of paradox, ambiguity, irony and other devices in language. Most critics of Aiken's times were not. Perhaps what Aiken really points to is the fact that his corpus has a characteristic that much contemporary poetry and fiction lacks: *a real coherence, a staggering thematic and symbolic unity, a philosophical argument, that stretches over forty years across novels, poems, short stories and a play, Mr. Arcularis*. Since the late twenties, he has made a single-minded and unwavering attempt to wrestle certain metaphysical themes to a solution and, as a result, all his work is one . . . Because Aiken's writings constitute *almost a system*, isolated works lose full significance when read alone.
>
> (Stepehen Tabachnick, "*The Great Circle Voyage of Conrad Aiken's 'Mr. Arcularis*,'" "*American Literature*, Vol, XLV, January, No. 4, !974; italics added.)

Tabachnick's observation and reflection on Aiken's prefaces and the poems for which they were written strongly suggest—and support the method employed in this study—that Conrad Aiken's poetic works should be regarded as a vast but essentially single poem, unified not only by its three basic themes but also by the method of composition outlined in his 1919 appendix to *The Divine Pilgrim*. This underlying unity encourages a 'synoptic' approach to studying Aiken's philosophy of consciousness, that is, an ahistorical approach which examines Aiken's poetry as if it were one vast work in which different portions of his philosophy are developed at different times but which, in the end, forms a single, coherent whole.

Using painting as an analogy, one might say that at the outset of his career, Aiken chose the limits of his canvas, that is, he established the philosophical boundaries of his work within epistemology. Without exception, each of Aiken's major poetic works is concerned with what human beings can know and how. He explores these questions in two directions: *inwardly*, asking what we can know about ourselves and how, as well as outwardly, asking what we can know about others and the world around us and how we can attain such knowledge. These two directions, in and out, form part of what shall be discussed later as the concentric (inward-focused) and eccentric (outward-focused) phases of our consciousness. Aiken approaches these questions, the very foundation of his poetic enterprise, from three points of perspective, that is, the three themes already listed: consciousness, the evolution of consciousness and identity. Over the years he filled in the details of his philosophy. This analogy suggests that it would be fruitful to study Aiken's philosophy of consciousness by studying his works the way we usually study a painting: *as a whole after it has been completed*, as opposed to the chronological or developmental approach that have dominated Aiken studies until now.

Chapter Two

The Meditative Stance

The first major problem in exploring Aiken's philosophy of consciousness is that nowhere does he explicitly define the term "consciousness". However, as already demonstrated, Aiken's prefaces and above all his major poems offer an excellent starting place for remedying this situation. Even a cursory reading of his long poems makes it clear that introspection, reverie, dreams, interior monologues and soliloquies play a vital and later predominant part in these works. In other words, almost all the action happens *within* the protagonists who are all embarked on an inward journey of exploration or involved in deep debate with themselves, or engaged in monologues wherein the female listener functions almost exclusively as an audience for the protagonist's philosophical ruminations. In short, Aiken's poems are primarily works of inward focused or concentric consciousness. This remains the case in virtually all of his major long poems throughout his entire writing career.

The nympholeptic pursuit of *The Charnel Rose* (1915) comes to us entirely through the mind, the impressions, feelings and thoughts of the protagonist who has an almost pathological inability to maintain a steady vision of an outwardly real person.

> But at times it seemed
> Walking with her of whom he subtly dreamed,
> That her young body was ringed with flame,
> Hover of fire,
> And that she went and came,
> Impalpable blossom of desire,
> Into his heart and out of his heart again,
> With every breath and every breath was pain.
> And if he touched her hand, she drew away,
> Becoming someone vast; and stretched her hair
> Suddenly like black rain across the sun.
> Till he grew fearful . . .
>
> (*The Charnel Rose*, II, 1, 35)

CONRAD AIKEN'S PHILOSOPHY OF CONSCIOUSNESS

The protagonist is constantly and completely overwhelmed by his feelings, ideas and imaginative perceptions which is why he is so utterly desperate:

> To shape this chaos of leaderless ghostly passions—
> Or else be mobbed by it—there was the question,
> Dry leaves above him whispered the slow question,
> Black ripples on the pool chuckled of passion
> And through the windows drifted his own white face,
>
> (*The Charnel Rose*, II, 3, 38)

Indeed, the protagonist of *The Charnel Rose*, despite his moments of turning outward towards the 'real' world, that is, despite his *moments* of outward or eccentric consciousness, never successfully escapes the inexorable gravitational pull of his psychological underworld. He simply wants to lose himself in his dreams and become part of an even larger, cosmic dream.

> To muse in the afternoon by a convent wall,—
> Here, at the bottom of the a vast blue well of sun;
> To watch the lizard breathe and crawl,
> And know yourself the world and lizard in one:
> Let us lose ourselves and all we meditate
> To melt, through dream, in the timeless dream of fate.
>
> (*The Charnel Rose*, IV, 5, 52)

Moments later he reduces the external world to "an old recollection" (ibid.) that "dissolves in darkness" (ibid.) and eventually concludes that "[w]e must escape this temporal flesh and place," (*The Charnel Rose*, IV, 5, 53) and "forget them all. / I must forget this sun,—myself,—this wall." (ibid.) and turn inward again:

> Here, then, at last, grown weary of long pursuing
> We find the perfect darkness!
>
> (*The Charnel Rose*, IV, 5, 53)

Unfortunately, the pursuit also continues in the darkness where finds himself "a part of the maniac laughter of chaos; / Rebellious chaos of unfulfilled desire."(ibid.).

The Jig of Forslin (1916), the second long poem in *The Divine Pilgrim*, is also dominated by the concentric phase of consciousness. At the beginning, Forslin, a circus juggler defeated in his attempts to achieve fame by balancing two balls on each other, reflects on the course of his life:

> In the clear evening, as the lamps were lighted
> Forslin, sitting alone in his strange world,
> Meditated; yet through his musings heard
> The dying footfalls of the tired day
> Monotonously ebb and ebb away
> And heard the dark world slowly come to rest.
> Now, as the real world dwindled and grew dim,
> His dreams came back to him . . .
> Now, as one who stands
> In the aquarium's gloom by ghostly sands,
> Watching the glide of fish beneath pale bubbles—
> . . . .
> He did not know if this were wake or dreaming . . .
> (*The Jig of Forslin*, I, 1, 55)

In the course of these reflections, Forslin not only reviews what has happened in his career as a juggler but also uses his fantasized dream egos to explore imaginatively other, in large part unrealised and often grotesque and bizarre, dimensions of his mind. In doing so, he struggles with the question of identity: "[t]he lights return / And we have silently changed . . . To what, to whom?" (*Forslin*, III, 3, 80). With a certain desperation, he asks, "Am I one or a million men?" (*Forslin*, IV, 4, 93). He also speculates about the nature of consciousness and the endless evolution of consciousness through an infinite regress of dreams and dreamers: "We dream our dreams but dream forever waking," (*Forslin*, V, 2, 102).

> We hold them all, they walk our dreams forever,
> Nothing perishes in that haunted air,
> Nothing but is immortal there
> And we ourselves, dying with all our worlds
> Will only pass the ghostly portal
> Into another's dream; and so live on
> Through dream to dream immortal.
> (*The Jig of Forslin*, V, 8, 115)

First appearances to the contrary, *The House of Dust* (1916) also displays the dominance of inward, concentric consciousness. The protagonist, a sort of Diogenes figure identified as "the inquisitive dreamer of dreams" (*Dust*, I, 1, 115) and "the eternal asker of questions" (ibid.) stands on a city street where he plans to ask people about their dreams:

> I will ask them all, I will ask them all their dreams,
> I will hold my light above them and seek their faces.
> I will hear them whisper, invisible in their veins . . .
> (*The House of Dust*, I, 1, 115)

CONRAD AIKEN'S PHILOSOPHY OF CONSCIOUSNESS

He is interested in people's inward lives, but more important, his pursuit of this quest, soon makes it clear that the outer conversations with others are little more than prompts for his own thoughts, feelings, dreams, and memories. Indeed, the outward city in which he seems to be acting and the inward city of his dreams have merged and blurred into one another:

> And, growing tired, we turn aside at last,
> Remember our secret lives, seek out our towers,
> Lay weary hands on the banisters, and climb;
> Climbing, each to his little four-square dream
> Of love or lust or beauty or death or crime.
> (*The House of Dust*, I, 5, 120)

According to Aiken's preface, the identity of the outer city of concrete and the inner city of consciousness is Aiken's main concern in this poem: "the entire poem is really an elaborate progressive analogy between the city, seen as a multi-cellular living organism, and the multicellular or multineural nature of human consciousness" (*Collected Poems*, 1021). The fragile and yielding nature of our identity and consciousness that make possible such a blurring of distinctions is expressed in one of the protagonist's beautiful lyrical outbursts:

> Weave, weave, weave, you streaks of rain!
> *I am dissolved and woven again.*
> Thousands of faces rise and vanish before me.
> Thousands of voices weave in the rain.
> (*The House of Dust*, I, 6, 122; italics added)

A similar blurring of identities occurs in *Senlin: A Biography* (1918) which, like *The Jig of Forslin,* begins with a man alone in his room.

> Senlin sits before us, and we see him.
> He smokes his pipe before us, and we hear him
> (*Senlin: A Biography*, I, 1, 195)

Before long, however, the seemingly clear identity of Senlin dissolves into the environment in which he finds himself.

> Has Senlin become a forest? Do we walk in Senlin?
> Is Senlin the wood we walk in,—ourselves,—the world?
> Senlin! we cry . . . Senlin! again . . . No answer
> Only soft broken echoes backward whirled . . .

> Yet we would say: this is no wood at all,
> But a small white room with a lamp upon the wall;
> And Senlin, before us, pale, with reddish hair
> Lights his pipe with a meditative stare.
>
> *(Senlin: A Biography,* I, 1, 196)

The rest of the poem is a series of imaginative adventures, memories and reveries as Senlin, and, by invitation, the reader, explore the intricacies of Senlin's own mind.

The Pilgrimage of Festus (1921), the last poem of the original poems of *The Divine Pilgrim,* also begins with the protagonist's plunge into inward, concentric consciousness. As in other poems, we find the protagonist in what may be called Aiken's 'meditative stance': a lone person, usually, but not always in-doors, has reached a critical juncture in life, and stands or sits observing both his own feelings and the surrounding world.

> And at last, having sacked in imagination many cities
> And seen the smoke of them spread fantastically along the sky,
> ....
> Festus, coming alone to an eastern place
> Of brown savannahs and wind-gnawed trees
> Climbed a rock that faced alone to the northward
> And sat, and clasped his knees.
>
> (*The Pilgrimage of Festus,* I, 1, 222)

Eventually, after pleading and tempting solicitations from various voices, Festus does what virtually all Aiken's protagonists do—begins a new inward journey of self-exploration: he "joyously into the *world of himself* set forward / Forgetting the long black aftermath of pain." (*Festus,* I, 1, 224; italics added).

Aiken's next major work, *Preludes for Memnon* (1931), wastes no time establishing the usual 'meditative stance'. After the introductory stanza in which the boundaries between inner and outer, the mind and the world are blurred—"Winter for a moment takes the mind" (*Memnon,* I, 1, 498)—readers find themselves in a familiar situation:

> The alarm clock ticks, the pulse keeps time with it,
> Night and the mind are full of sounds. *I walk*
> *From the fire-place with its imaginary fire,*
> *To the window, with its imaginary view.*
> darkness, and snow ticking the window silence,

> And the knocking of chains on a motor-car, the tolling
> Of a bronze bell dedicated to Christ.
> And then the uprush of angelic wings, the beating
> Of wings demonic from the abyss of the mind.
>
> (*Preludes for Memnon*, I, 1, 498; italics added)

The 'meditative stance' in *Preludes for Memnon* differs from that in *The Divine Pilgrim* insofar as in the earlier long poems, the protagonist takes the initiative and chooses to enter the concentric phase of consciousness whereas in the *Preludes for Memnon*, the angelic and demonic forces of the mind rush upward to engulf the protagonist, even though he has not willingly surrendered Himself to them. The essential situation however is the same as in the previously noted poems: a protagonist is suddenly overwhelmed by the 'forces' of the unconscious mind.

The Coming Forth by Day of Osiris Jones (1931) is also an inward journey, albeit one in which the usual framework of a meditating character and a specific location have been abandoned, leaving readers with the sheer play of the objects of one man's consciousness. The deliciously ironic twist in this poem is the fact that the man in question is dead! Readers are never told where Jones is; we can only be sure of the action of the poem, that is, the play of memory and consciousness and the testimony of the important objects of his life. All this takes place on

> . . . a stage of ether, without space,—
> a space of limbo without time,—
> a faceless clock that never strikes;
>
> and it is bloodstream at its priestlike task,—
> the indeterminate and determined heart,
> that beats, and beats, and does not know it beats.
>
> (*The Coming Forth by Day of Osiris Jones*, 574)

Despite the lack of a dreaming or meditating character, the essential action remains the same as in Aiken's other long poems: the exploration and play of a man's consciousness, in a setting that is ambiguously located in both the inner and outer world—and perhaps, as suggested in *The Coming Forth by Day of Osiris Jones*, in neither.

In *Landscape West of Eden* (1935), the location of the 'meditative stance' is moved to the deck of a ship where the protagonist finds himself with imaginary companions, Adam and Eve. The dialogue is what one would expect from an Aiken poem: an imaginary inner dialogue with various personified ideas, beliefs, feelings and attitudes:

> It was of a deck, the prow of a ship, uplifted
> by the wide wave of blue and whiteness, swung
> towards the star-side by a long wave from the west,
> then earthward dropped. And there, I, not alone,
> westward facing,
>
> and with me the two children,
> Eve and Adam, from Eden come with flowerbuds,
> (*Landscape West of Eden*, I, 1, 622)

The rest of the poem features the protagonist's dialogues with various dream egos or aspects of himself as he struggles to achieve a vision of the evolution of consciousness, symbolised by a westward journey. The protagonist also struggles to find a way of integrating the low, obscene, and even evil aspects of his and all human nature—symbolised by Lillith—into a coherent sense of identity and a viable Weltanschauung.

Like *The Coming Forth by Day of Osiris Jones*, *Time in the Rock* (1936) does without the lonely rooms that form the usual setting for Aiken's 'meditative stance'. The poem plunges directly into concentric consciousness, opening with a moment of a transformative vision in which a seed is metamorphosed into a star, and eventually into a god and laughter: "And there I saw the seed upon the mountain / but it was not a seed it was a star" (*Time*, I, 1, 665). It plunges readers directly into the flow and dialectics of the mind:

> and thus beneath the web of mind I saw
> under the west and east of web I saw
> under the bloodshot spawn of stars I saw
> under the water and the articulate laughter
> the coiling down the coiling in the coiling
> shot homeward foully in a filth of effort
> clotted and quick and thick and without aim
> spasm of concentration of the sea
> (*Time in the Rock*, I, 665-6)

Time in the Rock, significant parts of which are concerned with the theme of obscenity and evil already taken up in *Landscape West of Eden*, explores consciousness in what is essentially a long monologue covering a wide variety of metaphysical, ethical, evolutionary, religious and psychological issues. Even though she is explicitly addressed as a real and present character on occasion—"Woman, woman, let us say these things to each other / as slowly as if we were stones in a field" (*Time*, IV, 668)—the woman listener remains more than anything else, a background, or, alternately, an audience for whom the protagonist performs the exploration of his own consciousness. The fundamental stance is still inward or concentric, that is, focussed entirely upon inward events.

Because *A Letter from Li Po* (1955) is an extended soliloquy, a profound and complex revelation of a character's deepest feelings and insights, it, too, exhibits the inward focus of Aiken's works. Soliloquising requires, above all else, a condition of fine attunement to one's own inner states, though, ostensibly, the discourse may seem to be about the external world. Indeed, in a soliloquy, the primary use of images and references to the outer world is to provide objective correlatives for deep feelings and personal insights.

Even though one of the major themes in *A Letter from Li Po* is that man, language and the world are ultimately one, the fact remains that Aiken chose to present these ideas in a soliloquy—an inwardly focussed work, of concentric consciousness—when he might just as well have chosen a play or a narrative work such as *Punch: The Immortal Liar* (1930), or *John Deth* (1929-30), or *The Kid* (1947). A similar remark can be made about *The Morning Song of Lord Zero* (1963). At first reading this latter poem does not seem especially inward, but in fact, it is dominated by concentric consciousness insofar as it is a long philosophical self-revelation by Lord Zero.

Adopting 'self-consciousness' as Aiken's operative definition of consciousness, makes it possible to see and explain certain developmental trends in his poetry. It seems clear, for example, that the inward focus of Aiken's work became less intense as his career advanced, especially after he returned to America in the years just prior to World War Two. He wrote more poems like "*The Soldier,*" *The Kid* and "*Brownstone Eclogues*" in an effort to forge links between his original inward vision and the outer, more public world of simple and common people and occurrences as well as vast historical events such as the Second World War. This change was a part of his struggle with the solipsistic tendencies in his work and the difficulty he had in fully embracing their conclusion that no real meeting between people is possible since others are either not real or not knowable.

CHAPTER THREE

The Quest for Identity

Although critics have admitted the importance of the identity theme in Aiken's writing, its connection to the theme of consciousness has not been explored in the depth and detail it deserves. If consciousness is primarily self-consciousness, then to become conscious means to become self-conscious, that is, to become aware of one's own being as well as aware of one's own nature. The latter, of course, implies attaining self-knowledge. Gaining self-knowledge is, therefore, an essential part of the quest for identity, which is, in fact, merely another name for the quest for consciousness. This leads to a potentially serious difficulty: if a person does not know his or her own identity, how can he or she really be conscious? When such problems with self-knowledge arise—as is almost always the case in Aiken's long poems—difficulties inevitably follow. To become conscious, the characters in these poems are required to undergo a long and painful self-exploration, an undertaking that forms the substance of the poem.

The quest for identity as presented by Aiken is enormously difficult. In the first place, he does not believe there is such a thing as a 'stable' identity, once found and then taken home like a hunting trophy. Aiken consistently undermines any endeavour to attain an identity of this sort because such identities are false, betrayals of the perpetually changing nature of man and the essential self. In striving to deal with these changes, the seeker takes the first step in discovering the 'problem of identity'.

The problem of identity—and the impossibility of attaining a final conclusive identity—arises because Aiken believes that the Self is dynamic rather than static. By 'Self' he means the main character whose mind contains or encloses the action of the poem. Forslin, Festus, and the speakers of *Preludes For Memnon* and *Time in The Rock* are 'Selves', because virtually all the action occurs *within* them. When the Self seeks an identity, it searches for the unchanging essence or 'what' with which it can identify itself. However, if the Self is constantly changing, how can this condition be fulfilled? How could we ever find a stable identity in a Heraclitean universe in which everything is constantly subject to change?

Phases of the Self

In view of these problems, the logical starting point in the quest for identity is knowledge of the ever-changing Self. Such knowledge is not easily acquired because the Self is affected by more than one kind of change. Making matters still more complex is the fact that Aiken's philosophy does not permit problems to be 'solved', if by that term is meant 'a permanent end to the problem'. As shall be demonstrated, each solution leads to ever new difficulties that require solution.

One of the most important changes affecting the Self is an inward and outward 'motion' analogous to the diastolic and systolic movement of the heart (*Time*, V, 669). The two extremes of this rhythm represent states or phases of consciousness between which the Self oscillates, the phase of outward focus being "eccentric" (*Li Po*, V, 908) and the phase of inward focus being "concentric". Both terms are Aiken's, originating in *A Letter From Li Po*:

> Who knows but one day we shall find
> hidden in the prism at the rainbow's foot,
> the square root of the *eccentric* absolute
> and the *concentric* absolute to come
>
> (*A Letter from Li Po*, V, 908; italics added)

In the case of language, this rhythm is characterised as a collection and dispersal:

> Speak to me of Babel, that I may strive to assemble
> Of all these syllables a single word
> Before the purpose of speech is gone.
>
> (*Time in the Rock*, XIX, 684)

Syllables being 'assembled' or compressed into a single word corresponds to the concentric or systolic phase of human consciousness, whereas the dispersal, diastolic or eccentric phase of consciousness corresponds to the word's loss of unity, cohesion and purpose.

The movement between these phases is epistemological, a shift of attention by the poem's protagonist or the Self seeking an identity. In the concentric phase, the protagonist looks inward, paying no heed to the surrounding commonplace world where he usually dwells, and imagining a 'smaller' self or dream ego engaged in all kinds of actions. During the eccentric phase, the Self, or protagonist, is aware of himself as an identifiable character in the ordinary world, although he may still be fully aware of his inward life and the self or ego that he imagined. In the extreme eccentric phase, the Self identifies with the entire outward world, or, put into other words, becomes one with the world. The difference between the two phases is that one involves total self-absorption to the exclusion of all else, while the other is self-reflection on oneself *and* the world, and, at its farthest limits, identification with the world.

The opening lines of *The Jig of Forslin* are in excellent introduction to a more detailed discussion of the concentric state:

> In the clear evening as the lamps were lighted,
> Forslin, sitting alone in his strange world,
> Meditated . . .
> ....
> Now, as the real world dwindled and grew dim,
> His dreams came back to him . . .
> Now, as one who stands
> In the aquarium's gloom, by the ghostly sands,
> Watching the glide of fish beneath pale bubbles,—
> ....
> He did not know if this were wake or dreaming,
> He though to lean, reach out his hands, and swim.
> (*The Jig of Forslin*, 1, 1, 54-55)

This passage describes the absorption of the protagonist or Self into his dreams and his dream ego. As these lines indicate, in the concentric phase, the Self is unable to distinguish between dreaming and wakefulness, and between itself and its imaginative dream ego. More philosophically, one might say that the subjective and objective poles of perception are fused. The latter fact is illustrated by Forslin's attempt to swim like one of his dream-fish. Equally evident is the disappearance of the daily world and of Forslin, the failed juggler who is the protagonist of this poem. However, both the world and the juggler are replaced by a dream figure, which, despite the fact that it frequently goes by his name, is not to be confused with the juggler who produced it. As shall be seen, one of the major crisis in the quest for identity arises because the awakened Self, the eccentric dreamer, does not wish to be identified with his own dream egos. He tends to regard them as mere, often undesirable, fragments of himself.

In *The Jig of Forslin*, and in other poems of *The Divine Pilgrim*, the dream egos are simple insofar as they take the form of specific characters acting out the protagonist's often luridly violent adventures. However, in such later works as *Preludes for Memnon* and *Time in the Rock*, interaction among distinct characters is replaced by the dialectical interaction of ideas, feelings and points of view. In that sense, Aiken's poetry exhibits a mild development towards 'abstraction' insofar as actions are replaced with dialectic of ideas.

This trend to abstraction in Aiken's writing is not entirely unanticipated. In *The Pilgrimage of Festus* we find such a purely intellectual dialectic in the discussion between Festus, the protagonist or Self, and the Old Man, the dream ego, each of whom makes claims that undergo progressive transformation as the dialogue develops. These dialogues may be described as dialectic in nature because there is no denial or outright negation of any claim but rather a struggle to attain a transcending view that includes them both. Admittedly, in *The Pilgrimage of Festus*, the application of the method is partial and crude, relying on the explicit identification of each particular viewpoint with a distinct character. Such mechanics are rather clumsy when compared to the smooth, often nearly unnoticeable shifts in the dialectics of Aiken's mature work. However, this is not to say that Aiken's masterpieces, *Preludes for Memnon* and *Time in the Rock* are entirely without characters and dream egos, but rather that their occurrence is an exceptional interruption in the usually smooth flow of ideas and shifts in viewpoint.

From the point of view of the dream egos, the Self is the world, containing them just as the real world contains the actual Self. To the dream egos, the mind or Self may show itself as a forest, a city, a pool, a room, a house, a theatre, a net or anything else capable of functioning as a 'container'. Naturally, each of these things fulfils this function in a unique way; a house for example, does not hold a thing in the same way as a mirror.

In its outward or eccentric phase, the Self may reflect on inner imaginative events, but it is not completely absorbed in them. For example, the awakened Forslin, still recalls his dreams but he is sufficiently distanced from them to ask "Whence do I come, and why? And what's my name?" (*Forslin*, III, 3,80). The memories and imagined events serve as materials for conscious reflection about himself as a person *in the world*. Whenever questions of this kind occur in Aiken's poems, the protagonist asking the questions is, momentarily at least, in the eccentric phase of consciousness. From this we may conclude that the problem of personal identity—and, therefore, the problem of consciousness—belongs to the eccentric phase as the Self begins to examine its situation in the world along with its own inward condition. It undertakes its imaginative introspective activities in order to solve the correlated problems of consciousness and identity. However, consciousness and identity may not properly be ascribed to the dream egos themselves since they are merely the means by which the Self pursues its quest.

An examination of the Self in its eccentric phase also reveals that the relationship between it and the cosmos (the ordinary world we all share) corresponds to the relationship between the dream ego and the Self. Just as the dream ego is an inward projection of the introspective dreamer, the Self may be viewed as an inward projection or dream ego of the entire cosmos itself, an idea suggested when the protagonist tells the lady in *Time in the Rock*, "the world, creating, imagined you." (*Time*, LXXXVI, 746). Elsewhere we read,

> This whirling wheel, concentering on itself
> Produced and sought you, you yourself poor spider.
>
> (*Preludes for Memnon*, XII, 511)

Punch: The Immortal Liar also suggests this idea. Mountebank, who has dreamed an entire world of puppets / dream egos, speculates that he, too, may be the toy or dream ego of an even greater puppeteer. In turn, this greater one may be the plaything of a still greater master, and so on in a regress that, ironically, might well lead back to Mountebank himself! The situation may be diagrammed as a series of concentric circles, in which each circle is the dream ego, the inward projection of the one enveloping it in the following order. An alternate image of this situation might be a set of Chinese boxes or Russian dolls. Because the relationship between the Self and the dream ego, and between the world and the Self are essentially alike, we know that whatever applies to one applies to the other.

In this sense, Aiken conflates psychology / epistemology, that is, what happens inside human minds, with cosmology which studies the external universe and man's place in it. When the Self in its eccentric phase examines the outer world and its own position therein, it thinks in terms of cosmology whereas in its concentric, inward phase it thinks in terms of psychology. Aiken's Kantian premises makes such a conflation inevitable. In Kant's epistemology, the human mind organises the raw data from the external world into a coherent whole with its characteristics of time, space, causality and all other attributes; what the external world is 'really' like, we have no way of knowing. In short, our psychology is the basis for all knowledge, including our cosmology—and all knowledge about the outside world is, ultimately, psychological in nature. Even our most rigorous scientific knowledge does no more than tell us about how our minds work in shaping in-coming data; it tells us more about ourselves than about the universe around us. Consequently, because the mind always follows the same rules for organising data, the inner and outer worlds are structurally identical and whatever we discover about one applies to the other as well.

An image from *Preludes for Memnon* illustrates these ideas. Speaking to the lady, the protagonist says, "and in your heart I find / Orion in a cobweb and the World" (*Memnon*, VII, 506). The "heart" (ibid.) represents the Self enclosing Orion, the dream ego, not only in a "world"—since the Self is the only world that dream egos can ever know—but also in a "cobweb" (ibid.) which entraps Orion like a fly in a spider's web. As we shall have occasion to see later, the dream ego frequently regards the Self as a trap from which it seeks to escape just as the Self often has yearnings to escape or transcend the world in which it feels trapped. More importantly, this passage represents man's situation in the universe insofar as man is the dream-ego of the entire cosmos which is itself engaged in its own universal dream. Because it is ever-changing, the universe itself is also embarked on a quest for identity and human consciousness is the means whereby it conducts this search. Thus, we can conclude implicit in Aiken's poetry, the following analogy is at work: 'man' is to the 'dream ego' as the 'universe' is to 'man'.

Elsewhere Aiken writes that we must "know ourselves but as old stones that sleep/in God's midstream of wreckage" (*Memnon*, XXXVI, 542). Here, and in the line, "Man is but a leaf" (*Memnon*, XXII, 524), we see image of man as a natural object or as product of nature. In each case, there is a certain sense of diminishment because such an image cannot help but accentuate humans as objects of nature's action, not as empowered, subjective participants in their evolution. Knowing ourselves as "old stones" (*Memnon*, XXXVII, 542) or as a mere "leaf" (*Memnon*, XXII, 524) is conducive to moods of despair and helplessness. However, we must never forget that this diminished portrait of man is only part of the story. We are also an entire world to our dream egos, and, because of our microcosmic identity with the macrocosm, we are, in a sense, the entire cosmos itself. As already noted, our awareness of this identity with the cosmos occurs in the extreme eccentric phase of consciousness.

Many Worlds

Already at this early stage, the investigation of the Self and its quest for identity has grown exceedingly complex. The concentric dreaming Self is a containing world for its dream egos while at the same time, the cosmos is a containing world for the Self. Furthermore, the eccentric Self is able to expand beyond mere reflection about its own situation in the world and, in a sense, become coterminous with the world itself insofar as there are no inherent limits to consciousness. In effect, we are part of an infinite series of worlds, a situation which Aiken describes in these lines:

> World whorled in world the whorl of his thought,
> shape under series the godhead he sought:
>
> (*The Kid*, VIII, 862)

Elsewhere in his writing, Aiken speaks of a "coil of worlds" (*Memnon*, XXI, 522), an image which draws attention to the complexity of worlds within worlds. Noteworthy here is the circular imagery—"coil" (ibid.) and "whorl" (*The Kid*, VIII, 862)—which re-enforces an idea already encountered in *Punch: The Immortal Liar*, namely, that all of these worlds within worlds are connected and, like a spring coil, lead from one to the other until the first joins the last. This image, reminiscent of the Buddhist doctrine of "dependent-arising" in which all phenomena depend on each other, makes the universe inherently ironical since the inter-dependence of first and last confounds all hard and fast distinctions between them, and thus undermines any final and self-contained sense of identity. Yet it is precisely such a clear, final and self-contained identity we feel compelled to seek! Exploring this odd situation, and what it means for us intellectually, emotionally and socially is the focus of much of Aiken's work.

Aiken's beliefs about the Self becoming a complete world at the limits of each phase of consciousness, makes it easier to understand the such lines as "You are all things and nothing" (*Memnon*, VIII, 507). When we are "all" we are in the extreme eccentric phase of consciousness; however, at the same time, we are "nothing" because we are also a dream ego of the cosmos which is a larger Self.

In Aiken's interconnected universe, extremes meet: as indicated previously, the Self is destined to become a world at either end of its oscillations. From this it is evident that we have, in fact, discovered a universal constant in the midst of universal flux, namely, the essential identity of Self and cosmos. However, what is most important for understanding Aiken's poetry is that the discovery was made, not by a denial of change, but by a rigorous pursuit of it. Had the Self refused to explore its concentric and eccentric phases and clung to one or the other as its 'identity', it would have lost one of the very things it was seeking, an enduring fact. The simple humility of accepting things as they are and resisting the temptation to force our own schemata on the world even if doing so provides momentary comfort leads to truths that may be simple and seemingly mundane, but can at least be steadfastly relied on.

However, as already noted, Aiken does not believe in 'solving problems' in any final sense because in a Heraclitean universe of constant flux, there can be no final closure to any problem or situation whatever. Each solution is merely the beginning of a new problem and a search for new answers. While the discovery that the Self and cosmos are identical in their essential features represents progress in the quest for identity, it also creates as many new problems as it solves. When the concentric Self seeks knowledge, it turns outward—only to discover itself once again. Similarly when the eccentric Self seeks knowledge, it turns inward—and finds only itself—and this leaves the seeker caught in a thicket of thorny questions. For example, if the Self in its expanded, eccentric phase is also a world, then how is objective knowledge possible? Does this situation not condemn all knowledge to be hopelessly personal, subjective and, in effect, introspective? Indeed, how can anything but Self be known if the extremes of the concentric and eccentric phases are essentially identical? Finally, does this not make some form of solipsism inevitable insofar as we can never escape ourselves and, in that sense, are forever trapped in the subjectivity of all knowledge?

An incident in *Preludes for Memnon* illustrates the inevitable subjectivity or 'narcissism' of all knowledge. The protagonist exclaims that when his lady touches him, "I am no longer I: I am world" (*Memnon*, XVI, 518). He has been expanded by love, but that is not the end of the story. At first, he takes this development as a narcissistic confirmation of himself as he is at this particular moment for which reason he is described as "Narcissus, cunning with a hand-glass" (*Memnon*, XVII, 518). However, things do not quite go as he expected.

In the first instance, he finds his own image, thus re-enforcing the notion that all knowledge is subjective or narcissistic. He also discovers his lady, but not as she is, a distinct human being in her own right, but rather, as he sees her, as "Lesbia" (*Memnon*, XVII, 518), one of the stock female figures in the classical poetry of Catullus. Individual and distinct as she might be, she has inevitably become one of the 'fictions' created by the protagonist's mind. Most important of all, he discovers death, the fact that "we must die" (ibid.) which is one truth of which we can be absolutely sure in a Heraclitean universe of relentless change: "Alas, alas, / To think that so great beauty should be lost!" (ibid.). To his dismay, the protagonist also discovers himself as a shape "obscene, disastrous, huge,—/ Huge as the world and formless" (*Memnon*, XVII, 519).

In other words, after first discovering his bright 'Apollonian' mask or coherent identity, Narcissus finds himself as a 'Dionysian' chaos that undermines any attempt to establish a coherent and unchanging identity.

It is worth noting that even in the concentric phase of consciousness, he finds himself "[h]uge as the world" (ibid.), thus re-emphasising the point that the Self becomes a world in both forms of consciousness. The formlessness he encounters is not surprising since a universe of constant change naturally always verges on chaos and confusion which he later describes oxymoronically as a "mad order" (ibid.). This emphasises one of the most important themes in Aiken's poetry, namely, that lurking beneath the apparent order and beauty of the world, that is, beneath its Apollonian mask of order, there is chaos of the Dionysian element.

Equally important, perhaps, is the protagonist's discovery of "the inhuman god" (ibid.), within himself. In Aiken's poetry, God represents the inward potential we are striving to actualise. On one hand, we are one with this God which is our own potential, better, more evolved selves but, on the other, we are alienated from this God because it is not only us *in potentia*, but also, it is us as we are not or not yet. Indeed, we may never actualise this potential and, thereby, remain alienated from this God forever. In other words, the only thing the Self cannot completely assimilate in either of its phases of consciousness is its own, partially unactualised potential. This means that in Aiken's subjective world, if we are alienated from anything, it is ourselves—and not from the others we seek so desperately to know. Again, the ironic nature of Aiken's universe becomes clear: we are farthest and most removed from that which is closest to us.

Self and Cosmos

A further example of the kind of paradoxes caused by the interplay of concentric and eccentric viewpoints is found in *A Letter from Li Po*:

> We are the tree, yet sit beneath the tree,
> Among the leaves we are the hidden bird,
> we are the singer and are what is heard.
> (*A Letter from Li Po*, III, 905)

In these lines, so reminiscent of Emerson's poem, "*Brahma*," the Self sitting beneath the tree is a product of the concentric phase of the cosmos, while as the tree, the Self is expanded to its fullest extent and has become the world. The viewpoints from two opposite phrases have been combined. However, this explanation, which permits some understanding of what occurs, cannot obscure the fact that what happens is highly 'mysterious'. If the expanded Self is the world, and Self is also a product of the world, then, in effect, the Self is its own product, or conversely, its own creator. No wonder the next line asks in perplexity, "What is this 'world'?" (*Li Po*, III, 905). Here, too, the paradoxical nature of Aiken's universe comes to the fore. Logically, and physically speaking, self-creation is utterly impossible, since in order to create oneself one would have to exist before one exists! However, psychologically speaking, it is quite possible to undertake a program of self-actualisation and self-building as we make resolutions and strive to become more like our goal or, our God. In effect, we thereby create ourselves. Metaphysically speaking, it must be possible to create oneself. If nothing comes from nothing, if *creatio ex nihilo* (creation from absolute nothing) is impossible, then it follows that self-creation must be possible because in some way the new entity must already exist, even if only in potential. Otherwise we would have a case of *creatio ex nihilo*. Thus, in a sense, the Self already exists and is capable of creating itself.

This scenario produces a conflict between the demands of logic on one hand (there 'must' be some form of potential existence) and science on the other (there is no evidence for this potential pre-existence). While according to the image of the universe most humans subscribe to it is necessary to abandon one of these positions in order to resolve this conflict, in Aiken's universe there is really no conflict at all. Such conflicts are simply the result of our own intellectual short-comings because each viewpoint has its own undeniable truth and abandoning one or the other simply blinds us to one of the facts of our existence. If we seek to resolve the conflict, we must do so, not by denial but rather by seeking a still higher viewpoint capable of transcending the conflict and thereby uniting the contraries into one coherent vision.

The subject of impossibilities is taken up in, among other poems, *A Letter from Li Po* where, in a whimsical passage reminiscent of squeezing sunlight from cucumbers in Swift's *Gulliver's Travels,* Aiken suggests that someday we might find

> hidden in the prism at the rainbow's foot,
> the square root of the *eccentric* absolute,
> and the *concentric* absolute to come.
>   (*A Letter from Li Po,* V, 908; italics added)

From a purely scientific view point, there is little likelihood of finding a "prism at the rainbow's foot" (ibid.) but, from a psychological point of view, this odd image has its share of truth. In any endlessly changing universe, no one state of affairs is permanently true; it is, so to speak a temporary expedient, or, a momentary 'fiction'. Discovering "a prism at the rainbow's foot" (ibid.), in other words, discovering that rainbows are not signs of God's promise but rather the products of prisms, or products of light refraction through droplets of water suspended in the air is an apt symbol of the fictive—or deceptive—nature of the universe. Even this seemingly whimsical symbol has its truth if we care to look for it.

Furthermore, this odd image contains another truth: that which is deemed untrue now may be yet turn out to be true in a future evolutionary development. In Aiken's vision of the universe, we must discount nothing. We may even find the "square root" (ibid.), that is, the essence of the outer and inner limits of the Self, although we must not take that promise too literally in an ever-changing, or 'deceiving' universe. Perhaps we already know the secret essence of Self: change. How, and if, that knowledge helps us, depends on whether or not we choose to understand and accept its full—and sometimes frightening—implications.

The Nature of the Self.

The oscillations in consciousness that have been described as "eccentric" and "concentric" may also be interpreted as phases in identity because in Aiken's philosophy of consciousness, we become what we perceive whether the perceived object is inner or outer, a real object or one that is thought about or imagined. This is made clear in the following lines from the beginning of *Preludes for Memnon*:

> And you because you think of these are both
> Frost and flower, the bright ambiguous syllable
> Of which the meaning is both no and yes.
> (*Preludes for Memnon*, I, 499)

The identification of Self with its objects of perception is explicitly stated later in the line, "Your Helen of Troy is all that she has seen" (*Memnon*, XXIX, 535). In *A Letter from Li Po*, written near the end of his career, Aiken still maintains this idea, applying it man's dream-life:

> Did Chouang dream he was a butterfly?
> Or did the butterfly dream Chouang? If so,
> why then all things can change and change again,
> the sea to brook, the brook to sea, and we
> from man to butterfly; and back to man,
> This 'I', this moving 'I this focal 'I'
> Which changes when it dreams the butterfly,
> into the thing it dreams of;
> (*A Letter from Li Po*, V, 907)

The reference to the "focal 'I'" (ibid.) shows that the Self is the object or focal point of its dreams and / or perceptions. If Chouang dreams he is a butterfly, then, for the moment at least, that is what he is. He experiences himself as such, and for Aiken the Self is what it experiences, regardless of how ridiculous or otherwise untenable the situation may appear to an external observer.

Aiken's notion that the Self is what it perceives denies realist epistemologies in which subject and object are rigorously separated and distinct. In a philosophically realist epistemology, external reality is completely independent from perception, and, therefore, it is logically inconceivable that a person becomes what he or she perceives. Perception alters the perceiving subject but not in such a way as to dissolve the actual distinction between subject and object. However, Aiken does not subscribe to a realist epistemology. Rather, his epistemology may be described as 'dialectical', viewing all objects as being interdependent and inter-acting and, therefore, changing each other at least in some minimal way. The distinctions between them are relative and malleable, not absolute. Indeed, in a Heraclitean universe of ubiquitous change, such hard and fast distinctions cannot be permanent since everything constantly loses its present identity and changes into something else. There is no reason for the subject / object or perceiver / perceived distinction to be exempted from the law of change.

The notion that the Self is identical with its inner and / or outward perceptions raises a serious problem, namely, how many identities do we human beings actually have? The only logical answer is that we have many, and, indeed, this is Aiken's response from his earliest long poems to the latest. In *The Charnel Rose* (1918), the protagonist discovers, somewhat grandiloquently,

> 'I am the Christ, returned from the dead!
> It was I you wounded, I that you crucified,
> It was I who wept and bled.
> Did I not prophecy three days ago?
>
> (*The Charnel Rose*, IV, 3, 51)

Thirty seven years later, in *A Letter From Li Po* (1955), he recounts the old Chinese story of Chouang's dream of the butterfly to illustrate exactly the same idea. He describes the 'I' as wearing "many guises and disguises" (*Li Po*, V, 907) and being "nimblest of actors" (ibid.) who adopts and abandons countless names. The idea that we have multiple selves, that our lives are succession of selves emerges clearly from these lines.

However, the concept of multiple identities does not exhaust Aiken's beliefs about the nature of the Self. What, we might ask, happens to Chouang himself while he dreams? Does he actually disappear from the earth at this time? Does Forslin vanish from the room simply because he is identified with and lost in the dream egos of his reveries? The answer is that neither Chouang nor Forslin disappear while they are absorbed in their dream egos but continue to exist as the 'stage' on which these dreams are played out; the outer Self functions as the containing 'space' or the merely passive, non-interfering location of these inner dramas. This simultaneous existence of the Self or consciousness as its dream ego, and as the dreamer or 'stage', is one of the inherent self-contradictions which characterize the Self, a fact emphasized in the following lines in which the protagonist sees himself as a God in the mirror and, at the same time, observes himself objectively:

> Here is the God who seeks his mother Chaos,—
> Confusion seeking solution, and life seeking death.
> Here is the rose that woos the icicle; the icicle
> That woos the rose.
>
> (*Preludes for Memnon*, I, 500)

CONRAD AIKEN'S PHILOSOPHY OF CONSCIOUSNESS

Given the inherent self-contradictions of the Self, one might also describe its existence as naturally ambiguous since the nature of its existence is never precisely clear at any time. Aiken draws attention to the ambiguous nature of the Self and consciousness in his description of man as a "bright ambiguous syllable" (*Memnon*, I, 499), mixed with a "bright ambiguous nature in the blood" (*Memnon*, L, 557). In the foregoing passage, the protagonist sees opposites or contradictories seeking each other within himself, thereby, making his identity unclear and ambiguous. Later, in *Preludes for Memnon*, the same situation occurs and the protagonist reaches the identical conclusion about his nature.

> Wreckage I saw, but also I saw flowers,
> Hatred I saw, but also I saw love . . .
> And thus I saw myself.
>
> (*Preludes for Memnon*, XIV, 515)

Aiken never attempts to resolve or clarify the self-contradictions and ambiguities which constitute the Self, indicating, thereby, that he saw these as final, irreducible features of the Self and consciousness. These features define our essence or nature as a species and as individuals for which reason we must accept them much as we accept universal change. If, like the protagonists of *The Divine Pilgrim*, we choose to ignore or defy our natures, we risk madness by engaging on an impossible quest to find a single, clear, non-self-contradictory and final identity.

Aiken's apparent 'failure' to clarify the ambiguities and resolve the self-contradictions constituting the Self emphasises, yet again, the dialectical nature of the Self and the universe in general. All things are relative to one another, that is, they exist in relation to other things, they exist inter-dependently and are, therefore, at least partially defined by each other. There can be no black without white—and no good without evil. In a constantly changing universe, such a dialectical existence means that not only good and evil but also all other things, continuously define and re-define each other in ever new circumstances and, thereby, reveal new aspects of themselves. Furthermore, in true Hegelian fashion, this dialectic is driven by self-contradiction, not only within the characters themselves, but, by extension, within all things. This is all plainly visible in the four long poems of *The Divine Pilgrim*, in which, more obviously than in the later works, the protagonists' struggles are driven by the desire to overcome and transcend the anguish of their self-contradictory ambiguities and multiplicities. From a dialectical point of view, the result is predictable: the protagonists roam "forever unsatisfied" (*Rose*, I, 1, 27) because the very nature of the cosmos prohibits the solution they desire. In their struggles, they forge a new synthesis, a new Self capable of including the opposites in a new unity—and immediately face the same problem again at a higher level. The problem cannot be solved because the problem *is* the inherent nature of human consciousness, it *is* the very being of the Self and what we are. We are dialectical beings who live in a dialectical universe. To pretend to 'clarify' the ambiguities and 'resolve' the self-contradictions would be deceiving ourselves about the nature of human existence and consciousness, and thus, a betrayal of our mission to evolve consciousness.

The ambiguous and dialectical nature of man has important ethical consequences. Since, like everything else in the universe, good and evil are also involved in an ever-changing dialectical relationship with all other things, all human beings, like the entire cosmos, are inevitably a mixture of both. Purity of any kind is a chimera because in a dialectical universe, nothing can be only one thing or another. For example, after metaphorically 'dissecting' his lady and revealing her "ignoble blood" (*Memnon*, XXX, 536), the protagonist proclaims the morally mixed, ambiguous or self-contradictory nature or identity of everything.

> For so it ["the ignoble blood"] comes from God.
> Bears with it false and true and dead and dying:
> It is the sovereign stream, the source of all;
> The seed, the seedling; worlds and worlds to come.
> Is there a treason here that is not you?
> Accept this logic, this dark blood of things.
> There is no treason here that is not you.
> (*Preludes for Memnon*, XXX, 536)

All things in the "sovereign stream" (ibid.) of creation are mixed from their very source. Not unexpectedly, these lines strongly suggest that morals themselves are relative, a suggestion that is immediately adopted in the next section of the poem:

> Where is the noble mind that knows no evil?
> Gay insubordination of the worm?
> Discord of mishap, rash disharmonies
> Sprung from disorders in the spirit's state?
> If there is such, we'll have him out in public,
> And have his heart out too. There is no good,
> No sweet, no noble, no divine no right
> But it is bred of rich economy
> Amongst the hothead factions of the soul.
> (*Preludes for Memnon*, XXX, 536)

According to these lines, good morals, good motives and good thoughts are the result of compromises among a variety of inner impulses or "hothead factions of the soul" (ibid.) and, as such, are neither as pure as we might believe, nor as independent from lesser impulses as we might want. Anything that is born from the "rich economy" (ibid.; "rich" because it excludes nothing) of compromise is relative to and thus dependent on everything from which it originates. Thus, good has a part in evil, and evil a part in good.

CONRAD AIKEN'S PHILOSOPHY OF CONSCIOUSNESS

Such ethical beliefs naturally prevent Aiken from adopting a conventional morality constructed of specific, eternal prescriptions, which emphasise 'purity' or absolute consistency. Our own Heraclitean nature, and that of the cosmos, dictate that we can only practice 'situation ethics', that is, derive our ethical principles from concrete and specific situations as they develop in our lives and not simply take them as 'ready-made' from some immutable, transcendent source, as, for example, the Ten Commandments. Accepting such a pre-made and supposedly permanent moral code would be living in 'bad faith' because it violates our own and the world's changeable nature, and inevitably deforms us and increases our difficulties. Honest living in a Heraclitean universe requires rejection of any pre-determined, or rigidly prescriptive ethics.

A possible consequence of the Self's lack of a single, stable, and durable identity, is the denial of the existence of any such thing as human nature, or essence either as individuals or as members of a species. Aiken specifically explores this possible consequence of his philosophy in "*The Morning Song of Lord Zero*" (1963), one of his last and shortest long poems. The protagonist, Zero, personifies the idea of endless personal transformation:

> Gambler and spendthrift by nature,
> chameleon soul whose name is Zero,
> anonymous in headlines,
> nameless in breadlines
> nevertheless I am your hero.
> . . . .
> I am inscrutably someone else tomorrow
> . . . .
> I am your jack-and-jill
> of all trades dubious brother
> panhandler father Cassandra mother
> and yet in the end insidiously
> o indispensably and invidiously
> something more.
>
> (*The Morning Song of Lord Zero*, i, 966)

If we adopt the view that identity is of necessity something absolutely stable then, as the title indicates, we may think of the ever-changing Self as a 'zero', as being 'nothing' or 'no (one) thing'. However, the first stanza of this poem already makes it clear that such a view is untenable. Superficially, Zero is all things and none; he wears many disguises, but he makes it clear that he is "something more" (ibid.) than these appearances. In short, he has an identity, a nature, an essence, if we choose to recognise it. However, this essence is not the stable Self that many humans expect. Rather, for Aiken, man, the Self, *is* an ambiguity, an ever-changing dialectic of self-contradiction, in other words, not a thing but a process:

> at every instant of the perpetual intersection
> of one with another in bloodstream and firmament
> *you are again being born and again die,*
> only o Phoenix to arise again in flame
> immutable mutable of sunlight
> (*The Morning Song of Lord Zero*, iii, 972; italics added)

Describing himself as "immutable mutable" (ibid.) clearly suggests the paradoxical, ambiguous or self-contradictory nature of the Self, both changing and changeless, or, in terms of the poem's title, zero and not zero. Like everything else in the universe, our nature is Heraclitean, a process, a flux that maintains itself through all time. While this may not be the kind of stable identity we wish to have, it is what we are and the only kind of identity we shall ever get. Until we can accept that such is our nature, we shall, like the protagonist of *The Charnel Rose*, remain incurably restless and "forever unsatisfied" (*Rose*, I, 1, 27).

The Dominance of the Concentric Phase.

A survey of Aiken's long poems shows that the quest for identity and, thereby, the evolution of consciousness, is most profitably undertaken in the concentric phase of consciousness when the Self is absorbed in its dreams and thoughts. Consequently, this phase is far more common in Aiken's writing than its outward turning, eccentric counterpart, a trend already noticeable in *The Divine Pilgrim*. Forslin, Senlin, and Festus all sit introspecting as they pursue their adventures of self-discovery. First appearances to the contrary, this is true even in the case of *The Charnel Rose*, the apparent outward action at the beginning is really a vision which the protagonist pursues through his dreams and fantasies.

In Aiken's later, more mature works such as *Preludes for Memnon* and *Time in the Rock*, the Self is also absorbed, but not so much in dreams as in language and speech. To a considerable extent, these poems are long, highly complex soliloquies in which the protagonists twist, turn and explore arguments and images from a wide variety of viewpoints. They do so with an almost obsessive exclusion of others whose brief and sporadic intrusions into the stream of speech serves only as prompts for another soliloquy. A good example of this is *Preludes for Memnon*, XIV, which forms a question and answer session in which the protagonist asks the lady about her inner travels: "—You went to the verge, you say, and came back safely?" (*Memnon*, XIV, 514). She answers and he replies with more questions. However, this section, in which the lady is unusually active, returns us to another long stretch in which readers see everything through the medium of the protagonist's speech.

Though louder, soliloquising is no less introspective than meditation or dreaming. Whether the Self dreams or soliloquises, the essential fact is that others hardly appear in the flow of reveries or speech; they are either completely excluded or simply provide prompts for further soliloquizing. This is not to say that their words are unimportant, but they are significant only insofar as they form prompts for further speeches. Indeed, were it not for the dash introducing each part of the dialogue in *Preludes for Memnon* (XIV, 514), readers would hardly guess that anyone else is present and simply assume that, for a few moments, the speaker is talking with himself. Less charitably, one might say that Aiken's protagonists are so intensely egotistical, if not outrightly solipsistic, that other people have been reduced to interruptions in the flow of their consciousness!

Frequency alone does not indicate the importance of the concentric phase of consciousness. Aiken specifically recommends it as necessary to growth.

> No, without phrase of comfort or deceit,—
> no quondam star admitted by despair,—
> go forth poor fellow to that *inward air*
> which is your spirit's courage;
>
> (*Time in the Rock*, LII, 716; italics added)

Given Aiken's self-appointed task of using his poetry for the evolution of consciousness, the dominance of the concentric phase of consciousness in his work should come as no surprise. How else, except by inner intellectual, emotional and imaginative work, through the labours and explorations of our dream egos, can we develop or evolve our consciousness? Had Aiken chosen the body and action in the world as the basis of identity he would, in the final analysis, be no farther ahead because the body can only be known and know itself through the mind—which is precisely what such an out-ward turning strategy seeks to avoid. Of course, this is not to say that outward, bodily action in the world plays no role in self-discovery and our psychological evolution; the eccentric phase of consciousness exists for a reason. However, the dominance of the concentric phase shows that for Aiken, the quest for identity, self-knowledge and consciousness is primarily, though not exclusively, pursued through inward activities.

Chapter Four

Issues in the Pursuit of Identity and Consciousness

The Problems with Memory

The dominance of concentric consciousness gives memory a very powerful role in the psychological development of Aiken's protagonists, all of whom invest considerable energy and time in exploring their past. This is quite commonsensical: if we want to know who and what we are, the memories of our actions and external life history, not to mention of our feelings, thoughts, and dreams, are the most obvious, and easiest place to start. Yet this ease is misleading because it belies the inherent unreliability of memory. Aiken wants us to become aware of this fact and turn to other aspects of ourselves for identity.

The examination of Aiken's argument against memory may well begin with Forslin, who is clearly a man in search of himself. Having neglected an essential aspect of his life by rejecting love, he indulges in a considerable number of dreams which not only provide at least some compensation for lost experiences but also help his self-explorations in search of his true identity. This introspective strategy leads to an important question: could not Forslin pursue the goal of discovering his identity more effectively by recalling the actual events of his life instead of indulging his fantasies?

Such a strategy will not work for three reasons. First, were Forslin to recall his actual life, the need for compensatory dreams, for imaginary indulgences would merely be intensified as the memories of his mistakes and other inadequacies increase his pain. Memory would simply exacerbate, not heal his inner wounds. Anyone trying this strategy would face the same dilemma of being hurt by that which is intended to heal. Second, Forslin realises that the outward events and deeds in his life are not adequate in identifying him completely. They are necessary but not sufficient for providing a complete portrait of him because, like anyone else, he is not merely the sum total of the external, worldly events in which he has been involved. Something has been left out and the dreams are needed to make up the deficiency.

In Aiken's view, day-dreams and fantasies, in addition to thoughts and outward actions are integral parts of our identity and must not be ignored. Thus, what initially looks like a weak-willed foolishness in Forslin, is actually wise. The simple truth is that he has spent too much time—ten years—in outward action, single-mindedly perfecting an incredible trick:

> To balance one ball on another ball—
> Tossing the upper one, to catch it, falling
> In easy balance again—
>
> (*The Jig of Forslin,* I, 3, 58)

Ironically, while he struggles to balance one ball on top of another, he is unbalancing his life, neglecting his needs for companionship and love. Thus, his seemingly extreme indulgence in introspection and reverie is no more than a necessary counter-balance to his previous extreme outward focus. His overly long sojourn in the eccentric phase of consciousness, focused on his career as a circus performer, has already resulted in establishing one identity: failed circus clown. However, since this outward identity does not exhaust the potentials of his whole being, he must now seek another identity elsewhere. Being a 'failure'—he masters the trick of balancing two balls on each other but audiences do not recognise its difficulty and remain indifferent—he has nowhere else to turn but inward, to the phase of concentric consciousness.

The third problem with memory is as thorny as the first two: in introspection, how do we distinguish between a memory and a dream, a fantasy or a false memory produced by the imagination? Aiken's answer—and it remains consistent throughout his works—is that we cannot. In the first place, memory can verify nothing. One 'knows' a memory is true only by verifying it with yet another memory, either our own or someone else's. We, and / or others might be deluded, or, consciously or unconsciously deceptive, but whatever the case, we can never be sure of the truth because we are simply using memories to check on memories. As Aiken would have known from his considerable readings in psycho-analysis, purely imaginary events have often been mistaken for 'memories' of 'real' events. The 'feeling of truthfulness' that seems to accompany is not reliable.

Aiken's lack of faith in the powers of memory is plainly evident in the following quotation:

> Remembering also
> the memories of these things, and the deep magic
> wrought upon them by *the falseness of memory*
> ....
> .... ; wherever
> nimbly I sent my messengers, they return swiftly
> with that fantastic nonsense which feeds the soul.
>
> (*Landscape West of Eden,* III, 625; italics added)

The most obvious result of memory's embellishing powers is that "the past [is] changed, and strange as future—" (*Time*, LXII, 725). This refers to the fact that the imagination is not only able to create memories but also to re-create them, that is, take genuine memories and re-shape them to new purposes. In fact, this would seem almost inevitable in a Heraclitean universe in which everything, memories included, is subject to ceaseless change. Obviously, memories that are continuously re-created offer no reliable basis for the construction of a personal history in the commonly understood sense of providing a stable and enduring portrait of one's past. The random nature of memory is yet another problem.

> Memory . . . a flight of wind through the forest of mind,
> Prolonged, prolonged and strange.
> ....
> .... O singular miracle
> To see our universe so blow and change
> Obedient to this foolish wind from Nowhere.
> (*The Pilgrimage of Festus*, IV, 4, 271)

In other words, memory is sporadic: we remember some things but not others, and at certain times, we cannot remember even events, people, feelings or other information usually at our command.

Immediately after saying these things, Festus expresses a more positive attitude towards memory, but he does not succeed in dispelling the doubts he has raised. After all, it would be foolish to expect memories to remain unchanged in a Heraclitean universe. Unlike a photographic film, memory is a poor stabiliser. Memory's limited stabilising power is also indicated in *Time in the Rock*, where, summarising a long argument, the speaker says, "You will not remember the shape of a single word" (*Time*, LXIV, 728). This, too, re-emphasises the fact that memory is a poor tool in the search for knowledge whether it be of ourselves, of others, or of the external world in general.

Another related reason for the limited value of memory is that by nature it must deal with what is 'dead and gone' and, therefore, no longer available to serve as verification.

> Where is that drop of blood you knew last year?
> Where is that image, which you loved, that frame
> Of ghostly apparitions in your thought,
> Alchemic mystery of our childhood, lost
> With all its dizzy colours? . . . It is gone.
> Only the echo's echo can be heard.
> Thrice mirrored, the ghost pales.
> (*Preludes for Memnon*, XXI, 523)

CONRAD AIKEN'S PHILOSOPHY OF CONSCIOUSNESS

Only a little reflection is needed to realize that in a Heraclitean universe, perception suffers the same handicap. The very moment after we perceive something, it is already 'gone' insofar as it is irremediably different, and no longer available for evidence in its previous state. This condemns us to live forever in the past, because we remember and think of things as they were and not as they actually are at every moment. More radically yet, this means that there is no essential difference between a perception and a memory, since the former is, in actual fact, never more than a memory of how things were. Consequently, all of the problems associated with memory also apply to perception—an observation which has the unsettling consequences of leaving us lost and locked into a world of perpetually changing memories and perceptions none of which offer any final assurance of accuracy.

As if the previous 'case against memory' were not be sufficient to induce severe epistemological doubts and uncertainty, Aiken identifies two additional problems. The most radical of these is that a return to the past, even if possible, is immoral. This belief is part of his more encompassing theme of rejecting inheritances, that is, refusing to accept the world as 'ready-made' for us by the perceptions and opinions of others, especially ancestors. Aiken contends that to be ourselves to the greatest possible extent, it is necessary to create ourselves from 'scratch'. In his view, inheritances of any sort are merely a pre-fabricated past, and, for that reason, are utterly impersonal. This makes them unsuitable for the creation of a personal identity.

> Christ, and are we drowning men, to clutch
> At straws and leaves? Must we remember each
> Frolic of dust along the road that led us
> From there to here?
> . . . .
> Good God, we are not come to such weak softness
> That we must beg our very origins
> To bless us from the past! What we remember,
> Why that's ourselves; and if ourselves be honest
> We'll know this world of straws and leaves and hearts
> Too well to give it power.
>
> (*Preludes for Memnon*, LXI, 570)

In stating that humans are what they remember, Aiken is, of course, engaging in ironic play with his readers, since the issue of his entire case is that we cannot rely on memory at all. That is why he warns us by saying that if we are "honest," (*Memnon*, LXI, 570) we will not give our memories, "this world of straws and leaves and hearts" (*Memnon*, LXI, 570) the power to determine our identity for us.

Aiken's sceptical attitude toward the past and memory is virtually mandated by his philosophy of the evolution of consciousness. Evolutionary viewpoints are forward looking, future oriented and inherently incompatible with any undue emphasis on or hankering for the past. Such nostalgic yearnings are immoral insofar as they violate our own basic evolutionary nature and the evolutionary nature of the universe and, for that reason, lead to nothing but harm. Change is our nature and therefore, working against change or trying to deny it is the one 'misdeed' which cannot go unpunished because endeavouring to do so is the one thing that is actually impossible in a Heraclitean universe. It is a betrayal of oneself, and, indeed, of everything that exists.

Another, more complex reason for the rejection of memory is Aiken's belief in the value of forgetting. The necessity of forgetting is evident from the beginnings of Aiken's literary career. As early as *The Charnel Rose*, we can read passages such as the following:

> I must forget them. I must forget them all.
> I must forget this sun,—myself,—this wall.
>
> Here then, at last, grown weary of long pursuing
> We find the perfect darkness!
> The infinite spreads before us, and shrinks to nothing.
> Or must we always remember, always that sound of voices
> Our little cave of dusk?
>
> (*The Charnel Rose*, IV, 5, 53.)

The speaker feels that memory has become a terrible burden, if not an outright curse on his life. He gleefully finds "the perfect darkness" (*Rose*, IV, 5, 53) that will allow him rest from his memories and then—we can almost hear him groan—wonders if we must "always remember?" (*Rose*, IV, 5, 53), that is, if we are condemned to recall the past within our skulls, or "little cave of dusk" (*Rose*, IV, 5, 53).

In *Preludes for Memnon* almost all of section LXII is devoted to the importance of forgetting. "Praise Limbo, heart, and praise / forgetfulness" (*Memnon*, LXII, 571) says the protagonist, and adds, "Remember to forget / and have your rest" (*Memnon*, LXII, 572). Simply letting the past be past and accepting change, which is to say, surrendering and 'going with the flow' is the only way to attain even a moment of rest in a Heraclitean universe.

To understand Aiken's point about forgetting, we must be aware that for Aiken, 'forgetting' is 'assimilation', and not 'obliteration'. The difference between the two is indicated in the line, "Where are my lovers now?/ buried in me" (*Memnon*, LXII, 571). Because they are assimilated, "buried" in him, they can grow and develop as part of the speaker's own evolution of consciousness; they have become part of his life and not simply vanished as if they had never been. As is quite proper in an evolutionary universe, they are being used as resources for further growth without any nostalgic hankering to keep them as they were. This strategy involves a proper, healthy forgetting as distinct from the impossible attempt to obliterate something that has already been and is, irremediably, part of cosmic evolution.

Imagination in the Quest for Identity.

In Aiken's view, we have no choice but to accept that identity cannot be discovered by seeking evidence in our memories of the external world and must, therefore, turn inward to the imagination. During the concentric phase of consciousness, this faculty is used chiefly to create inner dramas featuring either the adventures of a dream ego, or, in the more intellectually sophisticated poems, the dialectical interaction of ideas, feelings and attitudes. These inner dramas have two distinct but closely correlated 'plots': the growth of consciousness and the discovery of identity. They are correlated because, as already seen, for Aiken, consciousness is by definition 'self-consciousness'; we cannot become more conscious without knowing our identity, not merely in the mundane, outer worldly sense but also in the inward, more personal sense of knowing our secret desires and motives, and as Forslin learns, our deepest, often neglected, needs.

It bears repeating that for both quests, it is essential to become conscious of one's ultimate, metaphysical identity as one of the dream egos created by the Heraclitean universe itself in its own quest for identity and consciousness. Without this vital next step beyond the limited human Self and its immediate world, even the eccentric phase of consciousness will not be enlarged much beyond the boundaries of the Self and will remain eternally frustrated because it will never attain the only satisfaction and rest available—the knowledge that in a Heraclitean universe, there is no final, stable, identity, and that the endless quest for identity and consciousness is the only identity we can ever achieve. If we find this discovery depressing, then there remains only the comfort of knowing that everyone and everything is involved in the same quest: our remaining consolation can only be that misery loves company.

In Aiken's work, the main strategy used to achieve a sense of identity as well as to pursue the evolution of consciousness is imaginative self-exploration in the concentric phase of consciousness. The only difference between the earlier and the later works in this regard is that the earlier works feature a variety of dream ego adventures ranging from the somewhat lurid to the romantic and tragic, while the later poems such as *Preludes for Memnon, Time in the Rock, A Letter from Li Po* and "*The Morning Song of Lord Zero*" pursue the same goals by means of a Hegelian dialectic of ideas, that is, a discussion, usually with themselves, in which the continuous negation of ideas leads to the formation of new ideas and attitudes that include but transcend what has been negated. *Punch: The Immortal Liar* (1921) is only apparently an exception to this rule. Although he is initially presented as a real character who seeks to develop his identity and consciousness by outrageous lies about super-human exploits, he is, as the Epilogue shows, simply one of Mountebank's puppets or dream-egos. (Mountebank in turn sees himself as a puppet or dream ego of "some greater dreamer" [*Punch*, Epilogue, 360] involved in his own evolution.) Like Aiken's earlier protagonists, Punch still seeks a sense of identity and the evolution of consciousness by means of imagination and dreams, but, at the same time, by telling others his dreams, he invites their commentary and thereby initiates a simplified dialectic of ideas. In later poems, it is the dialectic and not the narrative that will prevail. Thus, *Punch: The Immortal Liar,* stands not only as a chronological intermediary between *The Divine Pilgrim* and the later long poems, but also as a methodological intermediary between the earlier poems with their conspicuous narrative component and 'dialectical moments' to the later long poems that concentrate on a dialectic of ideas in the evolution of consciousness. *John Deth* (1930), of course, is presented as an outward narrative, and as such, represents an anomaly in the development of ways of evolving consciousness. However, Aiken subtitles *John Deth* "A Metaphysical Legend" (*John Deth,* 397), suggesting thereby that we should not read it simply as a tale of real world adventures but as something akin to a dream. In that sense, *John Deth* continues Aiken's line of inward-looking poems although, in its actual presentation, it marks a break with such works.

If we recall that for Aiken, the cosmos, too, is a vast Self engaged in the quest for identity and the evolution of consciousness through its own inward dream productions—known to us as 'the universe'—then it becomes clear that the Self and the cosmos are theatres featuring a wide variety of performances. This notion is one of the foundations of Aiken's work. It is implicit in the first five poems of *The Divine Pilgrim* and it becomes explicit in the sixth of that series, the very much shorter "*Changing Mind*" (added in 1949) where the protagonist sees himself as "a submarine orchestra, a telephone exchange of blue nerves and *a bare stage* on which something was about to happen!" ("*Changing Mind*", 283; italics added). The protagonist discovers himself in all the characters and concludes,

> All this was I and also the amphitheatre itself,
> All this, but also a small room, a forest,
> Trees full of birds walking down to the water's edge
> ....
> Hegel arriving on a sea-scallop accompanied by Venus,—
> ("*Changing Mind*", 284)

Hegel's presence is important here because it suggests that Aiken recognized the similarities between his ideas and those of the great German idealist who conceived of world history or evolution as the thoughts of the Absolute realizing themselves through the history of the human race, and especially through the actions of great 'world historical' figures such as Charlemagne and Napoleon. This concept is virtually identical to Aiken's belief that the cosmos develops or evolves itself through us as its dream egos and that we, in turn do the same with ours own dream egos. The fact that Hegel arrives "accompanied by Venus" ("*Changing Mind*", 284) indicates that Aiken had a good enough knowledge of this philosopher's masterpiece, *The Phenomenology of Spirit,* to know that desire plays a pivotal role in Hegel's theory of the development and evolution of consciousness.

The reason that we must explore, discover and develop our identities through imaginative dream egos is that each one of us possesses more potentials than we can ever actualize in the outer world. We are doomed to remain incomplete beings unless we find a way to bring our other potentials or selves to life, something we can do by seeing ourselves as a stage on which dream egos act, as well as actors in the performance of our lives. For example, the protagonist in *Time in the Rock* tells us

> And look and remember well, as with an actor,
> how each moment is that brilliant and particular
> stepping forward from the shadow to the stage
> where *all* will be seen;
>
> (*Time in the Rock*, LXXXVIII, 748; italics added)

Elsewhere in the same poem we are told to "Walk on the stage of your imagining" (*Time*, LXVII, 729). We must be like actors, who, for a time, give life to imaginary lives or dream egos and, in the process of doing so, develop otherwise un-lived aspects of their own identities. They enrich their outer world personalities by giving life to those aspects and potentials that would otherwise remain suppressed. Such suppression leaves us unbalanced in our psychological development and requires us to seek compensation elsewhere and by other means. However, while we cannot all become actors in real life, we can, through imagination, give life to our hidden potentials in the inward theatre of the concentric phase of consciousness. This idea, already evident in his early long poems remains with him throughout his career.

When Aiken asks which of these many "I"s is true, he eventually concludes that "[i]n every part we play we play ourselves" (*Li Po*, V, 908) and that "the only voice that answers is our own" (ibid.). He then proceeds to praise the "thousand eyes, the Argus 'I's' of love" (ibid.) that make up Li Po's identity—and, by implication, our own. What has happened between his earliest poems and *A Letter from Li Po* is that his attitude towards his multiplicity has evolved from a somewhat panicked awareness of those "leaderless ghostly passions" (*Rose*, IV, 1, 48) threatening to mob him and arrived at an enthusiastic acceptance and appreciation of this situation.

> This 'I,' the moving 'I,' this focal 'I'
> which changes when it dreams the butterfly
> into the thing it dreams of . . .
> . . . .
> . . . . this liquid 'I':
> how many guises and disguises this
> nimblest of actors takes, how many names
> puts on and off, the costumes worn but once,
> the player queen, the lover or the dunce.
>
> (*A Letter from Li Po*, V, 907.)

Reliance on the imagination in the quest for identity is not, however, problem free. First of all, the imaginative activities of the Self, the dream egos, and the cosmos, suggest that at both the personal and cosmic levels, the entire process is somehow 'fictional', and, thereby, less than 'real'. Indeed, the term 'fictional' carries with it the connotation of 'false', a connotation fully intended to be felt but not because Aiken wants us to believe that the universe is an 'illusion'. Rather, Aiken wants us to see that the distinction between 'fictional' and 'real' is a false distinction, that the products of the imagination are as real as anything else. His rationale for doing so is simple: if the cosmos which we accept as 'real' is the imaginative creation of a still greater Self, then why should we deny the reality of our dreams? However, regardless of rationale, there is a credibility problem in regards to his conclusion that dream egos are as real as anything or anyone else. Even though we may consent to this proposition intellectually, it is difficult to deal with other people as if they were dreams or with dreams as if they were other people.

A second problem is that someone sincerely seeking the 'real me' may well regard the fictional nature of the process as a mockery of his or her quest and is likely to be dissatisfied with the results. Indeed, since only 'fictions' or 'falsehoods' and 'untruths' are gained, the quest seems doomed and pointless even before it begins. Aiken is keenly aware of this problem because it haunted him throughout his poetic career. Speaking of the seemingly endless roles that he has played, Forslin asks

> Tired of change, I seek the unmoving center—
> But is it moveless—or are all things turning?
> Great wheels revolve. I fall among them and die.
> My veins are streets. Millions of men rush through them.
> *Which, in this terrible multitude is I ?*
>
> (*The Jig of Forslin,* IV, 6, 111; italics added)

Earlier, the protagonist of *The Charnel Rose* seeks to find the one, true Self that could provide inner order:

> To shape this world of leaderless ghostly passions,—
> Or else be mobbed by it—there was the riddle
>
> (*The Charnel Rose,* IV, 2, 48)

Albeit in different form, the same question occurs in *A Letter from Li Po,* where the protagonist asks, "which is the 'I' / of 'I's'?" (*Li Po,* V, 907) as well as in Aiken's last long poem, "*The Morning Song of Lord Zero* "where we are advised to

> Stoop and try the lock
> Hoping still to find
> Somewhere someday
> The sacred and the vulgar key
> To you or me
>
> (*The Morning Song of Lord Zero,* i, 967.)

Elsewhere in the same poem, he describes the challenge of finding a 'real' self:

> How in this whole magnificence to find
> Our own self-seeking and self-shaping phrase
> And so ordain our days.
>
> (*The Morning Song of Lord Zero*, ii, 967)

The persistent problem of finding a stable and fixed Self amidst our imaginative productions shows that Aiken himself is not entirely satisfied with the conclusion that all imaginative products are equally real. He still desires one "master cadence" (*Li Po*, V, 907) by which to organise them all into a unified and coherent identity.

A third problem in relying on the imagination in the quest for identity is that the identification of the Self with its dreams leads inevitably to the problem of how to establish a coherent, unified Self. What if the dream egos are unpleasant or even evil, or just plain contradictory? Would not the unity of Self be irrevocably undermined by conflicts among the dream egos or between a particularly unpleasant dream ego and the Self? Even more devastating is the question: can the notion of the Self as a unique and distinct being have any meaning if the Self is continuously absorbed in its own imaginative productions? Would not the Self be continuously lost, and, if so, what can it possibly mean to 'seek one's identity'?

Yet another problem related to the imaginary quest for identity is that the Self is bewildered not only by the variety of its own productions, but also by the fact that these productions perpetually change. Thought, for example, is affected by "weariness or weather, time or space or mood" (*Eden,* XIV, 640). These alterations tend to preclude the attainment of a stable identity and demand that the seeker cope with them in addition to the eccentric and concentric motions of his or her own consciousness. The possibility of 'thinking things out' has obviously been undermined because clear and consistent thought requires a certain minimum of stability that seem impossible to attain in Aiken's world.

The Problem of Alienation.

Frequently in Aiken's poetry, the eccentric Self feels alienated from the creations of its concentric phase, and is unwilling to accept all of them as equally valuable or proper to itself. Shock, shame and bewilderment are common reactions and show that the Self does not always want to recognise itself in its own dream egos. Compounding the difficulty is the fact that, despite its wishes, it cannot always do so. After all, it is difficult if not impossible to recognise something that is constantly changing in the midst of an entire universe of relentless change. The same dilemmas are operative when the Self regards its role in the world since both its roles and the world are subject to endless flux.

In this situation, the Self confronts two distinct but related tasks: to overcome its fragmentation and alienation and to identify, in an exclusive sense, either with one of its dream egos or with one of its worldly roles. Fortunately, both of these challenges can be met at one stroke. The endeavour to solve these twin problems is illustrated in the following lines:

> Which is the 'I'
> of 'I's'? Is it the master cadence who
> transforms all things to a hoop of flame where through
> tigers meaning of leap?
>
> (*A Letter from Li Po,* V, 907)

The "master cadence" (ibid.)—note the singular—is the longed for exclusive central identity to which all other lesser identities must adjust themselves, and, by virtue of doing so, bring order and unity to the multiplicity of inner and outer identities. However, as indicated by the question in the foregoing quotation, this central identity is difficult, if not impossible to locate, a situation that was already evident in Aiken's earlier works. Surrounded by a veritable host of dream egos, the agonising Forslin wonders, "Which in this terrible multitude is I?" (*Forslin,* IV, 111). Forslin finds no answer but the protagonist of *A Letter from Li Po* does; the problem is, that the answer is as mysterious as the question: "In every part we play, we play ourselves" (*Li Po,* V, 908). While this assures us that we never lose our identity no matter what roles we play, the fact remains that it does not tell us precisely who we are. This inevitably leaves the Self with feelings of dissatisfaction and alienation in regards to itself.

However, the alienation the Self feels in regard to its own dream egos in the concentric phase, must be distinguished from the alienation it feels towards its own activities per se, a distrust of the mind's activities as such. This is a second level of alienation experienced by the Self. In his quest for the "master cadence" (*Li Po,* V, 907), the protagonist of *A Letter from Li Po* finds that "the only voice that answers is our own; / We are once more *defrauded* by the mind" (ibid.; italics added). The word "defrauded" (ibid.) clearly conveys the intensity of the protagonist's disappointment with himself and his deep sense of self-alienation. Inevitably, he feels a profound and corrosive self-distrust that could easily lead to complete despair.

In the following stanza of *A Letter from Li Po,* Aiken explains the necessity of this fraud by which the mind acts almost like an autonomous character against our own deepest desires; however, the fraud itself, and the resulting moments of despair are not explained away. They are a part of the evolution of consciousness, and, indeed, such an important part that suspicions about the trustworthiness of the mind or thought in the quest for identity and truth are already evident in Aiken's earliest works. In *The Jig of Forslin,* the protagonist writes that he must

CONRAD AIKEN'S PHILOSOPHY OF CONSCIOUSNESS

> ... follow silently through my mind
> The *devious* paths that wind
> Among old forests *lamia-haunted,*
> Through silence enchanted
> (*The Jig of Forslin,* V, 1, 100; italics added)

The protagonist of *The House of Dust* refers to "coiling thought" (*Dust,* IV, 3, 182) and wonders, "Where have we been? What savage orgy of chaos / Whirls in our dreams?" (*Dust,* III, 12, 174). It would be difficult to miss the connotations of suspicion, deceit and destructiveness in these lines which strongly suggest that the mind is not necessarily a 'benign' entity. In *The Pilgrimage of Festus,* the Old Man refers "this goblin forest / We call our minds" (*Festus,* IV, 4, 268) indicating, thereby, that the mind is not to be trusted. In a later work, Aiken's protagonist exclaims

> Where then,—I said to the moon,—is honesty?
> can thought be trusted if it change its tune
> as weariness or weather, time or space or mood
> dictate the theme? If so, here's chaos come
> (*Landscape West of Eden,* XVIII, 640)

Here too, the protagonist expresses doubts about the "honesty" (ibid.) of the mind. Paradoxically, he concludes that confronted with the mind's alterations, the only policy is "honesty" (ibid.), namely, that we ourselves must be as honest as our inner weather and change

> minute by minute the bewildered compass;
> we'll change our minds, as change our moods; and die still changing
> and wisdom will be change and faith in change.
> (*Landscape West of Eden,* XVIII, 640)

What makes this resolution paradoxical is that such honesty and truthfulness to change makes us appear dishonest to those who still associate honesty with consistency and steadfastness!

The treachery and untrustworthiness of the mind is clearly indicated at the beginning of *Preludes for Memnon:*

> The mind too has its snows, its slippery paths,
> Walls bayoneted with ice ...
> (*Preludes for Memnon,* I, 498)

Here to we see the negative aspects of the mind brought to the fore: it has "slippery paths" (ibid.) on which we can fall and seriously injure ourselves, as well as sharp, icicle bayonets that could prove fatal to our commitments and beliefs. The theme of the mind's treachery is also pursued in *Time in the Rock*, where the mind, along with the heart, are to be framed and inhabited by a deceptive magician:

> Here's the *magician*
> come for his evening *tricks* with bags and sleeves
> marked cards and easy fingers. Here's the *illusion*
> come for the morning with an eye of sunrise
> and every grassblade golden. *Here's the deception*
> *who framed our hearts and minds and dwells there now*
> *as naturally as blood . . .*
>
> (*Time in the Rock*, LVII, 719; italics added)

From these lines one may conclude that the mind is deceptive by nature, is, in a sense, a 'con-man' whose tricks are forever beyond our grasp. What else can we conclude except that by trusting the mind, we are setting ourselves up for deceit and probably, heart-break?

Weaknesses of the Mind

The inherently deceitful nature of the mind is not the only reason we cannot trust it according to Aiken. Another reason for mistrust is that it cannot deal adequately with the world it perceives. In his first major long poem, *The Charnel Rose*, we can already discern the outlines of this idea; the protagonist

> . . . thought the minds of men were like black ripples
> Ripples of darkness, darkly huddled in night,
> Each of them with its image of lamp or star,
> Thinking itself the star.
>
> (*The Charnel Rose*, I, 5, 34)

If the mind is like transitory "black ripples" (ibid.), then obviously it cannot accurately reflect the surrounding world and is, therefore, unreliable. Indeed, in these lines we also feel the previously discussed negative, deceitful connotations associated with the mind in the reference to "ripples of darkness" (ibid.) that swamp and destroy the accuracy or truthfulness of images.

The notion that the mind is unreliable in its perceptual activities is explored in considerable detail in *The Pilgrimage of Festus*, one of the original long poems in *The Divine Pilgrim*. In a discussion between Festus and one of his dream egos, the Old Man, they develop the image of the mind or Self as a sea-pool which catches "the first star" (*Festus*, IV, 4, 269) while the agitated surrounding sea is "unconscious of the stars" (ibid.). The Old Man then adds the idea of a crab whose movements disturb the image of the star in the hitherto quiet pool. The crab represents the ego inhabiting the mind, which, without the ego's disturbance, would be a perfect reflecting surface. Festus quite accurately realises that to be a mind inhabited by an ego means, like the pool, "nightly to lose the image of one's desire / in one's own agitation like the sea" (ibid.) Perfect perception of the world as it 'really is', is obviously impossible in the situation as described here because the presence of a Self or an ego, frustrates any effort to see clearly.

The notion of the mind's unreliable perception of the external world is also found in *Time in the Rock:*

> What the mind touches is a ghost
> impermanent as wound in air
> which active memory cannot fill
> ghostly image of ghostly tree.
>
> (*Time in the Rock,* LXXXVI, 746)

As with memory, the mind works not with the object of perception directly as it is, but, rather with the object of perception as it has been, or, in other words, with a ghost. The latter term is appropriate for two reasons: the tree is dying, like any other living thing; the distance between subject and object ensures a time-lag between the two, thereby condemning the image to inaccuracy at least in regards to time. Evident in this passage as well, is an addition to Aiken's argument against memory. Memory is unable to fill the gap between the original reality and subsequent image and, thereby, bring about a meeting of mind and world.

An objection to the foregoing explication may be raised by pointing out two other lines in the same section:

> the hands reaching, imagine god,
> the truth is permanent in the mind
>
> (*Time in the Rock,* LXXXVI, 746)

If the truth is permanent or fixed in the mind, the mind cannot be wholly chaotic. However, we must not be seduced to any obvious understanding of these lines, since, according to Aiken, the only truth we can know is the self-contradictory truth that everything always changes. The only kind of fixed order that could develop from that truth is the permanence of change and, possibly, disorder. Those seeking a fixed order in the mind will get no comfort here. But all is not hopeless. If we understand the term 'God' as Aiken intended, namely, as a term for a more highly evolved, future Self, then these lines suggest that in any physical and / or mental action, man tends to over-reach himself, to strive for his 'God'. In philosophical language, man has a transcendental orientation and transcendental drives or ambitions. This orientation and striving, is "permanent in the mind" (ibid.), that is, is a permanent structural feature of the mind and, therefore, a permanent truth. This leads to the conclusion that truth is found not in the immediate apprehension of specific aspects of reality but in adopting an orientation or attitude, in a directed effort made in the midst of the perceptual inaccuracies or, to express it negatively, amidst the 'lies' to which we are subject.

Two observations are worth making at this point. The first is that these ideas are fatal to any correspondence theory of truth. We simply cannot define truth as the correspondence between perception and reality if our perceptions are indelibly flawed. Indeed, given this fact, how could we know what reality is really like? In effect, Aiken has imposed a Kantian structure on his world, that is, one in which we are limited or trapped within the phenomenal world of our own perceptions without any way of ever knowing what the external noumenal reality is really like. This means that if we are going to find solutions to our philosophical and psychological problems, they must be found within the phenomenal world without any appeal to externals truths or beings like God or gods. If this leads to paradoxes, contradictions and inconsistencies, then we must accept these as the unalterable conditions of our existence.

The second observation is the inevitable realisation that if the mind is inherently deceptive and unreliable, then we can be certain of absolutely nothing—except that fact. This makes self-alienation a permanent feature of human life, not a 'problem' to be solved but rather a 'mystery' to be understood and lived with as best we can. This conclusion—already available to Aiken at the outset of his career—helps explain the remarkable thematic consistency of his work from its beginnings near the start of the twentieth century to his death in 1973. He knew from the outset that we cannot 'solve' or change our existential situation, but can only achieve deeper, more detailed understanding of it in our ever-varying circumstances and that wisdom consists in understanding, accepting—and even enjoying—this fact however painful it may be to our pre-conceived notions of stability and self-satisfaction.

It should also be noted that the alienated relationship between the ego and the Self or mind shows that Aiken was confronted by a genuine choice in the nature of his philosophy. Rather than accept deficient perception as a fact of existence, he could have elected to 'solve' the problem by ridding the Self of its troublesome egos. Certain mystical philosophies have adopted this strategy, denying the egos and even the Self any real, that is, ultimate existence beyond being mere temporary conventions. However, Aiken refuses this strategy because he accepts the world and us as we are, deceptions and all, in his own version of the teaching that nirvana—the ultimate truth—and samsara—the deceptive conventional world—are one.

Alienated Dream Egos.

So far we have only considered the alienation felt by the eccentric Self towards its dream egos. These, however, may harbour similar feelings about the mind or Self they inhabit. To them, the mind is often a strange and dangerous place requiring careful exploration. This would be unnecessary were the mind a familiar place. Perhaps the best summary of this situation is found in *The Kid*:

> Dark was the forest, dark was the mind:
> dark the trail that he stooped to find:
> dark, dark, dark in the midnight lost,
> in self's own midnight, the seeking ghost.
>
> (*The Kid*, VII, 858-859)

The "seeking ghost" (ibid.) is a dual reference to the worldly quest of the Self as the Kid and the inner travels of the Kid as a dream ego journeying through the mind or Self. Similar references to the dream ego as explorer are found in *The Pilgrimage of Festus* where the dream ego enters the "net of himself" (*Festus*, IV, 1, 258) and the "forest of departed gods" (ibid., III, 1, 246). In *Preludes for Memnon* the dream ego travels to the verge of the mind and on a ship beneath the "mind of stars" (*Memnon*, XLI, 546); and in *Time In the Rock*, it passes through a room filled with confusing voices (*Time in the Rock*, LVI, 718-719). The dream egos, which act on the behalf of the eccentric Self, are alienated because the Self does not possess self-knowledge and is, therefore, a place of dangerous uncertainties. Their task, as will be recalled, is to remedy the situation and to help the Self gain at least some reliable self-knowledge. Because of the continuing uncertainties, the dream egos not only feel lost in the mind or Self, but also feel threatened. For example, the Old Man in *The Pilgrimage of Festus* is surprised that the mind "lays not hold of us / And flings us out and down like fiery dust-motes" (*Festus*, IV, 4, 268).

Because the relationship between the ego, the mind or Self and the cosmos are analogues of one another, that is, Self or mind is to ego as cosmos is to Self or mind, we may conclude that whatever is true in one set of these relationships is true in the other. Consequently, we should be able to predict that the concentric Self often finds the external world uncertain and threatening. Aiken's imagery indicates that such is indeed the case. In the early poems this idea is conveyed by such images as "spears of rain" (*The House of Dust*, IV, 5, 188) and the "savage forest of earth" (*Senlin*, II, 4, 210). Later works present the same concept by means of images of the Self trapped in the cosmos like an insect in a web, (*Memnon*, XII, 511) and as lost, bewildered by surrounding chaos, "lost in a roar of sea, [a] Rover[] of chaos"(*Li Po*, IV, 906).

The Secret of Identity.

In light of the enormous difficulties besetting the quest for identity, it seems an almost hopeless undertaking, a prolonged exercise in self-frustration. Aiken intentionally creates this despondent mood, intent on driving his readers into a corner so that in desperate circumstances his seemingly nonsensical, or, at the very least, highly unconventional solution will get a hearing. His concerns about the reader's willingness to explore his ideas is not without reason since much of Aiken's writing is nothing less than a drawn out—albeit disguised—challenge to the usual and conventional concept of identity as a collection of consistently stable characteristics.

His attack is 'disguised' because Aiken does not openly oppose this conventional concept; instead, he incorporates it into his dialectic and gradually reveals its untenability. Ultimately, his aim is to convince us that the problem is the solution: identity *is* change; it *is* the dramas which the dream egos and the Self enact. We are, personally and essentially as human beings precisely the thing—our seemingly endless quest for an identity—that we seek to escape and must learn to accept this fact. Ironically, the *real* problem of identity in Aiken's writing is not that it cannot be found but rather that it cannot be avoided. In short, as long as we seek our identity and act in harmony with our essential nature as a quest, we have it. Our difficulties arise because we reject what has been given us in favour of an impossible ideal, stable Self.

The suspicion that we might have to abandon the quest for a stable and permanent identity, occurs early in Aiken's writing. Forslin asks, "And am I one, or a million men?" (*Forslin*, IV,4, 93) and later says,

> Tired of change I seek the unmoving centre—
> But is it moveless,—or are all things turning?
> Great wheels revolve, I fall among them and die.
> My veins are streets. Millions of men rush through them,
> Which, in this terrible multitude is I?
>
> (*The Jig of Forslin*, V, 6, 111)

The protagonist of *The House of Dust*, experiences himself as "dissolved and woven again" (*Dust*, I, 1,122) in the rains, an image also suggesting that identity is neither stable nor permanent. An inner voice talks to Festus of "the multitudes within you" (*Festus*, I, 1,224) and later, in the image of the forest—"these trees / Which are yourself" (*Festus* I, 3,251)— we have an image communicating the idea that there is no single Self, and that, like the forest Festus saw rising and falling within him, (*Festus*, 1, 2, 225) no permanent self can be found. In later long poems, the image of the Self as an actor with multifarious roles is used to express this same idea, which is perhaps best summarised in the following lines:

> "This 'I', this moving 'I', this focal 'I,'
> which changes when it dreams the butterfly,
> into the thing it dreams of; liquid 'I'
> how many guises and disguises this
> nimblest of actors takes . . .
>
> (*A Letter from Li Po*, V, 907)

However, Aiken does not want us to conclude that because identity is fluid that it is, therefore, beyond our grasp. Quite the contrary, identity is omnipresent, both in the dramas enacted by the dream egos and in the roles played by the Self in the world. This idea is most directly formulated in *A Letter from Li Po* :

> In every part we play, we play ourselves;
> even the secret doubt to which we come
> beneath the changing shapes of self and thing,
> yes, even this, at last, if we should call
> and dare to name it, we would find
> the only voice that answers is our own.
> We are once more defrauded by the mind.
>
> (*A Letter from Li Po*, V, 908)

This statement is made in response to the observation that the Self is not stable and seems to be lost in an overwhelming welter of easily changing roles. It is not the concept of 'identity' per se that we must give up but rather the notion that we have a single *real* identity that is somehow primary to all the other lesser identities. Even if we think we are only acting, or faking our various roles, we must not despair because, paradoxically, the act is real; indeed, the act actually *is* who we are: we cannot lose ourselves even in a multitude of roles because we will find ourselves again in each part, albeit in a new transformation. The "poor king" in *Preludes for Memnon,* is advised to praise the queen's "false beauty which is richly true" (*Memnon*, XLVIII, 556). Her cosmetic and 'false' mask is as much hers as her supposedly 'real' face. In *Time in the Rock,* the speaker tells the lady that although she is a "character in a play" (*Time*, LXXX, 740), her lie "becomes a truth" (ibid.) and is a part of God's calculations. Each of us is an act and no matter how hard or how skilfully we call into the world, "The only voice that answers is our own." (*Li Po*, V, 908). Thus, if the problem of identity is anywhere, it lies in the fact that we cannot escape it!

A bewildering number of questions arise from this concept of identity. For example, if the act *is* our identity, then a 'play' entitled 'The Quest For Identity' is, in fact, what and who we are. But then, why do we seek what we already possess? Why do we feel compelled to seek the unrealistic goal of a stable identity knowing full well such a goal is forever beyond our grasp? Even more drastic, could we have an identity if we decided to stop all acting and cling to one limited version of ourselves no matter what? That would be living a lie, but then so is constantly changing from one identity to the next. Are we all condemned to be, literally, living lies?

Solipsism.

One of the most important consequences of the impossibility of escaping or avoiding identity is the seeming inevitability of solipsism. Of this philosophical position there are essentially two varieties: a metaphysical solipsism maintaining that Self is *all* that exists; and epistemological solipsism which holds that all perceptions are irremediably subjective and that in a sense, Self is all we can know. Evidence suggests that Aiken tends toward the latter, epistemological solipsism. Take, for example, the following quotation from *Time in the Rock* :

> Tired of the long soliloquy of the mind
> he walked into the wind and heard
> his own soliloquy magnificently abroad
> the wild original word around him flowing
> the word uttered without knowing
> framed by no mind, flying from no mouth
>
> the drowning one balanced breathless in the wind
> lost in speech
> striving in haste to know the ever from the each
> in vain to find
> the leaf of leaves the wave of waves
> the meaning of meaning
>
> (*Time in the Rock*, XLIX, 713)

There is no possibility of escape from identity here. Another quotation from the same poem puts the same idea in a different, more startling, perspective:

> 'this is 'you', this headline in the news,
> the news is 'you', is old already, undiscovered
> is 'you', too, long discovered. Greet your face
> dispersed in such terms, phrased and rephrased,
> speak to the farthest star, which is yourself.
>
> (*Time in the Rock*, X, 673)

Aiken draws attention to the "'you'" (ibid.) in single quotation marks so that readers will not take this term in its literal sense, that is, will recognise that this 'you' is no more than another role or fiction enacted by the Self. Indeed, even the audiences before whom we act are "flattering multiplications of [ourselves]" (*Time*, LXVII, 729) not in a metaphysical sense, but rather epistemologically because we see others in our own terms, from our own perspective and through our own thoughts and emotions. In that sense, any audience, metaphysically real or not, is "imaginary" (ibid.) because we have re-shaped it to our specifications.

The situation described in theses lines encourages the conclusion that the world functions like a mirror in which we constantly encounter ourselves because all our perceptions are re-shaped according to our personal specifications. The truth is that no matter from what angle we approach this subject, we cannot escape ourselves regardless of where we turn or what mood we are in. This idea is elaborated in a long passage from *The House of Dust*, that says, in part,

> This water says there is some secret in you
> Akin to my clear beauty, beauty swaying
> To mirror beauty silently responsive
> To all that circles you. This bare tree says
> . . . .
> There is some cold austerity in you
> A frozen strength with roots long gnarled in rocks
>
> (*The House of Dust*, IV, 8, 181)

and then adds, "And so all things discern me, name me, praise me" (*Dust*, IV, 8 182). In *Preludes for Memnon*, there is a reference to this "mad world of mirrors" (*Memnon*, XXIX, 535) and in *Time in the Rock* it is asserted that we see "ourselves in mirror of all minds" (*Time*, IV, 668). These lines reveal another aspect of Aiken's belief, namely, that we are what we perceive: it cannot be otherwise since we perceive what we are! In effect, each person is locked into a 'circle of identities' which he or she cannot escape.

Aiken conveys the same idea in another way. If we are always reflected by the world, then we may claim that the world repeats or mimics us. The theme of mimicry is especially prevalent in his later work. In *Preludes for Memnon* it is seen as an essential feature of the cosmos:

> O just God
> Remind us, with the mirror and the sea,
> With ice, and the bright parrot, and the moon,
> And the dear dream that shakes our limbs in sleep,
> How all of nature is shot through with this
> Sweet mimicry.
>
> (*Preludes for Memnon*, XI, 510)

If nature is a mimic, then it follows logically that humans will only encounter only echoes or parodies of themselves. We will always hear "own soliloquy magnificently abroad" (*Time*, XLIX, 713.)

Narcissus

Since our lives are inevitably self-centred in some way or another, it is quite appropriate that the figure of Narcissus, who, without exaggeration, may be claimed as his image of man, is common in Aiken's writing. Though not always explicitly identified as Narcissus, the self-centred nature of his protagonists is frequently revealed by their performances and thoughts before a mirror, as for example, Senlin, who poses grandly in front of a mirror and asks himself questions about his identity:

> Is it I who stand in question here,
> Asking to know my name?
> It is: yet I know whither I go
> Nor why; nor whence I came.
>
> (*Senlin: A Biography*, II, 10, 219)

In episodes too numerous to mention, throughout Aiken's poems readers will find references to Narcissus or to situations in which the theme of narcissistic self-attention is prominent. After all, everything reflects, or acts as a mirror for, everything else. Sometimes the emphasis will be on the previously discussed narcissistic nature of human knowledge and perception; sometimes on God as a narcissist looking into the mirror of His creation; and sometimes on the world as a mirror in front of which we posture endlessly in a variety of roles. The uses of this theme are virtually endless because for Aiken, the narcissistic nature of our very being is an article of faith—not because Aiken desires it so but because according to Aiken's philosophy, it is the logical consequence of the nature of the cosmos and the operations of human perceptive faculties.

Readers are bound to notice the ludicrous vanity occasionally displayed by the numerous Narcissus figures in Aiken's poems, and the silly and even grotesque performances they often put on for themselves. This is Aiken's way of suggesting the inherently comic structure of existence, that is, the notion that humour, satire, mockery and self-mockery are unavoidable in a universe of mimics and mimes, that nothing, not even God Himself is exempt from parody and caricature by His own creations. Gazing into the mirror, the Self soon discovers that it is somewhat ridiculous, both in its infinitely malleable being but also in its expectations for a single, dignified identity.

If everything in the world acts as a mirror, if "the only voice that answers is our own" (*Li Po*, V, 908), then the objective knowledge valued by science is impossible to acquire because all knowledge is inevitably subjective, a notion dramatically portrayed in *Time in the Rock*. The Self, arms spread out "godlike and fisherlike the world to gather" (*Time*, XCI, 752) finds that it cannot capture the water, that is, the substance of the cosmos, and that the net traps more junk than fish, that is, more trivia and nonsense than knowledge. Even more important is the fact that the net brings back, or reflects, the greatness or the weakness of the thrower himself which is yet another way of indicating that the fisherman captures only knowledge of himself.

A further consequence of this epistemological solipsism is the discovery of the apparently inevitable solitude of the Self. The belief that all beings are insurmountably alone is manifested in the kind of poems most commonly written by Aiken, dramatic monologues in which readers seldom encounter someone other than the protagonist. Most, if not all discussion partners are the dream egos created by the Self in its concentric phase of consciousness. The Heraclitean nature of the universe, in addition to the relentless changes to which the Self is subject, also have the effect of isolating each individual, making it difficult, if not impossible to identify something. How can one recognise something that is never the same? Consequently, the Self feels it always dwells among strangers, and is, therefore, more inclined to turn inward to its own resources, a strategy which in turn re-enforces the narcissistic and solipsistic trends inherent in the Self. Intensifying the solitude effected by change is the fact that we only see ourselves in others. We cannot see beyond ourselves and thus, are once again locked into a self-centred world. Under these circumstances it is, therefore, only logical to ask whether knowledge of others is even a possibility. How can we get to know others if "the only voice that answers is our own" (*Li Po*, V, 908)? However, despite the apparent hopelessness of our wholly isolated situation, Aiken does not seem to regard it as utterly unfortunate: "Sole pride and loneliness: it is the state/the kingdom rather of all things." (*Li Po*, III, 905). Difficult as this solitude may be, Aiken appears to regard it as a privilege.

Self as World and Music.

It might well be argued that the omnipresence of identity, and the absolute impossibility of escaping it, do not solve the problems faced by Aiken's protagonists. They want a specific, singular identity, not a myriad of temporary identities; they also want genuine knowledge about other things, not merely about themselves. Indeed, since Self is encountered everywhere, the problem of identity has been intensified with the discovery of Self in all things; furthermore, when Self is reflected from everywhere, unity, one of the essential conditions for acquiring identity, has not been achieved either.

Aiken's counsel in the light of these facts is that our inner and outer multiplicity should frankly be accepted; he tells us to "be yourself / the multitude you are" (*Memnon*, XLII, 548). The frequent occurrence of the image of the Self as an entire world suggests that Aiken takes his advice seriously. At no time in his writing does he indicate that humans are to reject any of the inner and outer roles, although his characters may mistakenly endeavour to do so. They quickly discover their error, since the 'drama of rejection' will simply be added to a list of roles and plays which they have enacted. Aiken, in other words, holds that Self should not strive to be less than it is, which is everything: "You are all things, and all things are your soul" (*Memnon*, VIII, 507). This doctrine, while perhaps unable to solve the problems of fragmentation, is capable of resolving the dilemma of alienation. The eccentric Self living in the ordinary world learns that it need not choose between images to express or roles to play since its essence is revealed in all of them as well as in its dream egos. One of the ways in which Aiken conveys this theme is by describing identity as the sum of our dreams, perceptions, thoughts and deeds:

> ... We are the sum of all these accidents—
> Compounded all our days of idiot trifles ...
>
> *(Preludes for Memnon*, XXIX, 534)

Elsewhere in the same poem, the protagonist refers to the lady as a "golden sum" (*Memnon*, II, 528). The concept of identity as a chord also contains the same idea of a multitudinous Self: "You and I / are things compounded of time's heart-beats ..." (*Memnon*, XXI, 522). Furthermore, man is no different than anything else in the cosmos since, according to Aiken, "all things are music" (*Festus*, IV, 3,264). Nowhere in Aiken's corpus of work is this idea stated more strikingly than in the following lines:

> The thing itself—by God, the thing is music.
> For when she touches me or when she speaks—!
> Then comes the little fly's wing of a flame:
> ....
> .... And the thing is music.
> It is a sound of many instruments—
> Complex, diverse, an alchemy of voices,
> Brass melting into silver, silver smoothly
> Dissolving into gold; and then the harsh
> And thickening discord ...
>
> (*Preludes for Memnon*, XVI, 571)

Later the protagonist adds,

> This is a wondrous thing, that if she touch
> My fingernail with but her fingernail
> ....
> I am become a music, chaos, light and sound,
> I am no longer I: I am a world.
>
> (*Preludes for Memnon*, XVI, 518)

The positive, joyous tone of these lines displays the relief and pleasure to be found in accepting ourselves as we are: many, multiple, a whole world, joined to all other beings by the same musical essence. One of the glories of love is that it is able to bring us to this realisation so easily.

Self as Zero and Time.

The solution of accepting one's multiplicity is not, however, as simple as it seems, for the sum total of our identity is frequently found to be zero: "You are all things and nothing" (*Memnon*, VIII, 507) says the protagonist and then adds:

CONRAD AIKEN'S PHILOSOPHY OF CONSCIOUSNESS

> All this is nothing, all that we said is nothing:
> Your eyes, your hair, are nothing, your grief, your tears,—
> Nothing, nothing as goldenrod is nothing
>
> (*Preludes for Memnon*, IX, 507)

Later in a grand finale, he proudly addresses the lady as

> Majestic instant,—
> Great golden sum of dream whose truth is zero,
> Zero of thought, whose truth is god, and life,—
>
> (*Preludes for Memnon*, XXIII, 528)

Not only is the sum of human identity often nothing, but that of the cosmos as well: "neighbours, I have come / from a vast everything whose sum is nothing" (*Memnon*, LIII, 560). Similar ideas are expressed in the prayer to Lord Zero in *Time in the Rock*:

> I saw all these things and they meant nothing
> I touched all these things and they meant nothing
> I saw all these faces Lord and they meant nothing
> Lord Zero they meant nothing
>
> (*Time in the Rock*, LXIX, 731)

Later, in the same section the protagonist proclaims that "we ourselves go forth again on that wind / to become Lord Zero" (*Memnon*, LXIX, 732).

That our identity should suddenly be zero, after the frequent emphasis that Self is all, is probably the central paradox in Aiken's conception of the Self. To understand this essential paradox it is necessary to return to our original speculations regarding the changeful nature of the Self. The seeker of identity, it must be recalled, is subject to a wide variety of changes: the eccentric and concentric rhythm of the Self and the random changes of thought, perception, role and dream. The inevitability of these alterations leads to the conclusion that the essence of Self and the world is change. Further consideration shows that change involves time. Aiken, too, is aware of this since in his writings the Self and time are often identified. The Self is always part of a movement, or an 'instant' if we choose temporal terms. The description of the lady as a "majestic instant" (*Memnon*, XIV, II, 528) makes this quite clear. The following quotation expresses the same idea:

> You are a clock
> Unique, absolved, ridiculous, profound,
> The clock that knows, if but it will, its tick
> To be a tick and nothing but a tick.
>
> (*Preludes for Memnon*, XLIII, 548-9)

Broaching the topic of identity, one of Aiken's speakers asks, "How shall we name/this instant which is you . . ." (*Memnon*, XXIV, 1, 527). Man and time may also be identified by images involving the heart as seen in the following sample of phrases: "his heart ticks out the hours" (*Forslin*, I,156); "time in the rock and in the human heart" (*Memnon*, XLIV, 551) and "Her heart is like an hourglass" (*Time*, LXXXIV, 743).

The identification of the Self with change and time leads naturally to the notion that Self is no particular thing, or, expressed more flamboyantly, 'nothing'. This means that we cannot properly identify the Self with any of its specific dreams, thoughts, or actions. Choosing one among the various dream egos and or the Self's worldly roles is not a viable option in the pursuit of identity. In the western philosophical tradition, this position, that is, the notion that Self cannot be identified with the contents of the stream of consciousness was advanced by the English philosopher Hume. Aiken, however, would say that Hume missed the significance of his discovery: while Self is not any of the contents of the 'stream of consciousness', the very movement of images, feelings and ideas *is* the Self we seek so desperately. Our identity is itself *the quest for identity* and not any one of the images inner or outer phenomena we encounter on this quest. The following lines express the paradoxical nature of this situation:

> Take comfort if you can in this mad waste.
> I am the leaf that dies upon your hand:
> Dismiss me with your dying. We are undone
> *With permanence in impermanence, the flowing*
> Of shape to shape which means all shapelessness.
> Is this my hand or yours? Ah, no such thing.
> It is the fog which curtsies to the fog:
> The god who finds himself a fraud: *the wind*
> *From nowhere blown to nowhere.*
> (*Preludes for Memnon*, XXII, 526-527; italics added)

Further consideration makes it obvious that if identity is the process, that is, if identity is the quest for identity itself, then it follows that the Self is 'nothing' insofar as it is a process sustained only by continuous acts of negation. After all, motion is the passage of things or states out of existence or from one place to another; in either case, a condition or situation or a place is being negated by being 'rejected' in favour of something else. Similarly, the existence of the Self depends on the continuous negation of previous feelings, dreams, ideas and perceptions or, to put in more spectacular language, identity or Self depends on the 'continuity of negation or nothing'. Aiken expresses this belief in several ways:

> .... how far more wretched we
> Who have no selves, who are but lyre and flute,
> Broken by him or blown upon or mute!
> Only in silence, only in nothingness
> We have our being ... Let silence be our God!
>
> (*The Pilgrimage of Festus*, IV, 4, 267)

Briefly reviewing the passage, one notes that "no selves" (ibid.) means 'no permanent selves' in the conventional sense; that the negating process is referred to in the word "broken" (ibid.); and that "silence" (ibid.) is equated with "nothingness" (ibid.). The silence or nothingness of perpetually being 'no fixed thing' is seem in this quotation as the very ground or basis of our being. A similar idea is found in *Preludes for Memnon*.

> Magnificent angel, treader of bright thought,
> Your being, which is nothing, in a nothing ...
>
> (*Preludes for Memnon*, XXIV, 1, 527)

If the ground of the Self's being is nothing, we may conclude that man, too, is nothing—a conclusion that makes sense as long as we bear in mind that 'nothing' refers to the negating necessary to keep any process going. This idea is explicit in the statement by the protagonist of *Blues For Ruby Matrix* that he is "the conscious No One, watching Nought from Nowhere" (*Ruby Matrix*, V, 618). In light of Aiken's belief that the Self is what it perceives, then this claim is quite reasonable; if he watches or focuses on the "Nought" (ibid.), the negation inherent in any process, then that is what he must be. Similarly, man is identified with Lord Zero, Aiken's symbol of nothingness and the negating process. At the end of his prayer in *Time in the Rock*, the speaker states that "we ourselves go forth again on that wind / to becomes Lord Zero" (*Time*, LXIX, 731). The same theme is expressed with great subtlety in *The Kid* where it is found in one of Aiken's the delightfully ambiguous phrase "that was no horse, that was no man" (*The Kid*, I, 847). The Kid, the ever westward striving frontier spirit, is the outer, specifically American historical counterpart of the endless inward quest for identity. In other words, the Kid is no man because he represents a historical and personal developmental process.

Creation Ex Nihilo

However, a process cannot live by negation alone because *something* must be created in order to be negated. This necessity impels Aiken to adopt one of the most controversial ideas in Christian theology: *creatio ex nihilo*, that is, creation out of nothing. This complex doctrine, which shall be considered in great detail in a later chapter, is referred to in *Time in the Rock* when the speaker, addressing Lord Zero, says, "yours was the conception" (*Time*, LXIX, 730). The impact of this line lies in the clash between Lord Zero as the symbol of negation and the notion of him conceiving, that is, bringing into existence. If Lord Zero gives birth, that is, is the origin of things, then obviously we have a case of *creatio ex nihilo*. This *ex nihilo* theme is especially important in relationship to Aiken's theory of self-creation as seen in the following lines:

> . . . *we are nothing:*
> and yet we speak.
>
> And thus in speaking come
> *to something*, which is yourselves;
> you in a row waiting for words, you who listen
> with round mouths to the round words;
> and I who speak them, an old man leaning forward,
> an old man leaning from an open mouth.
> (*Time in the Rock*, LXXXVII, 747. Italics added)

The belief that man is a process and, therefore, in a sense, nothing, has a number of associated themes, the most important of which is that all means nothing:

> I saw all these things and they meant nothing
> I touched all these hands and they meant nothing
> I saw all these faces Lord and they meant nothing
> Lord Zero they meant nothing
> (*Time in the Rock*, LXIX, 730)

Naturally, "meant nothing" (ibid.) is not to be understood as 'without meaning' but rather as 'intended nothing' which, in an ironic sense, is exactly what the Self intends as it grows and changes; it means to keep the negation, the nothing, in motion as a necessary part of its development. After all, there can be no growth without 'negation' of what has existed before. That Aiken intended the distinction between 'without meaning' and 'meaningless' is clear from the following line: "And all is meaningless . . . Or all means nothing?" (*Memnon*, IX, 508). The difference between these two possibilities is that the first means 'lack of meaning', while the second refers to the negating process, an intentional activity of 'meaning or intending nothing' that already exists. Later in the same poem, a similar distinction is brought to our attention in the line, "Nothing to say, you say? Then we'll say nothing" (*Memnon*, LIII, 561). Here, too, we cannot help but conclude that the Self continuously means, intends, aims at, nothing to maintain the process that it actually is.

The Endless Journey of Self.

If the Self 'means nothing' other than its negating process, then in a sense it is also true that Self has no purpose. At least such is the conclusion that Aiken draws and expresses most clearly in the poems of his middle period. In *Landscape West of Eden*, the speaker twice proclaims that the journey, the evolution of consciousness, has neither purpose nor reason: "and you will say, 'You went further,' and I will say, / But to no purpose' . . ." (*Eden*, I, 623). Aiken chooses to crush our hopes in this manner because the evolution of consciousness is to be undertaken for its own sake. We are not to seek any rewards extrinsic to the process itself, and if we do, we are setting ourselves up for disappointment because no such rewards will be forthcoming. On the positive side, however, is that the denial of purpose also means that there is no termination to the development of consciousness. Since it is the nature of a purpose to terminate once it is fulfilled, a process without an end may be said to have no purpose.

The fact that consciousness and the Self are a process, and specifically, a process of continuously seeking an identity, leads to one of the most startling paradoxes found in Aiken's work. If the seeker of identity believes he has attained it, and, therefore, halts the process which is his very essence, he has, in supposedly 'finding it', lost it. On the other hand, if he believes he lacks identity and strives to attain it, in the striving itself he has what he seeks. Yet to keep it, he must continue to pursue the identity he now has as if he did not have it! The struggle for identity may therefore be characterised as a 'lie' although without this 'lie' the Self could not exist. Those who do not realise this situation suffer agonies in the pursuit of what they already have, while those who do know these facts may suffer agonies in having to maintain a lie for the sake of existence. Aiken, however, would advise the latter group their pain is needless. 'Truth' in his view is not nearly as important as life: "the one thing the heart needs the need to live." (*Time*, XXVII, 692).

If identity is an endless journey in a Heraclitean universe of perpetual change, is there any way in which the Self can achieve a measure of stability and rest? Unlikely as it seems at first glance, there is: a measure of stable identity can be achieved by continuously duplicating or repeating one image or content of consciousness and referring to this as a 'fixed Self'. Perfect duplication is, of course, impossible and the fact remains that the Self exists only through the continuous acts of duplicating but for those who realistically accept the nature of the universe in which we find ourselves, the general similarity of the images, feelings, ideas and perceptions is sufficient. They are satisfied with a 'stable' identity that is, in actuality, only a convention but a welcome convention at that.

Satisfying as this discovery may be, it contains an inherent danger, namely, that repetition will become a habit that hinders future risk-taking and creativity. Such a turn of events runs against the grain of Aiken's philosophy of the evolution of consciousness: "the habitual hero is no hero" (*Time*, L, 713). Implicit in this notion is that everyone should at least try to be heroic, that is, a creative risk-taker in the quest for identity and further self-evolution. The ending of *Time*, also makes it clear that man should be open to the world and its changes:

> Simple one, simpleton,
> When will you learn the flower's simplicity—
> Lie open to all comers, permit yourself
> To be rifled—fruitfully—by other selves?
> Self, and the other self—permit them, permit them—
> (*Time in the Rock*, XCVI, 757)

The other selves" (ibid.) can refer both to the people we encounter in our daily lives and to the various identities we create in our pursuit of an ever-elusive identity. Rather than minimise changes—which are often experienced as violations or 'riflings'—we should remain open to them and, thereby, remain true to our essence or nature. We must, in other words, always be prepared to lose our apparent momentary identity so that his true identity can be maintained. The last stanza of *Preludes for Memnon* Aiken exhorts us to accept struggle and change:

> A trumpet blast, that calls dead men to arms
> The granite's pity for the cloud, the whisper
> Of time to space
> (*Preludes for Memnon*, LXIII, 573)

Those involved in the process of negation and identity seeking are always, in a sense, dead, 'passing away' but this process is the very essence of their lives. Their only duty is to continue forward and by doing so, they will attain more real identity and more consciousness than they would by opposing their own nature.

Chapter Five

Further Issues in the Pursuit of Identity and Consciousness

Terror of Chaos

Terror, fear and even horror play a significant role in the process of attaining the various types of consciousness because, as we shall see, in Aiken's view, consciousness cannot be attained without an extreme experience of fear. The first task in clarifying this idea will be to examine in some detail the sources of terror and the circumstances in which it occurs.

One of the major sources of terror is the sudden discovery of a threatening inner chaos. For example, *Preludes for Memnon* begins with the sudden realisation that the "mind too has its snows, its slippery paths / Walls bayoneted with ice." (*Memnon*, I, 498) This observation, with its unavoidable suggestions of injury, is followed by an experience of

> the uprush of angelic wings, the beating
> of wings demonic, from the abyss of the mind
> The darkness filled with leathery whistling wings
> Numberless as the flakes of angelic snow,
> The deep void swarming with wings and the sound of wings,
> The winnowing of chaos, the aliveness
> Of depth and depth and depth dedicated to death.
> (*Preludes for Memnon*, I, 498-9).

Here, too, the connotations of disorder, potential threat and danger are unmistakable in the diction and overwhelm the weaker, positive connotations of references to angels. A similar discovery of chaos forms the substance of an almost identical passage in a later part of the poem. Staring into the mirror, Narcissus finds himself in a horrific form:

> . . . . a shape he saw
> unknown before,—obscene, disastrous, huge,—
> Huge as the world and formless . . . Was this he?
> This dumb, tumultuous all-including horror?
>
> (*Preludes for Memnon*, XVI, 519).

This level of consciousness is the same as that at the beginning of the poem, where the speaker's phrase, "and this is you" (*Memnon*, I, 500) shows that he, like Narcissus, recognises himself in the chaos he experiences. In these episodes, both characters possess, and are, at least momentarily, caught in narcissistic consciousness which, ironically, is not as pleasant as some might think, especially when it reveals the Heraclitean nature of the universe and the Self.

Part of what makes this inner chaos so unendurable is that the Self encounters, among other things, the enormous mass of utterly inconsequential material which seems to be the very substance of its being. If the Self is really this flow of trivial perceptions, memories, thoughts and feelings, then perhaps the Self is not worth the enormous trouble required by the evolution of consciousness. Why bother to get such junk? Moreover, the Self cannot help but note the randomness with which these realisations of inner chaos occur. These realisations undermine its concept of identity, not only by showing the Self to be composed of trivia, but also as subject to random dissolution and consequently, as totally unreliable and perhaps unworthy of any effort to attain. However, the full significance of this encounter is that chaos is man's mother. In the opening incident of *Preludes for Memnon*, man is described as "the god who seeks his mother chaos" (*Memnon*, I, 500) and still later as a child who, like Macduff, is "untimely ripped from chaos" (*Memnon*, XI, 510). The idea that chaos is man's mother is also found in *Time in the Rock* where woman is described as the "winged body of delightful chaos" (*Time*, XXII, 685). Chaos is also embodied in the figure of Clytemnestra whose totally unforeseen murder of Agamemnon brings disorder into the world. It requires only a moment's reflection to see that if chaos is man's mother as well as his mate, then the fear of chaos is the fear of one's very source of being and of one's partner in future creativity. It is fear of the very thing which permits one to live. Those who find this terrifying—and all do at first—are wholly alienated from themselves and from the source of their freedom. It is, after all, the sudden ingression of chaos that dissolves the falsely static identity which hampers the growth of the Self and the evolution of consciousness. Chaos provides the vital 'freedom from self' needed to reform and thus, while initially terrifying, guarantees freedom and salvation. The unexpected eruption of chaos may cause pain, but as Aiken notes, "man's salvation rose through pain" (*Rose*, IV, 4, 51). What we observe, in effect, is the Self's fear of its destiny, that is, of all that would be helpful to it which the Self easily confuses with foes and fate.

That chaos can also be perceived positively is demonstrated in the following lines:

> .... Is it this?
> Yes; and the chaos, then—the chaos, then,—
> Ah, what a heaven of sweetness of pure sound
> It yields to God! A clear voice, like a star,—
> And farther off another,—then another,—
> Each like an angel, taking his own station,—
> (*Preludes for Memnon*, XVI, 518)

The Self perceiving chaos in this manner is in a different state of consciousness than the Self reacting with fear. In this quotation, it must be noted that chaos and music, "the thing itself" (*Memnon*, XVI, 517) are identified. Music, as there will be further opportunity to observe, is one of Aiken's metaphors for the cosmic process. This fact also supports the contention that the Self really has nothing to fear in the encounter with its own essence, since it is also an encounter with its inner creative powers.

Terror of Death

For the Self endeavouring at all costs to maintain a stable, static identity, the encounter with chaos also produces the terror of death. Belief in a static identity encourages the attitude that change is the equivalent of death, since, in change, something passes away. The encounter with inner chaos inevitably produces momentous changes in the Self. However, in Aiken's view, this 'death' is entirely natural, is required, in fact, for growth for which reason everything in the cosmos, including the mind and the Self are "dedicated to death" (*Memnon*, I, 500). Here, too, the terror experienced by the Self is directed towards that which offers a multitude of benefits if it is accepted in the proper way as an opportunity for further development. This same pattern shall repeat itself in almost every case of terror in Aiken's work. It may be accurately described as the 'terror of salvation', 'terror' because of the death of an old, comfortable and seemingly stable identity, but 'salvation' because it opens new vistas for the evolution of consciousness.

Terror of Facticity

In order to escape the horrors of inner chaos, the Self may turn outward to the world and attempt to take refuge in the apparent simplicity and stability of outer things and events. This strategy leads to the discovery of 'facticity', that all things and events are exactly what they are and nothing more or less.

> What the moon says is moon, and all compact;
> What the act says is act, and only act;
> What the clock says, with the algebra's cold face,
> Is times and time, spaces and space.
>
> *(Time in the Rock,* XXIII, 687)

Facticity, plain matter-of-factness, is seen here in that all things 'speak' or directly manifest their own being—and nothing more. This can be terrifying to the Self because it forces the realisation that other entities or processes exist in their own right, cannot be wished away, or simply used for one's own purposes and in that sense, other entities not only juxtapose but oppose or challenge and limit the very being of the Self. They compete and are, in that sense, rivals in being. The Self realises that there is no ultimate explanation, no reason as to why it or the other things exist. They simply do so as inexplicable and mute facts that communicate their existence and nothing else. Moreover, in this experience of facticity, the Self faces the indissoluble difference between itself and everything else, and, thereby, experiences its ineluctable isolation. Indeed, the Self easily feels utterly overwhelmed, for which reason it experiences terror. There is an incident in *Preludes for Memnon* in which a child is suddenly confronted with the facticity of its existence; he hears music which "touches him with hands, stroking his hair / Gently as if to say why here we are,—"(*Memnon,* LIV, 562). Then

> Suddenly he is frightened—for no reason—
> Something mysterious has chilled him, left
> Somewhere an open door to darkness—
>
> *(Preludes for Memnon,* LIV, 562)

The child feels terror because it learns that it is here without reason, that our existence is, in that sense, irrational, and that we must learn to accept this fact.

This lesson is an important step in the attainment of consciousness because, obviously, consciousness—which for Aiken is self-consciousness—cannot develop without an experience of the Self's own existence, of its own absolute reality in the presence of other entities equally real. This experience, however, is fraught with terror for the reasons cited above, a terror that is intimately associated with the very birth of consciousness itself. Indeed, terror and consciousness, like the two sides of a coin, are correlatives, each necessary to the other: terror makes us aware or conscious of ourselves and consciousness of ourselves makes us experience terror. Yet, from Aiken's point of view, this situation is not entirely negative since the attainment of consciousness is of such great value that any price is worth it.

Another example of facticity, this time in connection with change is found in the following lines:

> Watch long enough, and you will see the leaf
> Fall from the bough. Without a sound it falls:
> And soundless meets the grass . . . And so you have
> A bare bough, and a dead leaf in dead grass.
> Something has come and gone. *And that is all.*
>
> But what were all the tumults of this action?
> What wars of atoms in the twig, what ruins,
> Fiery and disastrous, in the leaf?
> Timeless the tumult was, but gave no sign.
> *Only the leaf fell, and the bough is bare.*
>
> This is the world: *there is no more than this.*
> The unseen and disastrous prelude, shaking
> The trivial act from the terrific action.
> Speak: and the ghosts of change, past and to come
> Throng the brief word. The maelstrom has us all.
> (*Preludes for Memnon*, XIX, 520; italics added)

As soon as Self tries to articulate the utter simplicity of these changes, it is plunged back to the chaos it sought to avoid because the simplicity of these events is actually an illusion: they are, in fact, exceedingly complex. If we try to reflect this complexity in language, we become lost ourselves.

Terror of Essential Ignorance

Moreover, as the protagonist in *Preludes for Memnon* shows, the Self does not really know objects or events in its world: "What is this suchness that we talk of, lady? / What is a 'such' that we should make it speak?" (*Memnon*, XXXII, 537). He then proceeds to prove the simultaneous simplicity and complexity of these things, thereby vitiating the possibility of any essential knowledge of them. The facticity of things and events causes fear because the Self cannot escape being aware of their strangeness and of its own ignorance. Borrowing a word from Martin Heidegger, we might say that the Self is "thrown" into world it does not—and cannot—understand, at least not without a radical change in perception and attitude.

Naturally, if the Self were to use this frightening situation to question the adequacy of its way of perceiving and understanding the world, it would soon make progress in the evolution of consciousness and, thereby, lose much of its terror. Indeed, according to Aiken, much of our terror is caused by our struggles to escape terror. That is why he advises us to

> Indulge your terror: let him have his claws,
> His goblin snout, his fangs, his huge grimaces
> Which eat the fog, your house, your heart, yourself;
> Entice him............................
> ....So only
> You'll keep the little candle of your wits,
> And rise at daybreak—
>
> To another terror;
> And this is better still . . .
>
> (*Preludes for Memnon*, LV, 563-564)

Terror of Inner Evil, and Filth

Another source of terror is the Self's encounter with its own filthy and murderous nature. This discovery is needed because the Self must learn that "there is nothing pure" (*Time*, LXI, 724), and that foulness is also a part of life. The same is true of evil, and, as we have seen, of terror. Judging by the poem *Evil Is The Palindrome* ('evil' and 'live' are palindromes), Aiken believes that life and evil, like consciousness and terror, are, in effect, correlative terms. Each needs the other, though we must not, of course, understand his endorsement of evil in any superficial and vulgar sense. The evils to which Aiken is referring are the evolutionary murders of old, comfortable seemingly stable Selves, or, from another point of view, their suicide. Only by giving up old identities can we forge new ones, only by consciously slaying one state of mind can we achieve a higher, broader and more inclusive kind of consciousness. The speaker in *Time in the Rock* clearly perceives in man a "plan for murder unadmitted" (*Time*, XLIV, 709). Of course, the plan is only "unadmitted" (ibid.) by those who are too fearful to face the truth about the necessities of our evolutionary destiny and, therefore, turn down his invitation:

> Come, rooted ones, come radicals, come trees,
> whose powerful tentacles suck earth, and join
> the murderous angels; and let us dance together
> the dance of joyful cruelty, whence thrives
> the world of qualities which filth ordained.
>
> (*Time in the Rock*, XXVIII, 693)

The protagonist of *Preludes for Memnon*, utters similar sentiments:

> Then take your heart out and devour it mortal,
> Eat out its shreds of bitterness and taste
> The god you were before dishonour hid you.

CONRAD AIKEN'S PHILOSOPHY OF CONSCIOUSNESS

>..................................
>...................Hold out your hand and stare
>At fingers, palm and fingernails, the wrist
>Supple and strong, and wonder whence it comes,
>And what its purpose
>
>It's aim is murder:
>
><div align="right">(<i>Preludes for Memnon</i>, XLIX, 556)</div>

In these lines, we see a suggestion of another key idea in Aiken's philosophy of consciousness, namely, that as long as we accept change and evolution, and engage in it consciously and wilfully, we are 'divine' because we have put ourselves at one with the very nature of the universe. Resistance, however, brings us dishonour because it is a cowardly denial of our own nature; in fleeing from the horrors of murder and / or suicide, the Self turns from the source of its salvation, its own nature or essence. We must face the fact that the world's filth and evil are in each person, including ourselves. As the protagonist tells his lady after enumerating all the sins of Helen of Troy, "there is no treason here that is not you" (*Memnon*, XXX, 536). Like the lady, we must learn to accept that evil and filth are part of the riches of the cosmos, resources like any others, designed for profitable use. Referring to our tainted, morally polluted blood, he says

>For so it comes, from god.
>It is the sovereign stream, the source of all;
>Bears with it false and true, and dead and dying;
>The seed, the seedling; worlds, and worlds to come.
>Is there a treason here that is not you?
>Accept this logic, this dark blood of things.
>There is no treason here that is not you.
>
><div align="right">(<i>Preludes for Memnon</i>, XXX, 536)</div>

On the basis of this statement, it becomes evident that any endeavour at establishing a 'pure' virtue would destroy not only the foundations of life, but would also destroy virtue itself by cutting it off from its origin among the lower aspects of our natures:

>................There is no good,
>No sweet, no noble, no divine, no right
>But it is bred of rich economy
>Amongst the hothead factions of the soul.
>
><div align="right">(<i>Preludes for Memnon</i>, XXXI, 536)</div>

Since vice and virtue are so intimately connected or correlated, it follows that any effort to abandon vice paradoxically demands the abandonment of virtue as well. In more startling terms: to be a moralist, it is necessary to be an immoralist. Nature has made a shambles of humankind's conventional ethical standards which depend on one-sided definitions that ignore the inherent relativity of all human concepts. In a sense, the Self aware of these facts faces an ethical chaos which challenges it to use chaos and evil for positive growth.

Terror of Perception

Because perception can be terrifying to the Self, it can also be a starting point in the development of consciousness. This seems to be the point made in the following lines:

> Perception is the beginning, sweetheart, perception
> opens the window from which we view
> terror fluttering toward us down an empty road
> delight screaming on dark wings over the hill.
> Shall we run? Shall we stand still?
>
> (*Evil is the Palindrome*, 869)

Whether we run from evil or stand still makes no difference: obviously, there is no hope whatever of escaping the terror if perception is one of its sources. However, why would we want to flee? Without the terror resulting from our perceptions of the world, it would be impossible to attain consciousness. For this reason, we are asked to "praise the dreadful fountain of all blaze, . . . / of ethereal violent living and death-dealing powers" (*Evil is the Palindrome*, 869). Praise, intentional celebration is a more daring alternative than flight or denial since the Self will be subject to the facts of the universe no matter what it decides. Elsewhere in this poem, Aiken advises us to "live for the frontier of the daily unknown, of terror" (*Evil is the Palindrome*, 870), advice already given by suggesting that we "indulge our terror: (*Memnon*, LV, 563-564) and repeated in *Time in the Rock*:

> To face the terror in this rain that comes
> across the drowned world to the drowning window;
> be ignorant of rain, this unknown rain;
> unknown and wild as the world was to god
> when first he opened eyes—ah surely this
> were nobler answer than the glib speech of habit
> the well-worn words and ready phrase, that build
> comfortable walls against the wilderness?
> *Seeing, to know the terror of seeing:* being,
> to know the terror of being: knowing, to know
> the dreadfulness of knowledge:
>
> (*Time in the Rock*, XXV, 690; italics added)

Naturally, we cannot help but ask ourselves what makes perception so terrifying. To answer, it is necessary to recall that, according to Aiken, the Self is what it perceives, and since everything changes, alterations in perception cannot be avoided. In other words, the perception of an ever-changing universe confronts us with our own changes and 'deaths,' with the end of one identity and the birth of another which is itself soon doomed to die. Perceptions, then, brings us face to face with our inevitable mortality as well as with the understanding that our powers to change this situation are non-existent. Those unwilling to face this fact naturally fear perception and yet, how can perception be avoided?

One of the ways in which some people try to avoid all perception is by using language to build "comfortable walls" (*Time*, XXV, 690) against the flux of the world. This strategy is also mentioned in *Preludes for Memnon*, where the speaker notes the efforts to "comfort [their] panic hearts with magic names" (*Memnon*, II, 501). They endeavour to blind themselves to inherent, universal change, by naming things or events and relying on the apparent stability of words. This tactic, known in philosophy as 'reification', leads them to treat words as if they were the things referred to and the things referred to as if they were words. Thus, in an effort to create an artificially stable world and identity, the Self surrounds itself with illusions that blind it to its own—and everything else's—real nature.

Such undertakings obviously represent a serious misuse of language which, being part of the Heraclitean universe, should not be employed against its nature. The speaker in *Landscape West of Eden* is well aware of this danger, realising "how language too / leads one perforce into the south of worldmake." (*Eden*, XXI 648). Language can 'make' a world, albeit a temporary one, because it provides at least the illusion of stability and permanence. As illustrated in the following passage a similar linguistic strategy may also be used against chaos:

> But I have speech saved up against that demon
> And I will fend her off and kept her from me
> ....
> why from the hell of memory I'll summon
> the lightning word, the word of fire, and speak
> once and once only—
>
> (*Time in the Rock*, XXXVI, 700)

The protagonist feels he can overcome the "demon" (ibid.) chaos, change and meaninglessness by fixing the cosmic flux in words which he describes as "lightning" (ibid.) The image is aptly chosen. A flash of lightning reveals things as they are for a moment and imprints them on our vision as they momentarily are when we saw them; they are fixed in our vision just as words try to fix them in language. However, this strategy ultimately fails and the reason is simple: "word [is] only self" (*Time*, XXXVI, 701). Just as we always play ourselves in every act, so we speak ourselves in every word and the inevitability of change is an integral part of what we are. Similarly,—our illusions to the contrary—change is also a part of language, built into the flexibility and creativity of daily speech. Language doesn't stand still either and, therefore, cannot 'fix' things into a permanent state. The endeavours to use language as a way of avoiding the perception of flux, is therefore doomed to fail.

The idea that perception is a source of terror is sometimes also found in Aiken's early works. For example, in *The House of Dust* we read of the "sharp shaft of insight [that] dazzles my eyes and [pierces] me" (*Dust*, IV, 5,188). However, the notion of employing the stabilising powers of language to blind the Self is not developed in the early poems.

Terror of Wounds and Murder

The final source of terror is the fact that for the Self to grow, it has to be broken, wounded or hurt. This theme is already a part of Aiken's early work, indicated as early as Aiken's first major long poem, *The Charnel Rose*, when the protagonist wonders, "How could he make it clear . . . / That man's salvation rose through pain?" (*Rose*, IV, 4, 51). In a later poem, the protagonist refers to "the one dark wound that guides me." (*Dust*, IV, 3, 186), a rather bizarre image that nonetheless highlights the positive role that wounds and even murder can play in Aiken's poetry. The same idea is also encountered in *The Pilgrimage of Festus* in which the "lightning, sevenfold / Smoking clangs from a star, and splits / The eternal rock apart." (*Festus*, I, 6, 233). In this case, the rock is Festus, whose Self, having reached the highest point of a certain stage of consciousness, needs to be broken, wounded or murdered in order to continue his advance to still higher levels. It is precisely this blow, the sudden chaos from an unexpected influx of power that permits his advance to the next level of development. With this added power, he can evolve further but to do so, he must first overcome his fears by realising that chaos and filth are also potential energy which can be harnessed by the Self for its own purposes. The breaking or wounding is necessary also because it provides the suffering needed for growth. Suffering, too, is a kind of energy that may be used in the evolution of consciousness.

According to Aiken, being wounded, broken or killed is inevitable at every stage in the life of the universe simply because for growth to take place, the old identity or the old order must be destroyed. "God take his bowels out, and break his bones" (*Memnon*, XXXV, 540) says the protagonist in one especially striking image, and then adds,

> God take his conscience out and set him free
> And break his mind to rapture, and delight
> Those that would murder him, and those that love,
> And those that love mankind.

(*Preludes for Memnon*, XXXV, 540)

To be free to grow, we must lose our conscience, that is, get rid of the inner forces of convention that restrain us from pursuing our thoughts and goals to their greatest development. Only when we have left convention behind will we be able to discover the true "rapture" of being free in a Heraclitean universe. However, to achieve this freedom, the mind must be broken, something that will delight our enemies—"[t]hose that would murder him" (ibid.)—, our personal friends and those who break us for the good of human evolution in general.

The theme of wounding is also found in *Time in the Rock*, where it is given strong expression in numerous passages. One of the most unusual is the following:

> Then the red edge of sunlight spoke alone
> Graving the stars until their granite grieved
> And groves of grandeur grew along those grooves
> (*Time in the Rock*, XXXII, 696)

The phrase "red edge of sunlight" (ibid.) clearly conveys the idea of wounds, breakage, pain and even murder, a chain of associations continued in the idea of grieving granite. However, these lines also make it clear that such suffering is a necessary part of the creative process, the "groves of grandeur" (ibid.) that blossomed from the suffering. In a later stanza, the protagonist of the poem adds,

> Then the red cry of murder spoke alone
> and carved the silence into shapes of meaning
> out of the blood magnificent cry of meaning
> (*Time in the Rock*, XXXII, 696)

Here the protagonist also makes it clear that meaning too must grow out of suffering.

Uses of Terror

Having established in a wide variety of contexts the role of terror and pain in the process of becoming conscious as well as in the evolution of consciousness, it remains to be answered why these negative experiences are necessary. One of the more obvious reasons is that terror is the most direct and effective means of undercutting the habitual concepts upon which the Self has come to rely. The most dangerous of these conventions is the notion of a single stable Self because allegiance to this notion discourages the willingness to grow beyond it. In the face of terror, the Self experiences the unreliability of its identity and the consequent disappointment and devaluation make it easier to surrender the idea of a permanent Self. Important, too, is the fact that in the experience of terror, a division arises between the old Self identity and the new one.

Brief reflection on this passage reveals that wounding or breaking is necessary for the speech that will come from the resulting pain to provide the Self w"the one who knows his wings" (Time, V, 669), that is, knowledge of its powers. In an earlier part of this section, the speaker has already identified the angel as the "one who knows his wings" (ibid.). Thus, through terror the Self discovers its inherent potentials for greater growth, an idea symbolised by the angel. From this point of view, the process of becoming conscious may be characterised as increasing awareness of our God-like nature. However, in doing so, we must be sure to recall that for Aiken, God is not a distinct metaphysical entity but rather simply the goal for which we aim. Growth is our worship of this God. This is suggested in the last line in which we bring "the Thing from thing" (Time, V, 669), that is, we transform the current, seemingly stable 'thing'—whatever it is—into its next, more advanced development, its 'God' so to speak, that is its "Thing" (ibid.).

There is still another way of describing the process of becoming conscious. To understand this process, it should be recalled that in *Time in the Rock* Aiken puts special emphasis on the powers of language to heal the wounds required to become conscious: "Out of your sickness let your sickness speak—" (*Time*, V, 668). That speech and language have a healing function is made plain by the speaker's later call to praise the "saltatory fool" (*Time*, XXVII, 692), who makes of bitterness a "healing word" (ibid.). By placing the Self's discovery of its linguistic powers in the context of healing, Aiken makes it clear that the history of becoming conscious can also be the history of being healed. Consciousness in other words is health; unconsciousness is disease.

Terror and Ethics

The experience of terror is to be regarded as the start on the road to the total self-mastery which is a birthright of all conscious human beings. The experience of evil occupies a similar place, although in the case of evil the challenge is not issued to the existence of a supposedly, stable Self, but rather to inherited moral beliefs. When these are stripped away, a genuine morality emerges, based on the Self's own powers and potentials and not imposed by parents, tradition or society.

From the foregoing discussion, we may conclude that Aiken is by no means the complete amoralist as some might take him to be. The most fundamental ethical category to which Aiken subscribes is self-reliance, and its twin, courage.

> are we the angels who must heal ourselves
> condemn ourselves and then reprieve ourselves
> is it ourselves who must give absolution
> to hand to claw to root to leaf . . . ?
>
> (*Time in the Rock*, XXIX, 694)

CONRAD AIKEN'S PHILOSOPHY OF CONSCIOUSNESS

The answer to this rhetorical question is positive: humankind is required to do all these things for itself. However, the radical nature of Aiken's self-reliance should not be overlooked. If the process which is the Self's true identity is also the cosmic process, then self-reliance also means 'cosmic-reliance.' There is no need for support of social conventions when the Self is supported by the entire cosmos: "No gods abandon us, for we are gods" (*Memnon*, XLVII, 554). Elsewhere he writes,

> We dispense
> With all authority; and what we have and are
> In our own godhead, and in that alone.
> (*Preludes for Memnon*, IX, 508)

Because the Self embodies all cosmic processes it has at its disposal nothing less than the resources of the entire universe. There is no possibility of 'losing' if the Self submits to the cosmic laws however difficult to understand they may be at first. Aiken is clearly not at all the pessimist he is sometimes thought to be. He is, in fact, a 'cosmic optimist' whose optimism increased rapidly as he approached the end of his career. That is why the more positive, even religiously optimistic poems found at the end of the *Collected Poems* do not represent a break with his former views but are their logical fruition. Indeed, they represent the triumph of his philosophy. At an age when most writers grow pessimistic about the prospects of mankind, Aiken was still able to see the positive potentials in what at first appeared to be an unmitigated evil: the atomic bomb.

> Yes, and we with it, godlike everywhere,
> the regicide, the Kilroy, always there:
> ourselves—we know!—the god-destroyers and god-makers,
> idol and soul-idol breakers:
> ....
> O joyous laughter and derision
> *Gaia scienza* of the always first
> (*Everlasting*, V, 901-902)

The recognition of Aiken's essential optimism also requires us to admit that the ability to laugh is one of his virtues. The startling 'mad-song' in *Time in the Rock* (XIV, 677) leaves no doubt that for Aiken the proper reaction to horror is humour.

> When madness comes with yellow eye
> and thrusts with thumbs the skull awary
> so that its crooked scenes destroy
> the one hope left from childhood's joy:
> then *har har har har har* cry
> and give the fig to madman's day

(*Time in the Rock*, XIV, 677)

The reason for this belief has nothing to do with mere defiance. Humour is a sign of pleasure and enjoyment. If we enjoy the terror, pain and chaos which seem to threaten our existence, if we experience "merriment" (*Time*, XIV, 678) and "*fee, fi, fo, fum* merrily cry" (ibid.), we not only overcome their challenge but change their character from threat to a stimulus. A stimulus can only increase the powers of the Self and consequently, help such a Self continue seeking other vitality enhancing experiences. The humorous reaction does not, of course, mitigate the terror but it does make the terror serve the interests of the Self's vitality.

CHAPTER SIX

The First Stage of Consciousness: Divisive Consciousness

The aim of this chapter is to begin explicating the history of consciousness, that is, to explain the stages by which the Self achieves the main types of consciousness noted in Aiken's poetic works. Although this chapter covers some ground similar to what has already been discussed, this will be done from an entirely new viewpoint. The matter may be explained in the following way. As seen so far, the Self has asked the question "Who am I?" and focused its attention on discovering the nature of the mysterious 'I'. In this chapter we deal with the same question but rather than concentrating on this aim—the discovery of identity—we shall explore how the Self focuses on the types of consciousness through which it is led by the search. For example, the knowledge that its true identity is a process comes in or manifests itself as, a certain type of consciousness; moreover, the eccentric and concentric phases of Self have their corresponding states of consciousness. Understanding these states and how they are attained is the goal of this chapter.

Divisive Consciousness: The Beginning of Consciousness.

The Self's experience of terror and pain, from whatever sources they come, leads directly to the first stage in the development of consciousness. In the emotion of terror, the Self responds to a threat to its existence and this fear for its own existence implicitly asserts that it exists. Moreover, terror, by throwing the Self back on itself, creates a gulf between the Self and its surroundings. As the following quotation from *Time in the Rock* demonstrates, this divisive consciousness begins with the assertion of Self.

> The miracle said 'I' and then was still,
> lost in the wing-bright sphere of its own wonder:
> as if the river paused to say a river
> or thunder to self said thunder.

> As once the voice had spoken, now the mind
> uttered itself, and gave itself a name;
> and in the instant all was changed, the world
> *two separate worlds became—*
>
> The indivisible inalterably divided;
> the rock forever sundered from the eye;
> henceforth the lonely self, by self anointed,
> *hostile* to earth and sky.
>
> Alas, good angel, loneliest of heroes!
> Pity your coward children, who become
> afraid of loneliness, and long for rock
> as sick men long for home.
>
> (*Time in the Rock*, LI, 714; italics added)

This passage deals with divisive consciousness which is the first form of consciousness we develop. In reviewing this passage, several noteworthy matters are raised by Aiken. The first is that for Aiken, the existence of the Self is a "miracle" (ibid.) and is not something that can be explained; its existence is simply a fact from which we must begin. We note that after the initial statement of 'I', the Self is lost in astonishment or wonder at its own existence. The second point to note is that after the first, initial act of self-consciousness, the mind brings itself into existence from the initial act—"uttered itself"—(ibid.) and instantly, by its mere existence, divides the world into the perceiving subject and the perceived world of objects. Thus "two worlds" (ibid.) are created, the inward subjective, microcosmic world, and the outer, 'objective' macrocosm. Not only are these two worlds "unalterably divided" (ibid.), but the "lonely self" (ibid.) experiences its loneliness, at least in part, as hostility to competing existences. Finally, the protagonist addresses the Self as "loneliest of heroes" (ibid.) because to consciously endure its inevitable loneliness in regards to creation is itself a heroic act. This epistemic heroism makes the Self worthy of description in divine terms, as a "good angel" (ibid.). Unfortunately, this initial act of divisive consciousness is not always followed through; many people stop with this first act and, fearful of further loneliness, they cease their explorations and self-development. They seek stability of "rock" (ibid.) not realizing that this is not something they can have.

Even in his earliest work, Aiken recognises that man is essentially self-centred, a "whirlwind of speed that centres on itself" (*Time*, VI, 670), and that all consciousness must necessarily begin as self-consciousness which divides the Self from the world.

> You see me moving, then, as one who moves
> Forever at the centre of his circle:
> A circle filled with light.
>
> (*The House of Dust*, IV,3, 182)

CONRAD AIKEN'S PHILOSOPHY OF CONSCIOUSNESS

The circle, of course, divides the inside of itself from the outside, and, thereby divides the world in two, the subject from the object. Later, Aiken describes the Self as a spider at the centre of its web (*Memnon*, XII, 511). In either case, the protagonist stands irrevocably at the centre of its circle of consciousness. These simple but effective images clearly communicate not only the idea that all consciousness is, first of all, self-consciousness but also the idea that consciousness begins with an act of division. The Self must be distinguished from the not-Self. However, lest we be tempted to over-value the significance of discovering a seemingly unalterable fact, we must bear in mind that the Self at the centre of the circle is as subject to change as anything else in the universe.

At its simplest level, the 'I' asserts bare existence, and in this respect, humankind does not differ from other creatures. Nature is "shot through with . . . / Mimicry" (*Memnon*, XI, 510), and all things repeat "unknowingly the disastrous word" (*Memnon*, XI, 511) with which self-consciousness begins. The word "disastrous" (ibid.) is used because once the self has been asserted, then all kinds of difficulties such as loneliness, hostility and fear arise. These are the new challenges the Self will have to overcome if wants to pursue the evolution of consciousness.

There is no doubt that according to Aiken, all things possess a measure of consciousness. The potential difference between the consciousness of man and the consciousness of other created things is our ability to transcend the mere assertion of Self, either by word and / or act, and to wilfully recreate ourselves. We should not confine ourselves to the habitual repetition of only the one self-assertive word much less of a single identity. Our special duty is to change the meaning of the assertion by imitating the ever-changing universe and, thereby, altering the meaning of the word 'I'. We must change our identity and by doing so, pursue the evolution of consciousness no matter how frightened we might become.

As already seen in the previous lengthy quotation from *Time in the Rock*, one of the most dramatic results of the initial self-referential act is to divide the world into subject and object. For this reason we refer to this type of consciousness as 'divisive consciousness', and to the initial Self, that is, the Self of which we are first aware, as the 'divisive Self'. Another example of divisive consciousness is to be found in *The Kid*.

> Now I am waking: now I begin:
> writhe like a snake from the outworn skin:
> and I open my eyes: and the world looks in!
>
> (*The Kid*, VII, 859)

Here too a unity has been broken since a world that looks in is obviously no longer a world completely at one with the Self.

Because the initial or divisive consciousness does not recognise itself in the world which it confronts as "the loneliest of heroes" (*Time*, LI, 714), it easily feels alienated and slips into a hostile attitude towards the surrounding world. It finds itself "hostile to earth and sky" (ibid.). This stage, however, is not permanent.

> Then say: I was part of nature's plan
> Knew her cold heart, for I was consciousness
> *Came first to hate her, and at last to bless;*
>
>   (*Preludes for Memnon*, XLII, 548; italics added)

During the Self's development to higher levels of consciousness, this hatred will be overcome and increasing emphasis placed on love and the Self's identity in the world. Nonetheless, the negative phase must be experienced and recognised before it can be overcome. From this we may conclude that the growth of consciousness is also the growth of love and compassion for all things, including oneself. In addition, one should be aware that the first divisive act bequeaths a legacy of various divisions (between Self and the egos, for example) that must be overcome before the final unifying state of synoptic consciousness is attained. This matter will be discussed in greater detail later.

Consciousness, Language and Action.

One of the most important points to notice in the 'divisive I' section of *Time in the Rock* (LI, 714) is the simultaneous origin of consciousness and language. As soon as the initial word, 'I' is spoken, consciousness comes into existence. This shows that for Aiken, consciousness is not only at bottom self-consciousness but also that, like two sides of a coin, consciousness and language are correlated: one implies the other. While this does not allow the conclusion that consciousness and language are identical, it does indicate that they have at least some similar features. Activity is one of the characteristics they share. As shown in *Time in the Rock* (*Time*, LI, 714), the active nature of consciousness is readily apparent in its origin as part of an *act* of speech. Moreover, this characteristic fits into the general tendency of Aiken's thought to regard the cosmos as a dynamic process. The active nature of consciousness is also seen in the fact that its 'twin', language, is explicitly identified with action.

> Be then of madness all compact—
> singular soul whose *word is act*—
> singular act whose word is sole
> embassy of angelic whole—!
>
>   (*Time in the Rock*, XIV, 678; italics added)

The context of these lines is the already quoted 'mad song' (*Time*, XIV, 677). Its purport is that we should enjoy our madness or at least take advantage of the opportunities it offers and not let it ruin our lives. These lines indicate that by expressing our madness, we take action because "word is act" (ibid.) and that through the unity and coherence inherent in any communication—otherwise it would be non-communicative—we can become "whole", that is, unify and / or harmonise the various inner forces that threaten to fragment us. This will heal many of the inner conflicts that disturb us.

CONRAD AIKEN'S PHILOSOPHY OF CONSCIOUSNESS

Because in Aiken's poetry, angels symbolise a higher level of consciousness, these lines also suggest that by taking expressive action through language and becoming an "angelic whole" (ibid.), we can achieve unity at a level of consciousness higher than we had previously.

The identity of speech and action expresses itself in several ways throughout *Time in the Rock*, the long poem in which most of Aiken's philosophy of language is found. At one point, the protagonist notes that "word is action" (*Time*, XXX, 695) and that "act is speech / the kiss a word" (ibid.) since both, like language, communicate ideas and feelings. Elsewhere he discovers, albeit too late, that "Word is only Hand" (*Time*, XLII, 707). The unity of act and word can also be seen in Aiken's belief that a word "breathed all things to motion" (*Memnon*, VIII, 506). If words can cause motion, they must bear some resemblance to actions. Like actions, they are also capable of radically altering the world:

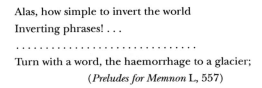

The speaker's lament about the possibilities of misusing language is based on his awareness of its enormous powers. At this point, we might object that while words and actions may be equated metaphorically, to assert that words can "invert the world" (ibid.) is simply fatuous. After all, actions affect material things and words do not. However, we must recall the philosophical idealism that characterises Aiken's thought, namely, the belief that what we call 'the world' and 'things' are our perceptions of our surroundings, our consciousness of them. Since words are equally capable of producing changes in perception and, thereby, in consciousness, they are capable of changing the only world we can ever know—the one we perceive. First appearances to the contrary, we can, if we wish, change the world by changing our mind.

However, as already noted, language and action, while similar, are not wholly identical, for which reason the protagonist of *Time in the Rock* prays, "Teach us to know the action from the word— . . . / never to confuse the one with the other—" (*Time*, XXX, 695). We must remember that although both words and actions communicate and affect our consciousness, they do so in different ways. Words do not physically change or displace things by the use of physical energy; rather, words change our interpretations of things, that is, their meaning. On the other hand, actions—walking, pushing, lifting, sitting, eating, moving away—all have an undeniable physical aspect in addition to whatever message they may communicate. This real difference between actions and words notwithstanding, in Aiken's work, which focuses on inward, imaginative rather than on outward action, the emphasis is on the ways in which words and acts are similar and affect consciousness.

Consciousness, Self, Language and Freedom.

Consideration of the next consequence of the initial, divisive act of consciousness reveals another aspect of the extremely close relationship between language, Self and consciousness: the three came into existence at the same time. It must now be understood that the origin of consciousness is also the origin of an independent, wholly self-made Self. To be conscious means to be free and to be free means to be self-made, that is, unconditioned by limitations that others, such as one's ancestors may have imposed. The Self in *Time in the Rock*, (*Time*, LI, 714) has achieved this aim: it springs into existence *ex nihilo*, seemingly out of nowhere and nothing, for which reason it is correctly associated with miracles. "The miracle said 'I'" (*Time*, LI, 714). Anything that comes into existence *ex nihilo* is, by definition, not subject to previously imposed limits. The result of this doctrine is that whenever the Self attains total freedom, that is, whenever it becomes truly independent, consciousness begins. From this we may conclude that consciousness, in Aiken's philosophy, is, therefore, not something attained merely by being born.

One of the major reasons why the Self may not achieve independence and consciousness is that it has adopted for itself a prefabricated language from others. It has failed to speak its own first word, 'I'. Of course, the Self in daily life may be saying the word 'I' but this does not mean it has made the word truly its own. Having adopted another's language, the Self exists in the mental framework devised for it by others, and consequently can be neither truly conscious nor free. The reason for this lies in the fact that such a consciousness is not yet actively creative; it has not yet begun to act according to its own nature as a dynamic and inventive entity. The entire problem is presented in the following quotation from *Preludes for Memnon*:

> Come let us take another's words and change the meaning,
> Come let us take another's meaning, change the words,
> Rebuild the house that Adam built, with opals,
> Redecorate Eve's bedroom. *We were born*
> *With words*, but they were not our words, but others',
> Smacked of the kitchen, or of gods, or devils,
> Worn and stained with the blood of centuries,
> The sweat of peasants, the raw gold of kings.
> *Shall we be slaves to such inheritance?*
> No; let us sweep these skeleton leaves away,
> Blow them beyond the moon; and from our anger,
> Our pride, our bitterness, our sweetness too,
> And what our kidneys say, and what our hearts,
> Speak with such voice as never Babel heard;
> And bring the curtain down on desolation.

CONRAD AIKEN'S PHILOSOPHY OF CONSCIOUSNESS

> Was this rich tongue of ours shaped by our mothers?
> *Has it no virtue of its own?* says nothing
> Not said before at church or between sheets?
> (*Preludes for Memnon*, XXXVIII, 541; italics added)

"Adam's house" (ibid.) refers to the linguistic and mental framework constructed for us by the first name-giver of Biblical mythology. To rebuild "Adam's house" (ibid.) is, therefore, to find or make one's own language, to speak with a "voice never as Babel heard" (ibid.) so that we shall be free and not slaves to the consciousness developed by others. Of special interest is the word "virtue" (ibid.) in the second stanza. Its original Greek meaning is '*arete*' or skill, ability, power. Obviously, if we do not possess language in which to embody our own special personal virtues, we shall be unable to use our own powers and shall, in effect, remain slaves to the consciousness of others. Lord Zero sums up this idea most succinctly by saying that it is necessary to find "our own self-seeking and self-shaping phrase / and so ordain our days?" ("*The Morning Song of Lord Zero*", ii, 969).

Several passages in *Time in the Rock* present similar ideas.

> Brought them with him and put them down as if
> to come from nowhere with a random burden
> of odds and ends, and quids and quods and surds
> whatnots and whiches—as if to put them down
> were tantamount to saying he had thought them
> and thought the bringing and thought the putting down
> and thought himself who thought he brought them there
> (*Time in the Rock*, LXVI, 728)

According to Aiken, this character has merely inherited his language, and is, therefore, unable to think for himself because he has passively received his consciousness from someone else. Having failed to speak his own creative word, and, therefore, being unable to write down his own "bright beginning" (ibid.) for himself, this person naturally feels despair at being wakened only to "face a self made ready while [he] slept / shaped in world's shape by the single voice." (*Time*, XXIV, 688). As a result, he is not self-made and, consequently, is neither conscious nor independent but lives as a "sleep walking shadow" (ibid., 689) who is not yet fully awake to his own existence. In a certain sense, such a Self has no real existence and is real only in a secondary sense from which we may conclude that for Aiken to be truly conscious means, in effect, to be truly existent and vice versa. Consciousness and existence are correlated like the two sides of a coin.

Moreover, we cannot help but conclude that the creative word imposed on us by others is a cause of self-alienation because it breaks and alters "that strange dream" (*Time*, XXIV, 689) of self-creation, of being *sui generis*, and, therefore, at one with ourselves. It is a form of *false consciousness* because, through language, others impose their consciousness on us, and, thereby, prevent us from genuinely becoming ourselves. Despite the interruption of our "dream" (ibid.) by other voices, we must choose to continue the dream and continue making ourselves by taking possession of our own language. Since the possession of our own language is so vital, it is not without reason that the protagonist of *Time in the Rock* asks, "where are we come, if neither word nor action / speak for ourselves?" (*Time*, XXX, 695). He feels that life has no meaning if our language does not adequately represent us as separate and distinct beings.

The most obvious way of solving the problems caused by the lack of one's own language is to make one by altering the meanings of the words we inherit. This strategy has already been indicated in the previous long quotation from *Preludes for Memnon* (*Memnon*, XXXVII, 541). However, Aiken has another method for accomplishing this aim, namely, what he calls 'murder'. The 'murderous alternative' is presented in the following quotation from *Preludes for Memnon*.

> When you have done your murder, and the word
> Lies bleeding, and the hangman's noose
> Coils like a snake and hisses against your neck—
> When the beloved, the adored, the word
> Brought from the sunrise at the rainbow's foot
> Lies dead, the first of all things now the last—
>
> Rejoice, gay fool, laugh at the pit's edge, now
> Heaven is come again, you are yourself
> As once you were, the sunrise word has gone
> Into the heart again, all's well with you,
> Now for an instant rapture you are only
> The sunrise word, naught else, and you have wings
> Lost from your second day.
>
> (*Preludes for Memnon*, XLIV, 550)

The word mentioned in the first line of this quotation refers to the pre-fabricated language (and Self) which prevents the attainment of consciousness. In order for the Self to be free to become fully itself, it has to overcome these and other ancestral gifts, a process that is so difficult and may entail such emotional violence that it may well be described as 'murder'. The imposed language, and perhaps those who bestowed it, have to be destroyed, that is, to be made unimportant or meaningless so that the Self can be its own "sunrise word" (ibid.). Only then will the Self be able to speak its own 'I' and therefore be the originator of itself, its consciousness and its language. In that moment of self-creation the Self will experience "all known, all good, all beautiful"(ibid.) because it will be obeying and giving expression to its own active nature. However, the acquisition of consciousness is not a one-time act, is not a permanent achievement. Indeed, the freedom gained in that first moment is "lost from your second day" (ibid.) That is because on the second day, the Self is no longer free from the conditions and consequences of the first day. It is subject to the consequences of its first action, one of which is the division of the world into subject and object. Thus, it is clear that in Aiken's vision, consciousness, Self and language are continuously limiting themselves, which is one of the reasons why Aiken insists that they must always be renewed. Without renewal, they would eventually reach a stage where nothing new could be said, and we remain stuck in the endless repetition of the same things. Such a state of affairs violates the natural change and creativity of the soul.

The need for a new language is also noted in *Time in the Rock*.

> come heart, invent a new world, a new thought:
> feel with new heat, new brightness, *a* and *b*
> may thus become a glass through which we'll see
> new worlds lost in the old world's alphabet
>
> the sudden light, the sudden breaking, the sudden whirl—
> come light, come light, let the heart be a bird
> whose single being is a single word
> brightness beyond soul or alphabet.
>
> (*Time in the Rock*, LXVIII, 730)

The new language will permit the Self to see new potentials or worlds that have been obscured, 'lost' in a worn out language.

The Meaning of Freedom.

Since freedom and independence play such important roles in Aiken's theory of consciousness, their meaning requires explanation. One aspect of Aiken's concept of freedom has already been noted: freedom from ancestors, that is, the freedom from being imposed upon by the ideas and actions of our predecessors. In various guises this theme is found throughout Aiken's work. It is, for example, specifically linked with the attainment of consciousness in *The Kid*: "now I am born, for the king is dead: / now I awake, for the father is dead . . . / Now I am waking, now I begin" (*The Kid*, VII, 859). Only when the king or father is 'dead', when we have learned all we can from him and struck out on our own do we really come into existence as genuinely independent beings. Until then, we are under the spell of his ideas, his customs and ways of thinking and his values. Even if we agree with our ancestors on many issues, Aiken, like Goethe, believes we cannot simply accept their ideas without thinking them through for ourselves and, thereby, making them our own. His negative attitude towards such intellectual laziness is clearly apparent in *Changing Mind* where the twice uttered word "Inheritor" (*Changing Mind*, 280; 287) is used pejoratively as accusation against the speaker.

However, Aiken's belief that each person should endeavour to be his own ancestor does not mean that we should forget our forefathers. Rather, he means that we should not depend on them and their language to provide us with answers to great questions or a sense of meaning; we must not expect them to have done our intellectual work for us. Instead, they should live in our awareness as examples of real people who have struggled with their own questions and problems to find their own answers; in this way they can live through us as fellow beings involved in the struggle for consciousness, identity and personal evolution.

> They move
> into another orbit: into a time
> not theirs: and we becomes the bell to speak
> this time: *as we become new eyes*
> *with which they see, the voice*
> in which they find duration . . .
> (*A Letter from Li Po*, X, 913; italics added)

When the ancestors live 'through us', that is, as part of our lives (rather than we living in theirs), then we have a positive relationship with them without having them impose upon us.

If to be fully conscious and fully existent the Self needs freedom from ancestors and their imposed ideas and language, it also needs freedom from itself. As we have already observed, the Self is not free on the second day because it is constrained by the consequences of its own first actions. In effect, the Self has become its own ancestor and, thereby, limits its future evolutionary growth, a negative situation that must be overcome by an act of 'creative suicide', or Self slaying. However, as we shall see in the next chapter, creative self-slaying is a difficult strategy and certainly far beyond the powers of the Self at the low level of divisive consciousness.

Freedom, in Aiken's view, is also associated with the ability to change and to achieve something new. Throughout his works, he advises readers that "wisdom will be change and faith in change" (*Eden*, XV, 640), and that they should "learn the alphabet of change" (*Memnon*, LVIII, 567). In *A Letter from Li Po*, he says that change is needed to bring us "new birth, new life" (*Li Po*, V, 907), that is, to a novelty, which, to Aiken, is worth almost any price.

> Pawn to king four; pawn to king four; pawn
> To king's knight four—the gambit is declined.
> The obvious is declined; and we adventure
> For stranger mishap than would here have fallen.
> . . . .
> Or at the table, where he carves his fowl;

> The king is murdered in his counting house,
> Stabbed by his light-of-love; drowned in his bath;
> And all that he might know—
> Why, something new.
>
> (*Preludes for Memnon*, XLVIII, 555)

These lines refer to the story of Agamemnon and Clytemnestra, an incident also brought up in the same context of change and novelty in *Time in the Rock* (XLV). Aiken associates change and novelty with death because from the point of view of a static entity, or an entity seeking stasis, change ends or 'kills' the present state that is supposed to be preserved.

The association of change and death is a constant throughout Aiken's work. For example, the speaker in *The Jig of Forslin* suggests, "Let us drown, then, if to drown is but to change." (*Forslin*, I, 56). In a later poem, Aiken praises death, writing, "O death, in shape of change, in shape of time." (*The Coming Forth By Day Of Osiris Jones*, 604). The close connection between freedom and death will be discussed in greater detail in the next chapter because it leads again to the theme of creative suicide. Briefly, the matter stands thus: the freest of all persons is the one who can overcome or slay himself and thereby become the master of his own change and death. Punch, the protagonist of *Punch: The Immortal Liar* tries to become the 'master of death' by fighting death rather than accepting it as an opportunity to change and grow. As a result of this unsuccessful strategy, he engages in the mere appearance of growth by using incredible and outrageous lies to aggrandise a single static identity. However, the fabulous adventures for which he takes credit are not genuine growth resulting from inner change and development but merely external, superficial changes that leave Punch essentially the same. Consequently, although his efforts may have their heroic aspects, Punch suffers from a failure of nerve because he cannot accept and make creative use of the inescapable facts of change and death.

Language, Consciousness and the World

In previous discussions we have already seen that the Self and consciousness begin simultaneously with language or the word. However, according to Aiken, the word creates not only consciousness (which for Aiken is always self-consciousness) but also, as in *The Book of Genesis*, the world itself. The earliest clear statement on this issue is found in *John Deth* (1930) where the line "In the beginning was the Word!" (*John Deth*, I, 10, 405) is repeated several times as a mocking parody to the *Bible* amidst Deth's 're-creation' of the world. *Landscape West of Eden* also explicitly shows the connection between language and world-creation.

> It was when Lilith became an angel that I learned
> (as before from Eve I guessed) how language too
> leads one perforce into the south of worldmake.
>
> (*Landscape West of Eden*, XXI, 648)

In Aiken's view, language always leads us to the creation of a world insofar as language fixes or reifies a certain moment in the flow of changes and identifies this momentary image as 'the world'. However, this linguistic 'world-making' is not without potential danger since the 'fixing' or reification of one particular moment of change distorts the essential nature of a Heraclitean reality. There is no harm in using language to create a world so long as we resist the temptation of thinking that the world we create is all there is to reality.

The idea of world creation by language is also pursued in *Preludes for Memnon*, where we read,

> You have no name:
> And what you call yourself is but a whisper
> Of that divine and deathless and empty word
> Which breathed all things to motion . . .
>
> (*Preludes for Memnon*, VIII, 506)

The connection between speech and creation of the world is also clearly present in *Time in the Rock* albeit in an almost gruesome passage:

> Then the red edge of sunlight spoke alone
> graving the stars until their granite grieved
> and grooves of grandeur grew along those grooves
>
> then the red edge of sunlight spoke alone
> and graved the stars and etched upon them voices
> voices of leaves and then the voice of hands
> the cry of murder answering to that edge.
>
> then the red cry of murder spoke alone
> and carved the silence into shapes of meaning
> out of the blood magnificent cry of meaning
> silence and speech silence and speech silence
>
> (*Time in the Rock*, XXXII, 696)

In the first two of these highly metaphoric stanzas, we see how by means of its speech, sunlight created not only life-supporting worlds from stars but also various "voices" (ibid.) speaking their own languages. The "red-edge" (ibid.) of the sunlight's speech is specifically linked to violence and murder, an initially grotesque idea until we realise this is Aiken's metaphorical way of saying that every creative act or word is preceded by a destructive act through which we free ourselves from slavery to the 'worlds'—ideas, beliefs, attitudes, customs—inherited from our parents. The voices and speech and the world that is truly ours grow out of the pain that inevitably accompanies the destruction of our inheritances. Once we have freed ourselves in this way, we can begin the task of developing our own meanings, our own interpretations of the world and our lives instead of living in a world made for us by others. The enormous effort and courage needed to do this explains why Aiken says that our own "magnificent cry of meaning" (ibid.) came "out of the blood" (ibid.).

Elsewhere in *Time in the Rock*, Aiken associates language and world creation in a less violent manner built on the metaphor of plant growth.

> But let us praise the voice the lonely voice
> but let us praise the leaf that is the first
> but let us praise the syllable the only
> that syllable which is the seed of worlds
>
> (*Time in the Rock*, XXXIII, 697)

Here, the creation of the world by language is portrayed not as a result of violent struggle and suffering but rather as the gentle and natural process of actualising potentials that already exist. The enormous creative capacity of language is suggested by the fact that the syllable produces "worlds" (ibid.). Its natural and gentle mood notwithstanding, the reference to the "lonely voice" (ibid.) suggests that the creation of worlds is not necessarily easy.

Because Aiken also describes consciousness as beginning with a word, it is difficult to resist the conclusion that the origin of consciousness and the origin of the world are one and the same. '*My* consciousness' and '*my* world' are identical, sharing not only the same origin—the word—but also the same essence. After all, for each Self, consciousness can mean nothing except his or her own consciousness of the world he or she inhabits. That being the case, how could consciousness and the world be different? This conclusion also harmonises with the self-centred nature of Aiken's philosophy in which, as already noted, the primary meaning of the term 'consciousness' is always 'self-consciousness'. From this it not only follows that there are as many worlds as there are conscious Selves but also that those who never attain their own genuine self-consciousness by overcoming their ancestral inheritances are doomed never to have their own world and their own meaning. They are simply destined to remain lost.

The notion that the world is created by word leads naturally to the concept of the world as a book. Such a motif is extremely common throughout Aiken's writing. References to this theme of the world as a book, that is, as a language, can, for example be found in *The Kid*.

> Stealth under stars, and stars to be read,
> lying on his back, the Book overhead—
> the Plow, the Pole . . .
>
> (*The Kid*, III, 850)

'Reading' the stars may be understood in two ways: it may simply be interpreted as the act of recognising the various constellations, but, at a deeper level, it may also be seen as genuine 'reading', that is, as perceiving physical objects (stars or words) in order to apprehend their meaning. This second view is supported by the image of the Kid "lying on his back [reading] the Book overhead—" (ibid.) If the sky is a book, it is not too much to think that the world beneath the sky is also a book of sorts communicating its own meanings by means of various objects or 'words.'

The notion that things are words or symbols is also prominently present in *Preludes for Memnon*, where for example, the protagonist asks, "What is a symbol?" (*Memnon*, V, 503) and answers his own question,

> . . . . It is the 'man stoops sharp
> To clutch a paper that blows in the wind';
> It is the 'bed of crocuses bending in the wind,' the
> Light that 'breaks on the water with the waves'
>   (*Preludes for Memnon*, V, 503)

In each case, we see that a symbol is an actual object in the world, from which it follows that the entire world must be a language and a book. The following section expands this idea to include the protagonist's lady as a language or book, of whom he says, "I find you many times, in many terms" (*Memnon*, VI, 504) to which he later adds,

> Yet you would have me say your hair is Helen's,—
> Your gait angelic; while I turn from these
> *To the vast pages of that manuscript*
> *On which the stars are stars, the world, a world;*
> *And there I find you written down, between*
> *Arcturus and a primrose and the sea*
>   (*Preludes for Memnon*, VI, 505; italics added)

Time in the Rock also makes use of the idea that all things in the world are actually part of a language or a book. For example, at one point the protagonist describes the world inherited from one's ancestors as "the picture world, / the lost and broken child's book . . . / the picture world, which is ourselves" (*Time*, XXV, 689). His point in this section, which describes how the words of others shape our worlds for us, is that we must find our own unique word in order to create our own world, our own consciousness and our own values. Later, the protagonist again emphasises the idea that objects are words and 'spell' out meanings: "our little alphabet of sand / our little alphabet of flowers" (*Time*, LIV, 717).

However, the strongest and most direct expression of the notion of things as a language and world as a book is found in *A Letter from Li Po* where Aiken states that "all is text" (*Li Po*, VIII, 910), a notion elaborated in the following way:

CONRAD AIKEN'S PHILOSOPHY OF CONSCIOUSNESS

> ....Yes, all is text, the immortal text
> Sheepfold Hill, the poem, the poem Sheepfold Hill,
> as we, Li Po, the man who sings, sings as he climbs,
> transposing rhymes to rocks and rocks to rhymes.
>
> (*A Letter from Li Po*, VIII, 910-11)

The identification of language and things could not be clearer than here or in the following passage:

> The landscape and the language are the same.
> And we ourselves are language and are land,
> together grew with Sheepfold Hill, rock and hand,
> and mind, all taking substance in a thought
> wrought out of mystery:
>
> (*A Letter from Li Po*, XI, 913)

The close association, indeed, identification of language, self-consciousness, the land and the world we create for ourselves, makes it virtually impossible to resist the conclusion that Aiken's philosophy of consciousness embodies strong idealistic tendencies, or is, in fact, a form of philosophic idealism. The trademark of all idealistic philosophies is the belief that the 'mental' takes priority over the 'material' insofar as the latter is interpreted as ultimately being 'non-material' in nature and may, perhaps, be nothing more than a mental impression or sensation. Since for Aiken, the world, the land, and self-consciousness are all fundamentally linguistic in nature and / or in origin, they are essentially mental phenomena. In other words, whether it be in regards to our own consciousness, our identity, our world or even the land on which we live, for Aiken the linguistic or mental aspects of existence play the decisive role in shaping who, what and even where we are.

A question still remains as to Aiken's adherence to a metaphysical or epistemological idealism. Metaphysical idealism asserts that entities in the world are actually immaterial in their very constitution, that matter itself does not really exist as such but is only a particular kind of appearance of a non-material 'stuff' often described as 'thoughts' or 'ideas' of some superior creative entity. Epistemological idealism, on the other hand, does not profess to know what matter is 'really' made of, but holds that whatever it might be, we can know nothing but our own sensations, impressions and feelings. We are only able to know mental phenomenon. Whether or not there actually is anything beyond the phenomena, that is, whether Kant's noumenal realm actually exists, remains pure speculation. It is doubtful whether or not any absolutely decisive answer is possible about Aiken's philosophical preferences on this score. However, given the overwhelming emphasis on consciousness and the evolution of consciousness in his work, the most likely answer is that he supports an epistemological idealism concerned with what we can or cannot know rather than with what is or is not supposedly 'really' there. To that extent, Aiken may be seen as a 'Kantian'.

Knowledge and Consciousness

Our discussions about the origin of consciousness do not exhaust Aiken's beliefs about the process of becoming conscious. Indeed, he has several versions of how this event actually takes place. One of the keys to understanding these versions lies in the meaning of the word 'knowledge'. Usually, 'to know' is associated with intellectual knowledge that we can articulate in conscious speech. Aiken, however, chooses not to limit the concept of 'knowledge' in this way, even in his early works. The dissection scene in *The Pilgrimage of Festus*, (II, 3, 238) makes it clear that identity, the Self, along with other aspects of existence such as "the passion men call life" (*Festus*, II, 3, 239), "the cry of pain itself" (ibid.), the existence of gods, hearts and love cannot be found and known in simple scientific and intellectual ways, that is, cannot be known as objective perceptions in the manner of material objects. Festus' inability to find any of these things suggests not that they do not exist, but rather that he seeks the wrong kind of knowledge in the wrong way. The wisdom of the gods—if it exists and can be gained at all—cannot be learned or known intellectually, from the outside, the way we know ordinary things like flowers; it must be gained by deep personal feeling and experience, which is how Festus eventually succeeds in gaining it. This suggests that purely intellectual knowledge of the facts is not sufficient for the attainment of consciousness of them.

The notion that for Aiken 'knowledge' is not just intellectual knowledge but also experiential, 'feeling knowledge', helps us understand numerous passages where an intellectual concept of knowledge would make no sense. Death, for example, cannot be known in this way, as suggested, for example, by the line "knowing the rank intolerable taste of death" (*Memnon*, XLV, 551). Death is something we can only experience for ourselves personally, or, to an extent, vicariously through imagination. Nor can an intellectual and objective definition of knowledge be applied in the following instances: "I have known / Such sunsets of despair . . ." (*Memnon*, LIII, 561); "This too to know, the moment of disruption—/ the cloud broken. The rain falling, the mind / emptied in foulness and distaste" (*Time*, VI, 669) or, "This too to know, death before death" (*Time*, VI, 670) and finally, "death-knowledge whispered, death-knowledge guessed" (*The Kid*, VIII, 860). In each of these examples, the knowledge referred to is best understood as experiential and / or imaginative and not objective, intellectualised knowledge.

Imagination and Knowledge

Earlier in this study it was noted that the Self seeking to know its identity is unable to rely on the powers of memory, and consequently, turns to the imagination to discover its true identity as a process. However, according to Aiken, the imagination is also important in the task of becoming conscious because it is the agency through which knowledge is transformed into the experience needed to attain consciousness.

One of the clearest examples of this process is found in *Landscape West of Eden* which begins with a protagonist standing "here at the western window, looking / across the red marsh" (*Eden*, II, 624) at a beautiful sunset. Though outwardly still, "from the window eastward faring in thought he went . . . / . . . spreading imagination's widening wings" (*Eden*, XVIII, 643) until in his reveries he encounters Adam, Eve, Lillith, the angels and the dream ego that he explicitly identities with himself. All the subsequent action in the poem is part of an internal monodrama in which all characters are really only various aspects of the protagonist. The poem's inner action begins just after the fall and expulsion from Paradise which is why we find Adam, Eve, and the protagonist's dream ego are already west of Eden, planning to recreate Eden in the post-lapsarian world which they are doomed to inhabit.

> What now is Eden? Eden was for our childhood.
> Are we forever children? Do we grow?
> Have you learned nothing, in this journey westward
> save that you want once more the fruits of Eden?
> must you go back and play with acorns, grass blades, fern leaves?
> *Is nothing learned, with loss of innocence?*
> (*Landscape West of Eden*, XIX, 645; italics added)

Adam and Eve's naiveté in wanting to recreate Eden suggests that while they know of the Fall intellectually, they lack a real understanding of their situation; their intellectual knowledge is deficient. In other words, they have superficial awareness but lack experience and, consequently, genuine consciousness of their circumstances. The protagonist is in a similar position; like Adam and Eve, he, too, has his "stubborn seeds and shoots" (*Eden*, II, 624) that is, plans and hopes for what he will do next after some unspecified dramatic change which has ended one phase of his life. Like them, he stubbornly wishes to recreate or resurrect the world he has just left—his familiar 'Eden'—showing, thereby, that while he has knowledge of his situation, he lacks full understanding and consciousness of it.

With this basic situation in mind, we are able to see that by means of various internal dramas enacted by Adam, Eve, and his dream ego, the speaker gains the inner experience that allows him to attain genuine consciousness of evil and the fall. In other words, this poem may be characterised as a rite of passage from knowledge to consciousness by means of the experience provided by the imagination. For example, the protagonist has such difficulty understanding that he cannot return to Eden again that, by means of the inner dramas, he has to experience this impossibility twice. Initially at least, he simply cannot comprehend the impossibility of returning to a former stage of consciousness or to a previous level of development; in the words of Heraclitus, he has trouble accepting the fact that no man can step into the same river twice. Both times he learns experientially that it cannot be done. At the end of Adam and Eve's futile attempt, the protagonist seems finally to understand, a change symbolised by the fact that he is no longer the recipient of the angel's lecture, but rather playing chess with him as an equal. Since the angel who symbolises his higher or more advanced consciousness accepts him as a peer, the protagonist has obviously arrived at a new, higher, level of consciousness, this time outside the gates of Eden. Naturally, he seems quite content outside of Eden and shows not the slightest hankering to return. Only one more step is required to take the next step in the development of consciousness—the experience of evil.

Logically enough, evil is represented by Satan and Lillith, who, according to Gnostic mythology was the first woman God created for Adam, but who turned evil as a result of her refusal to lie beneath Adam in the sexual act. The protagonist (through his dream ego) and the angel discuss the role of positive role of evil in existence:

> This peach-blossom is visited by innumerable
> bees and flies and butterflies (faithless wantons);
> it is their faithlessness that makes them welcome.
> Thus, she is fertile; thus, the mind is fertile; why then
> must love be sterile, in pure faithfulness?'
> (*Landscape West of Eden*, XIV, 638)

The phrase "thus, the mind is fertile" (ibid.) refers back to an earlier point that body and mind are unfaithful to one another, each with their own inclinations and each of them 'wandering' in different directions. Nonetheless, the fact that the "thought / runs westward, while the body leches eastward! / Thought will want fractions, body will want flesh!" (*Landscape*, XIV, 639) incites a creative tension between the two. The conflict between the abstractions or "fractions" (ibid.) of thought and the desires of the body leads to new experiences and insights, which is why the angel says,

> 'Thou sayest it? Thou knowest? Then thou growest!
> And soon, thou wilt learn to laugh."
> (*Landscape West of Eden*, XIV, 639)

At this point, the protagonist merely knows about the positive role of evil in our existence, but this knowledge will culminate in the laughter of experience only after he encounters Lillith. Now he will not merely know the positive role of evil in an intellectual manner, but also be able to appreciate it experientially. Once he has undergone the experience of evil with her, he is fully conscious of the fall and is able to seal off permanently the temptation to return to Paradise. Merely intellectual 'knowledge of' has become 'consciousness of' by means of experience created by the imagination.

The importance of the imagination in becoming conscious is also evident in *Preludes for Memnon*, especially in sections LIV and LV. In the first of these two, a child "goes out at evening, stands / Cold on the cobbled street, and claps cold hands / To frighten the pigeons . . ." (*Memnon*, LIV, 562). Suddenly, the child finds himself alone:

CONRAD AIKEN'S PHILOSOPHY OF CONSCIOUSNESS

> If, from an opened window, music falls
> And touches him with hands, stroking his hair
> Gently, as if to say Why here we are,—
> The ivy leaves of green, the earth is brown,
> The sky is red, but darkens—and if hearing
> *Suddenly he is frightened—for no reason—*
> Something mysterious has chilled him, left
> Somewhere an open door to darkness—
> (*Preludes for Memnon*, LIV, 562; italics added)

Here, too, consciousness is attained not by the mere thought of 'isolation', 'loneliness' or 'vulnerability' but rather by the direct experience of these feelings. This experience leads to a consciousness he cannot escape, despite the efforts to "[c]lose the door / Against the sunset and the flying pigeons" (*Memnon*, LIV, 563). The only result is that we shall find ourselves locked into the same room as "such darkness as we know is ours" (ibid.) and eventually learn to "warm our hands above our private terrors" (ibid.), that is, to make a pleasure out of experiencing—and not just intellectually knowing—our fears. Such experiences will help us attain full consciousness of our own, particular existence which is why the protagonist advises us to "[i]ndulge your terror: let him have his claws . . . [e]ntice him: let the cold mist creep upon you:" (*Memnon*, LV, 563).

Aiken's advice to "indulge" (ibid.) our terrors is accompanied by an elaborate description—of some sort of 'thing' stretching "his foul and sweaty reptile body" (ibid.) beside us—that suggests the imagination turns mere intellectual knowledge into consciousness at least partly by means of intense imaginative embellishment and subsequent intense emotional responses. Aiken does not seem to think that vague fears or 'angst' can achieve this effect equally well. Hence, in the first stanza of *Preludes for Memnon* LV, the fear has been given a definite form, grisly, lurid and visceral, and therefore, is not something to be brushed aside into unconsciousness with an easy explanation or convenient platitude. However, giving the fear a definite form also means that it has been limited, that is, defined. Once such a limitation is achieved, it is possible for the Self and its imagination to possess the fear rather than be possessed by it because the 'shape' of the fear is now determined by the Self which has begun to play with its own terror. Fear has become part of an actively, that is, consciously self-created experience of horror. The Self is now consciously rather than unconsciously horrified; it truly knows its fear both intellectually and experientially.

Furthermore, in constructing and embellishing this drama, the Self also becomes aware of its own powers as it experiences them in action and, thereby, increases its degree of *self*-consciousness. Terror has changed from being a merely external danger to the Self recognised by the intellect into an opportunity for the growth of consciousness and the Self. Of course, the first fear experienced by a child in this episode will not be its last but is only the beginning of the process of achieving consciousness. The greatest of these fears is death, "the very fashion-plate of horrors" (*Memnon*, LV, 564). The result of consorting imaginatively with death and terror is that the Self becomes "like wisemen / ghost before [its] time" (ibid.) What this means is that the Self imaginatively masters the many deaths involved in growing and changing deaths, before its actual physical death.

CHAPTER SEVEN

The Second Stage of Consciousness: Narcissistic Consciousness

The Beginnings of Narcissistic Consciousness

The foregoing pages explained the various means by which the first stages of consciousness may be attained. The essential identifying attribute of this "divisive consciousness" is the division between 'subject and object', between 'Self and world', and between 'me and not-me.' However, as subsequent discussion will reveal, in Aiken's view, there is an innate tendency for consciousness to dissolve these divisions and to join subject to object, Self to the world, and me to not-me. This is because consciousness is a unifying activity that accepts division only as an initial state from which it endeavours to advance until Self and the world become one in the final stage of synoptic consciousness.

For this development to occur, it is necessary to dissolve the subject-object dichotomy, a goal best-achieved not by rejecting or resisting the dichotomy but rather by altering its nature, by turning inward, by adopting a radical subjectivity that makes the Self its own subject and object. When this happens, as it does in the concentric phase of consciousness in which Self and its dream egos, while distinct, are nonetheless still one, the subject-object division continues to exist, but is no longer equivalent to a me / not-me division. Aiken represents the resulting type of consciousness by the man in the mirror, Narcissus.

The self-consciousness or self-experience gained by Narcissus, who is the object of his own perception, will be more intense than the experience of a Self facing a distinctly 'other' or even hostile external object. In the consciousness of Narcissus, both 'poles' of the experience belong to him: he is both perceiver and perceived, both actor and the audience. This development is important because progress through various levels of consciousness requires an ever increasing intensity of self-experience which suggests that the narcissistic phase is an essential part of our psychological evolution.

At this point, the question arises whether or not divisive consciousness belongs to the concentric or eccentric phase of the Self. In fact, it belongs to neither because it is the pre-condition for any sense of Self whatever. The Self only comes into existence with the achievement of divisive consciousness, an event Aiken calls a "miracle" (*Time*,

LI, 714) because it is essentially inexplicable by any rational means. It simply happens, and only after this occurs do intellectual problems about the origin and nature of our existence and identity begin.

> The miracle said 'I' and then was still,
> lost in the wing-bright sphere of its own wonder:
> as if the river paused to say a river,
> or thunder to itself said thunder.
>
> As the one voice had spoken, now the mind
> uttered itself, and gave itself a name;
> and in that instant all was changed, the world
> two separate worlds became—
> (*Time in the Rock*, LI, 714; italics added)

Only after the separation of these two worlds is the Self able to distinguish itself from the rest of the world, and, thereby, wonder about its identity. The miraculous, that is, wonderful but rationally inexplicable, nature of this event is evident in the language used here—"miracle", "wing-bright" (ibid.)—which obviously alludes to the Biblical creation story in Genesis, albeit it with some Aikenesque twists. For starters, consciousness is self-created and not created or given by any external, omnipotent God. We are, in this manner, our own self-creating God. This act creates not by making something in the traditional sense but rather, by an act of perception, by separating the Self from its surrounding environment and, thereby, establishing itself as a separate identity. It opens a space or 'void' between itself and the surrounding world. Moreover, the original creative act does not 'make' a world in the ordinary sense of making a 'thing', but rather, it creates self-consciousness, that is, a state of being that is aware of its difference from others; creation, or at least self-creation, begins with an act of differentiation or alienation and, in this sense, may be tinged with hostility as well as with "wonder" (ibid.).

Once the difference between Self and the world is established, the pre-condition for consciousness has been attained and the Self has the ability to develop two kinds or phases of consciousness. Looking outward, it enters the eccentric phase in which it simply sees itself objectively as one part of the world among others. In this phase, like all other human beings, it may wonder about its destiny or fate, its relationship to others and its proper social role. However, looking inward, it can study itself, in the concentric phase and its corresponding narcissistic consciousness.

A Look into the Mirror

In Aiken's poetry, the narcissistic consciousness encountered in the concentric phase of consciousness is most often symbolised by a man or women gazing into a mirror, a situation in which the Self takes the role of observer and observed at the same time. The subject-object dichotomy found in divisive consciousness still exists, but has been partially overcome because this division no longer corresponds to a division between the 'me and not-me.' The man or woman in the mirror is both subject and object at once. The same holds true for the Self in the concentric phase in which the dream egos function as mirror images of the original Self.

One of the earliest examples of narcissistic consciousness is found in *The House of Dust*:

> She rose and stared at her own reflection
> The dark-eyed ghost, waiting beside her,
> Or reaching from behind
> To lay pale hands upon her shoulders.
> Or was this in her mind?
>
> (*The House of Dust*, II, 10, 142)

In this poem, Aiken does not develop the philosophical questions that could arise out of this situation but in his next poem, *Senlin: A Biography*, he does:

> I wait in the dark once more,
> Hung between space and space,
> Before the mirror I lift my hands
> And face my remembered face.
>
> Is it I who stand in question here,
> Asking to know my name?
> It is I: yet I know not wither I go;
> Nor why; nor whence I came.
>
> (*Senlin*: A Biography, II, 219)

After some initial doubts, Senlin re-affirms his original identity, his "remembered face" (ibid.) only to discover that knowing who he is does not answer his questions about his origins or his ultimate destiny. Without at least some knowledge of these matters, his sense of identity is bound to remain incomplete and unsatisfactory. Whatever other knowledge Senlin may have about himself, it is not sufficient to satisfy him and he decides in the end to "forget these things once more / In the silence of sleep." (ibid.)

In *Preludes for Memnon*, the intellectual development of the man-in-the-mirror image is not only poetically more powerful because of the strength of Aiken's blank verse, but also because Aiken explores the philosophical potential of the situation in greater detail.

> Here is the tragic, the distorting mirror
> In which your gesture becomes grandiose
> Tears form and fall from your magnificent eyes,
> The brow is noble, and the mouth is God's.
> Here is the God who seeks his mother Chaos,—
> Confusion seeking solution, and life seeking death.
> Here is the rose that woos the icicle; the icicle
> That woos the rose. Here is the silence of silences
> Which dreams of becoming a sound, and the sound
> Which will perfect itself in silence. And all
> These things are only the uprush from the void,
> The wings angelic and demonic, the sound of the abyss
> Dedicated to death. And this is you.
>
> *(Preludes for Memnon,* I, 500)

This grandiose and self-affectedly splendid performance touches on several themes that inevitably arise in narcissistic consciousness. First of all, there is the question of accuracy or truth; the mirror in which the "gesture becomes grandiose" (ibid.) is "distorting" (ibid.), and leads, therefore, to doubts about reliability and trustworthiness about the knowledge provided by the mirror. Can we trust it? Can we trust our perceptions in the concentric phase of consciousness in which the Self is both the observer and the dream egos it observes? Can we avoid the fact that in such doubt a new space or 'void' arises between the Self and what it perceives and that an infinite number of new possibilities—symbolised by the "uprush from the void" (ibid.)—arise? These new possibilities, whose extremes are portrayed as the "wings angelic and demonic" (ibid.) inevitably complicate and confuse the development of identity and the search for consciousness. Our ability to rely on narcissistic consciousness in our evolutionary development is, thereby, called into question.

What makes matters even more complicated in this passage is the reference to our apparent divinity: "Here is the God who seeks his mother, Chaos,—" (ibid.). According to Aiken, we are divine insofar as the processes constituting the Self, are the same processes that constitute the very being of everything in the entire universe. The essence of this process, be it in us or in the things around us, is the dialectical quest for wholeness, for the union with our opposites, so that we can become greater wholes and begin the quest for still greater wholeness. God seeks his mother "Chaos" (ibid.)—that is, seeks unification with both his source and his opposite. We also see "[c]onfusion seeking solution, and life seeking death" (ibid.), in other words, opposites seeking each other to complete themselves. Once they have become unified with their opposites, these things become whole; they become themselves at their highest and fullest potential, which, in Aiken's view is divine. In a Heraclitean universe, this process is endless because when one divine synthesis is achieved, the quest begins for a still higher level of wholeness. Everything desires to become a greater synthesis with its dialectical opposite and is, therefore, inherently seeking self-transcendence.

According to Aiken, the distinguishing characteristic of narcissistic consciousness is the intrusion of self-mockery. Although narcissistic consciousness unifies the 'me and not-me' in one person, it divides itself against itself because one part of the Self passes judgement on another, deprecating the emotions it feels even in the very act of feeling them. Thus, "Narcissus, cunning with a hand-glass" (*Memnon*, XVII, 518) and "preening with a curl" (ibid.) says,

> God's pity on us all! he cried, and turned
> The guileful mirror in a guileful light;
> Smiled at the fair-curved cheek, the golden hair;
> The lip, the nostril, the broad brow the hand;
> Smiled at the bright young smile . . . Alas, alas
> To think that so great beauty should be lost!
> This gold, and scarlet and flushed ivory
> Be made a sport for worms!
> (*Preludes for Memnon*, XVII, 518-9)

Here we have the typical characteristics of narcissistic consciousness: a protagonist who is simultaneously actor and audience, subject and object, 'me and not-me' engaged in monodramatic performance for his own benefit. Despite his apparent unification of dialectical opposites, he has, paradoxically, re-created the 'void' or space that separate the observer and the observed through the self-mockery with which he observes his own performance. The obvious affectation and self-aggrandising gestures, in addition to his barely suppressed laughter at the thought of death, make it clear that the protagonist does not take himself too seriously. He feels there is something innately silly about this form of consciousness. Yet this stage is unavoidable in the evolution of consciousness because it is through this stage that the higher level of synoptic consciousness will eventually be attained. We must exhaustively explore all our various potential forms of consciousness until at least a climactic moment in synoptic consciousness. Naturally, in a Heraclitean universe, the entire process begins again after attainment of this supreme moment.

Narcissistic performances of this kind are also to be found in *Time in the Rock*. For example, in one striking passage, the deceitful husband puts on an excellent show for himself, grinning "at [his] own grin" (*Time*, LXXV, 735) by way of self-congratulation for having successfully deceived his wife. In this way, albeit it without an external mirror, he re-creates the exact situation in which Narcissus finds himself. The perceiver and perceived are one and yet still psychologically divided because he feels somehow ridiculous in the performances he puts on for his own benefit. Later, *Time in the Rock* features a variation of such a moment of narcissistic consciousness

> What's there? What virtue, or what truth? Hatred
> glares back at you; the dulled eye is stupid;
> but not too stupid, or too dull for hate.
> You hate each other; you lean and hate; the light
> shows deeply into hate. Who is that man?
> His face is meanness, and should be destroyed!
> But then the mouth—
>
> For suddenly the mouth
> begins to smile; and smiles and smiles; and grins
> maudlin affection; . . . .
> . . . .
> Who is that man? His face is strange, and good!
> unknown, and therefore god . . .
>
> (*Time in the Rock*, LXXXV, 745)

This passage shows the divided nature of narcissistic consciousness in which a character performs for and passes judgement on himself. He is one, yet paradoxically, divided and lives in an ontologically ambiguous condition of being both one and many. Furthermore, this passage reveals that even the character's self-loathing and self-hatred are manifestations of an underlying current of self-love without which he would not spend so much time and energy on himself and his own short-comings. This self-love, shown in the smile which the protagonist describes as divine, paradoxically joins the perceived and the perceiver into a unity in the very act of dividing it. Of course, at some places, this division undercuts itself, thereby re-enforcing the character's ontological ambiguity. When he says that the man in the mirror "should be destroyed" (ibid.), the context—a melodramatic performance for himself—suggests that we not take this judgement seriously, and that, perhaps, we should interpret it to intend back-handed praise. Thus, at one and the same time, narcissistic consciousness is both established and undermined.

Noteworthy, too, in the foregoing passage is the identification of the unknown with God. Not only do we see, once again, the Self characterised as divine, but also, we see how the "unknown" (ibid.), namely, that which in some way epistemologically transcends the Self, is identified with the divine. In Aiken's Heraclitean universe, this "unknown" (ibid.) will be the transcendent goal—or God—with which the Self tries to achieve a new and more complete unity because the Self can never be or feel complete if anything is beyond it. For this reason, Aiken's Self is truly an imperial self, that is, a self driven to include all existence within its own boundaries, a process which always appears to have an end but never does.

Two other passages from Aiken's works reveal the significance of these narcissistic monodramas. In *Preludes for Memnon*, the speaker hears Christ dying on the cross and is fully aware of his own actions while performing them. His actions near the cross are highly calculated, thus re-creating the basic situation of narcissistic consciousness in which the Self is unified as both subject and object and yet divided by his awareness of the performative nature of what he is doing. He admits, for example, that he is "studious not to turn" (*Memnon*, XXVI, 530) to the dying Christ. The whole scene contains a large deceptive element that leads again to an inevitable realisation of the innate ridiculous nature of narcissistic consciousness.

> I heard him die: I knew that he had died.
> And instantly I stooped and touched the grass,
> Tenderly, yet with hands self-conscious too,
> And with one finger touched the daisy, moved
> Its frightened face against a chickweed leaf
>
> And all the while I smiled.—But why was this?
> Was there no rash profundity to say?
>
> (*Preludes for Memnon*, XXVI, 531)

Here, in the midst of what is commonly regarded as one of the central events in the religious history of humankind, Aiken finds narcissistic consciousness in his sincere yet "self-conscious" (ibid.) actions at the foot of the cross. He is not fully absorbed by the momentousness of the event as others might be, but rather, he is focussed on himself, and smiles: "But why was this?" (ibid.). Even in the midst of a scene of such cosmic importance, the protagonist is unable to overcome the inevitable presence of self-consciousness which undermines the sincerity of his response to this occasion. This strongly suggests that we are unable to overcome the limits of our own self-consciousness regardless of our situation. Self-consciousness with its inevitable suggestions of acting and contrivance will always mock us even in our sincerest and even holiest moments. It is difficult, if not impossible, for human beings to take themselves completely seriously.

The following passage illustrates a similar set of ideas. Speaking to his lady, the protagonist says,

> Lady, you are a character in a play, you walk
> westward towards the window with just such taking
> of the strange light upon your face, the effect
> *conscious and calculated*, but none the less
> deep in the evening's beauty.
>
> (*Time in the Rock*, LXXX, 740; italics added)

Here, too, we observe the explicit association between consciousness and calculation. When people calculate and perform for others, they are in a divided state of narcissistic consciousness because part of them is putting on a show for the benefit of the audience, while another part watches and judges their own performance. This cannot help but make them intensely self-conscious. The concept of 'calculation' also implies that the process is contrived and, in that sense, unnatural. This leads to one of the major paradoxes in Aiken's poetry, namely, the notion that the contrived and unnatural is as much a part of nature as anything else. Despite being part of a calculated pursuit of an "effect" (ibid.) the lady's act is "nonetheless / deep in the evening's beauty" (ibid.), that is, a part of what is going on naturally—which suggests that the contrivance does not necessarily rule out an element of sincerity in the situation.

Is there any way to resolve this paradox? Perhaps, but to do so, we must first accept the notion that nature has two levels, the pre-conscious level, which we think of as 'natural', at which events happen without any conscious thought or intervention, and the post-conscious level at which to one degree or another everything is knowingly contrived and which we may associate with the 'non-natural', or 'unnatural'. Consequently, the 'natural' or 'pre-conscious' is contrasted with the 'unnatural' or 'post-conscious'. However, in the passage quoted above, Aiken is saying that the natural / pre-conscious and the unnatural / post-conscious are really one and part of each other. After all, how could anything that happens in the natural world be 'unnatural'? Consequently, we conclude that the purpose of the paradox is to reveal the untenability of this distinction by forcing us to examine it closely enough to see that it does not work. In other words, the paradox is not so much resolved as dissolved by discovering that it is based on a false distinction.

This affects the attitude with which we approach our own actions. Since, according to Aiken, we cannot escape being self-conscious actors and contrivers, let us make a virtue of a necessity and, in Nietzschean fashion, do with a good will and with full intention that which we must do in any case.

> Walk man *on the stage* of your own imagining
> peel an orange or dust your shoe, take from your pocket
> the soiled handkerchief and blow your nose
> as if it were indeed necessary to be natural
> and speak too if an idea should recommend itself
> speak to the large bright imaginary audience
> the flattering multiplication of yourself
> (*Time in the Rock*, LXVII, 729; italics added)

The truth is that our "role" (ibid.) and what we 'actually' are turn out to be "much the same thing" (ibid.) and we should not even pretend otherwise. However, as the succeeding stanza makes clear, we must at all costs avoid simply repeating ourselves, that is, simply being a "[d]ecrepit inheritor" (ibid.) of our former role and carrying it into the future. That would be a denial of our duty to make things new and to be original or creative. Even if we only act for ourselves, we have a duty to be original like the universe itself.

At this point it is possible to draw two conclusions about the second, narcissistic level of consciousness. In the first place, consciousness is a performance, an act. This last word can be used to mean both an activity and a stage act. The first of these refers to Aiken's belief in the active nature of consciousness; being conscious is something we must choose to do and intentionally continue doing or it will be lost. The second meaning of 'act' is associated with the deceptiveness, calculation and contrivance. The implication is that at the level of narcissistic consciousness the Self lives a lie—but it is a lie that is *really* being lived, and, in that sense, becomes real. What the actor or the Self does is not unlike a work of art which, in one way, is real as a work of art per se but in another is contrived and, in that sense, unreal.

The second conclusion is that narcissistic consciousness is more advanced than the first level of divisive consciousness which split the world into, 'I' and 'other,' as well as subject and object (See *Time*, LI, 714). The reason this level of consciousness is more advanced than divisive consciousness is that while the origin of divisive consciousness is an essentially inexplicable miracle (*Time*, LI, 714), the origin of the narcissistic consciousness is a calculated, explicitly willed undertaking to explore and find one's identity. This intentional state of consciousness is a project rather than being an inexplicable miracle and is clearly related to the concentric phase of consciousness. This latter may also be described as a project undertaken to find identity as the Self creates its various dream egos in the same way the man creates his reflections in the mirror.

Another reason why narcissistic consciousness is superior to divisive consciousness is that it is more intense than its predecessor. At the first level of consciousness, the Self still lives in a world divided into 'me' and 'not-me', 'I' and 'other.' Consequently, all experience is divided between the Self and alien entities. Such is no longer the case with Narcissus, who literally has the whole experience to himself, performer and critic. He has not only these roles but also the distinct pleasures associated with them. Imagining his own feelings, as well as the audience's and a critic's demands intense imaginative activity, which in turn raises the intensity of self-experience. This in turn broadens the basis on which consciousness may develop.

A Deeper Look into the Mirror

The foregoing discoveries notwithstanding, it is necessary to look even deeper into the nature of narcissistic consciousness.

> Here is the tragic, the distorting mirror
> In which your gesture becomes grandiose
> Tears form and fall from your magnificent eyes,
> The brow is noble, and the mouth is God's.
> Here is the God who seeks his mother, Chaos,—

> Confusion seeking solution, and life seeking death.
> Here is the rose that woos the icicle; the icicle
> That woos the rose. Here is the silence of silences
> Which dreams of becoming a sound, and the sound
> Which will perfect itself in silence . . . .
>
> (*Preludes for Memnon*, I, 500)

In this performance, the subject-object dichotomy still exists, but it is no longer a me/not-me division. The actor is both at once. As already noted, the same holds true for the Self in the concentric phase of consciousness in which the dream egos are the equivalents of images in a mirror. In reflecting about the dream egos, the Self realises that they are itself, but, at the same time, views them as objects. The Self is thus engaged in a kind of "double-think" in which it holds two contrary views about the dream egos at the same time. One might, of course, also describe this state of consciousness as "dialectical" insofar as it embraces opposites. However, because—as the above passage makes clear—Aiken chooses to emphasise the "grandiose" (ibid.), affectedly self-centered aspects of this frame of mind, it has been labelled as 'narcissistic'.

Several aspects of this passage call for further analysis. Why, for example, is the mirror "tragic" (ibid.)? The answer lies in the word "distorting" (ibid.). Despite the fact that we so desperately seek truth—and perhaps even expect the mirror of consciousness to be 'truthful'—the truth eludes us because consciousness is inherently distorting. Our dream of truth is a dream of something that we can never attain, at least not in the sense of an absolutely clear and undistorted truth. Here too, Aiken's tactic of making a virtue of a necessity plays its role. If the mirror of consciousness gives us nothing but distortions, then we must remind ourselves that these distortions are as 'true' as any other reflection. As Aiken writes in his last major long poem, *A Letter from Li Po*, "In every part we play we play ourselves" (*Li Po* V, 908). We need the courage to accept the truth that *all* of the images—including the so-called 'distortions'—are images of ourselves. When we realise this, the mirror will no longer be tragic because we know the distortions are as real as anything else.

Another feature that draws our attention is the 'God-like' character the protagonist assumes in the mirror. This portrayal is, of course, mocking and ironic, an indication of the protagonist's supreme ego-mania. However, like all other reflections in the mirror, it reveals at least some truth, in this case, the divine elements inherent in humankind. This must not be understood in the context of traditional Christian, Jewish or Muslim manner. For Aiken, God is our own future form, our own unused potential, that which we strive for and struggle to actualise. Consequently, the mirror image reveals God insofar as it reveals a role or image the protagonist lacks in the present but is striving to attain or, at least, is capable of attaining in the future.

The mocking tone of this passage is also intended to remind us, that in our divine aspects, we are only a small part of a whole cosmic process which is itself equally creative and divine. If we think we are the only gods in existence, we inevitably become "grandiose" (ibid.) that is, pretentious and showy, and arrogate to ourselves a status we cannot truly claim. Here Aiken makes a theological point by capitalising 'God', something he rarely does. We become "grandiose" and self-aggrandising if we become like the traditional Judeo-Christian God Who claims that He is the only true God in existence instead of admitting that He is one of an infinite number of gods all of whom are evolving to something better. When we adopt such an exclusionary attitude, we become somewhat silly even in our most serious moments, as seen, for example, in the line, "Here is the God who seeks his mother, Chaos—" (ibid.). The tone of this, and the subsequent line is ambiguous; there is an element of mockery in the notion that God, the maker of heaven and earth, would feel the need for comfort from His mother. This idea also exudes a pathetic quality insofar as God is identified with "[c]onfusion seeking solution" (ibid.), thus reinforcing the idea of a lacking and inadequate God subject to desperate needs. The idea is sad and, simultaneously, laughable because such a God does not differ from us—which is exactly Aiken's point: in some sense, we and God are the same kinds of beings. The notion of praying to such a God can only be a sorry joke.

What is also made clear in this moment of narcissistic consciousness is dialectical nature of the Self, which is constituted by entities struggling to achieve their opposites. The rose "woos the icicle" (ibid.) and silence "dreams of becoming a sound" (ibid.). This quest for the opposite is also described as "the uprush from the void" (ibid.), that is, things coming from their opposite, i.e. nothing, as do the "wings angelic and demonic" (ibid.). Aiken ends the stanza with a simple conclusion, "And this is you" (ibid.). Thus, he leaves us to contemplate the notion that not only are all things dialectically constituted as a struggle towards and from their contraries but also that the rhythm of existence is an alternation between opposites. Because he sees these as final, irreducible features of the Self, Aiken never attempts to resolve or clarify the self-contradictions and ambiguities which constitute the Self. These ambiguities define our essence or nature as a species and as individuals for which reason we must set aside whatever dissatisfactions we feel and accept them as much as we accept universal change. If we choose to ignore our inherently changeful nature and deify one of our particular identities, we risk madness by engaging on an impossible quest. It is simply impossible for us to achieve a single, clear, non-self-contradictory and final identity.

The dialectical nature of existence suggests that all things are relative to one another, that is, they exist in relation to other things, they exist inter-dependently and are, therefore, at least partially defined by them. There can be no black without white—and no good without evil. (See Aiken's *"Evil is the Palindrome"* for a witty expression of this idea.) In a universe of constant change, such a dialectical existence means that not only good and evil but also all other things, continuously define and re-define each other in ever new circumstances and, thereby, actualise and reveal new aspects of themselves. Furthermore, in true Hegelian fashion, this dialectic is driven by self-contradiction, within the characters themselves, and, by extension, within all things. Once again, this is all plainly visible as early as in the four long poems of *The Divine Pilgrim*, in which, more obviously than in the later works, the protagonists' struggles are driven by the desire to overcome and transcend the anguish of their self-contradictory ambiguities and multiplicities. From a dialectical point of view, the result is predictable: they roam "forever unsatisfied" (*Rose*, 1, I, 27) because the very nature of the cosmos prohibits the solution they desire. In their struggles, the protagonists forge a new synthesis, that is, a new Self capable of including the opposites in a new unity—and immediately face the same problem again at a higher level. The problem cannot be solved because the problem is the inherent nature of all things. To solve it would mean to cease being what they are, dialectical beings in a dialectical universe. For Aiken to pretend to 'clarify' the ambiguities and to 'resolve' the self-contradictions would be lying about the essence of man, and thus, a betrayal of his poetic mission. Such untruths would hinder, not help, the evolution of consciousness.

Dialectical Ethics

The ambiguous and dialectical nature of man has important ethical consequences. Since, like everything else in the universe, good and evil are also involved in an ever-changing dialectical relationship with all other things, human beings, like the entire cosmos, are inevitably a mixture of both. Purity of any kind is a myth because in a dialectical universe, nothing can be only one thing or another. In a scene that is more fully developed in the later *Preludes for Memnon*, Aiken portrays a grotesque vivisection in which Festus dissects a beautiful princess to see whether or not the sources of her beauty are also beautiful.

> Is this the golden eyebrow we have loved?
> Let us discover if its roots are gold,
> That they be also praised . . .
> . . . .
> Shall we explore it to its secret source,
> To some black smoking pool? . . .
> (*The Pilgrimage of Festus*, II, 3, 240)

Already in this early work, we see Aiken's awareness that human attributes and, by extension, all things, are based on their opposites. In the later work, the dissection is metaphorical, but nonetheless, the protagonist reaches the same conclusion about the morally mixed, ambiguous or self-contradictory nature or identity of everything.

> For so it ["the ignoble blood"] comes from God.
> Bears with it false and true and dead and dying:
> It is the sovereign stream, the source of all;
> The seed, the seedling; worlds and worlds to come.

> Is there a treason here that is not you?
> Accept this logic, this dark blood of things.
> There is no treason here that is not you.
>
> (*Preludes for Memnon*, XXX, 536)

All things in the "sovereign stream" (ibid.) of creation are mixed from their very source which is God Himself. Not unexpectedly, these lines strongly suggest that morals themselves are relative, a suggestion that is immediately adopted in the next section of the poem:

> Where is the noble mind that knows no evil?
> Gay insubordination of the worm?
> Discord of mishap, rash disharmonies
> Sprung from disorders in the spirit's state?
> If there is such, we'll have him out in public,
> And have his heart out too. There is no good,
> No sweet, no noble, no divine no right
> But it is bred of rich economy
> Amongst the hothead factions of the soul.
>
> (*Preludes for Memnon*, XXXI, 536)

According to this passage, good morals, good motives and good thoughts are the result of compromises among a variety of inner impulses, and, as such, are neither as pure as we might like to believe, nor as independent from lesser impulses as we might wish. The "economy" (ibid.) of the soul is "rich" (ibid.) precisely because it includes all ethical possibilities and not merely those we might find attractive.

Such ethical beliefs naturally prevent Aiken from adopting a conventional morality constructed of specific, eternal prescriptions, emphasising 'purity'. Our own Heraclitean nature, and that of the cosmos dictate that we can only practice 'situation ethics', that is, derive our ethical principles from concrete and specific situations as they arise in our lives and not simply take them as ready-made from some immutable, transcendent source. To do the latter would be living in 'bad faith', violating our own and the world's innermost nature, and inevitably deforming ourselves and increasing our difficulties. Honest living in a Heraclitean universe requires rejection of any pre-determined, or prescriptive ethics.

The Essence of Man

Because the Self always changes and, therefore, never really possesses a single, stable, and durable identity, it might be concluded that Aiken denies human beings have any nature or essence, either as individuals or as a species. There can be no doubt that Aiken wrestled with the issues of a definable essence and stable identity from the very outset of his career. Already in *The Charnel Rose* he shows awareness of the multiplicities that dwell within us and their challenge to our conventional concepts of identity and to our individual and species essence. Having discovered his multiple nature, the protagonist has a clear understanding of the task he faces: "To shape this world of leaderless ghostly passions,—/ Or else be mobbed by it—there was the riddle" (*Rose*, IV, 1, 48). In other words, the protagonist understands he must find a way to "shape" (ibid.) that is, form into coherent unity and identity the multiplicities within himself. He longs, albeit in vain since in a Heraclitean universe no such final completion can ever exist, for the moment when "the infinite soul [is] made complete" (ibid.). By the end of the poem, he still lacks an essence or stable identity, but has at least achieved awareness that despite his apparently multiple nature, he will continue to exist:

> We are struck down. We hear no music.
> The moisture of night is in our hands.
> Time takes us. *We are eternal.*
> (*The Charnel Rose*, IV, 5, 54; italics added)

The Jig of Forslin develops the same ideas. The protagonist is also haunted by the ephemeral nature of his essence or identity: "Are we real, or must we perish?—/ We blow in the air, like leaves our words are blown" (*Forslin*, V, 4,108). He is also acutely aware of his internal multiplicities and seeks "the unmoving centre—" (*Forslin*, V, 6, 111) of a stable identity or essence. However, he realises that his quest is impossible when he says,

> Great wheels revolve. I fall among them and die.
> My veins are streets. Millions of men rush through them.
> *Which, in this terrible multitude is I?*
> (*The Jig of Forslin*, V, 6, 111; italics added)

He cannot find a single identity because he senses that in some way, he *is* all of that "terrible multitude" (ibid.). However, unlike the protagonist of *The Charnel Rose*, Forslin develops a much clearer concept of the evolutionary nature of his essence or identity, that is, of himself as a process that continues through many forms.

> We hold them all. They walk in our dreams forever,
> Nothing perishes in that haunted air,
> Nothing but is immortal there
> And we ourselves, dying with all our worlds,
> Will only pass the ghostly portal
> Into another's dream; and so live on
> Through dream to dream immortal.
> (*The Jig of Forslin*, V, 8, 115)

CONRAD AIKEN'S PHILOSOPHY OF CONSCIOUSNESS

The theme of stable identity and essence remained with Aiken throughout his career. In *The Morning Song of Lord Zero* (1963), one of the last and shortest long poems he ever wrote, the protagonist, Zero, personifies the idea of endless personal transformation through many identities, that is, the continuation of the Self through change and its essential identity as change itself.

> Gambler and spendthrift by nature,
> chameleon soul whose name is Zero,
> anonymous in headlines,
> nameless in breadlines
> nevertheless I am your hero.
> . . . .
> I am inscrutably someone else tomorrow
> . . . .
> I am your jack-and-jill
> of all trades dubious brother
> panhandler father Cassandra mother
> and yet in the end insidiously
> o indispensably and invidiously
> something more.
>
> (*The Morning Song of Lord Zero*, i, 966)

If we adopt the view that identity is necessarily stable, then, as the title indicates, we may think of the ever-changing Self as a 'zero', as being 'nothing' or 'no [one] thing'. However, the first stanza of this poem already makes it clear that such a view is untenable. Superficially, Zero is both all things and none; he wears many disguises, but makes it clear that he is "something more" (ibid.) than these appearances. In short, he has an identity, a nature, an essence, if he chooses to recognise it. For Aiken, man, the Self, *is* the ambiguity, the ever-changing dialectic of self-contradiction and evolution; in other words, man is not a thing but a process:

> at every instant of the perpetual intersection
> of one with another in bloodstream and firmament
> you are again being born and again die,
> only o Phoenix to arise again in flame
> immutable mutable of sunlight
>
> (*The Morning Song of Lord Zero*, iii, 972; italics added)

Describing himself as "immutable mutable" (ibid.) clearly suggests that the nature of the Self is to be paradoxical, ambiguous or self-contradictory, both changing and changeless in the fact of its perpetual change, or, in terms of the poem's title, zero and not zero. Like everything else in the universe, our nature is Heraclitean, a process, a flux that maintains itself through all time. While this may not be the kind of stable identity we wish to have, it is what we are and the only kind of identity we shall ever get. Until we can accept that such is our nature, we shall, like the protagonist of *The Charnel Rose*, remain incurably restless and "forever unsatisfied" (*Rose* I, 1, 27).

The Case Against Memory

The dominance of concentric consciousness gives memory a very powerful role in the psychological development of Aiken's protagonists, all of whom invest considerable energy and time in exploring their past. This is quite common sense. (Although we have dealt with this issue before, a review will be useful at this point.) If we want to know who and what we are, the memories of our actions and external life history, not to mention our feelings, thoughts, and dreams are the most obvious and easiest place to start. However, this ease is misleading because it belies the inherent unreliability of memory. Aiken is keenly aware of how memories can be distorted by "deep magic/ wrought upon them by the falseness of memory" (*Eden*, III, 625). Aiken wants us to become aware of this fact and turn to other aspects of ourselves for identity.

The examination of Aiken's argument against memory may well begin with Forslin, who is clearly a man in search of himself. Having neglected an essential aspect of his life by rejecting love, he indulges in a considerable number of dreams which not only provide, at least, some compensation for lost experiences but also help his self-explorations in search of his true identity. This introspective strategy leads to an important question: could not Forslin pursue the goal of discovering his identity more effectively by recalling the actual events of his life instead of indulging his fantasies? In other words, do we really need imaginative, poetic work and deep introspection in the evolution of consciousness?

A strategy based on memory will not serve the evolution of consciousness well for three reasons. First, were Forslin to recall his actual life, the need for compensatory dreams would merely intensify as the memories of his mistakes and other inadequacies increase his pain. Memory would simply exacerbate, not heal his inner wounds by recalling they very events and decisions that hurt him in the first place. That which should be healing him, memory, would instead become a new source of hurt and pain.

Second, Forslin realises that the outward events and deeds in his life are not adequate in identifying him completely. They are necessary but not sufficient for providing a complete portrait of himself because, like anyone else, he is not merely the sum total of the external, worldly events in which he has been involved. Something has been left out and the dreams are needed to make up the deficiency and to provide some kind of compensatory life to his unlived potentials. Such is the case because, in Aiken's view, day-dreams and fantasies, in addition to thoughts and outward actions, are integral parts of our identity and cannot be ignored if we are to know ourselves. They allow us to a far wider range of experience than the outer world and, thereby, reveal what this 'real' world has left undeveloped in us. Unhindered by physical and social restraints, the imaginary world does not labour under the same limitations as external reality and, for this reason, what initially looks like a weak-willed foolishness in Forslin, is actually a display of wisdom, especially given the fact that he has spent ten years in outward action, single-mindedly perfecting an incredible trick:

> To balance one ball on another ball—
> Tossing the upper one, to catch it, falling
> In easy balance again—
> (*The Jig of Forslin*, I, 3, 58)

Ironically, while he is learning to balance one ball on top of another, he is unbalancing his life, neglecting his needs for companionship and love. From this perspective, his seemingly extreme indulgence in introspection and reverie throughout the poem is no more than a highly necessary counter-balance to his previous extreme of neglect of his inner being. His overly long sojourn in the eccentric phase of consciousness, focused on his career as a circus performer has already resulted in establishing one identity: failed circus clown. However, since our 'outer', worldly identity does not exhaustively show who we are, he must now seek another identity elsewhere. Being a 'failure'—he masters the trick but audiences simply do not recognise its difficulty and remain indifferent—he has nowhere else to turn but inward, to the phase of concentric consciousness.

The third problem with memory is as thorny as the first two: in introspection, how can we distinguish between a memory and a dream, a fantasy or a false memory produced by the imagination? Aiken's answer—and it remains consistent throughout his works—is that we cannot. In the first place, by itself memory can verify nothing. One 'knows' a memory is true only by verifying it with another memory, either one's own or someone else's. We, and/or others might be deluded, or, consciously or unconsciously deceptive, but whatever the case, we can never be sure of the truth because we are simply using memories to check on memories. As Aiken would have known from his readings in psycho-analysis, purely imaginary events have often been mistaken for 'memories' of 'real' events. The 'feeling of truthfulness' that seems to accompany 'real memories' is not a reliable indicator of their actual truth, a phenomenon well known to court room lawyers who must question witnesses who mean well, but who, in fact often offer contradictory evidence of events they have seen first hand. For this reason, memory is not necessarily a good way for Forslin to learn about his true identity.

Given Aiken's emphasis on the evolution of consciousness and implicitly, thereby, on the mind, it is paradoxical that his attitude towards the mind and its powers, such as memory and imagination, is highly ambivalent. While recognising the mind's strengths, he is also wary of its weaknesses. In the early poems, his wariness is indicated by the ambivalent imagery associated with the mind. At one point, he refers, for example, to the "devious paths" (*Forslin*, V, 1, 100) that "wind" (ibid.) through the "lamia-haunted" (ibid.) forest of his mind. Later, less luridly, the protagonist finds himself on "the windy corner of the mind" (*Forslin*, V, 1, 102) and still later, he describes a dream figure as wandering "through the corridors of his brain" (*Forslin*, V, 3, 106). In a subsequent poem, he refers, for example, to "the vagaries of the brain" (*Dust*, III, 165), "the caverns of the mind" (ibid., 167) and "coiling thought" (*Dust*, IV,3,182). Elsewhere, he mocks "the dull garden of my mind" (*Senlin*, I, 5, 201). Like Forslin, Festus finds himself wandering "the brain's enchanted forest" (*Festus*, II, 3, 241) which he later describes as "this goblin forest / We call our minds" (*Festus*, IV, 4, 268). In *Landscape West of Eden*, he describes the mind as "a little coral island" (*Eden*, III, 625) that is "broken upon with all the foams of nescience; / now bared, now glittering, now almost overwhelmed and drowned" (ibid.). This ambivalent imagery and diction associated with the mind culminates in *Time in the Rock* where the mind is described as having been framed by a deceitful magician (*Time*, LVII, 719) and in *A Letter From Li Po*, in which we are told that in seeking our true Self amidst our many roles, "[w]e are once more defrauded by the mind." (*Li Po*, V, 908). This brief survey illustrates that Aiken never overcame his fundamental suspicions about the human mind.

CHAPTER EIGHT

The Third Stage of Consciousness: Synoptic Consciousness

The narcissistic stage of consciousness attained by 'actors' (which is what all of us are, in Aiken's view) is by no means the highest type of consciousness available to humankind. The incompleteness of narcissistic consciousness is seen in the continued existence of the subject-object relationship, a relationship which must eventually be overcome in a higher unity. This dissolution can only happen in what we may call *synoptic consciousness* in which the Self and the world become a single conscious unit, when we and the world have, in a sense, become one. Synoptic consciousness, which seems to resemble some kinds of alternate or mystical states of consciousness, is the type of consciousness attained by the Self at the outer limits of eccentricity when all barriers between the Self and 'other' have been dissolved. To understand how consciousness becomes one with the world it is important to understand the role played by love.

Aiken's theory of synoptic consciousness is closely related to what is undoubtedly the most important pun in his work: "sum". This word has a variety of meanings: sum total in the mathematical sense; to summarise, to complete, to finish; most crucially, however, it means 'I am' in Latin. The latter is an assertion of existence as shown in Descartes' famous statement, "*Cogito, ergo sum*", 'I think, therefore I am', by which he thought to put philosophy on a logically certain foundation. As shall become clear, in synoptic consciousness, all meanings of the word 'sum' are involved.

The Role of Love

According to Aiken, love enables us to attain the highest level of consciousness because it is love that expands the Self and, thereby, broadens the basis from which consciousness grows. All of us know this instinctively, which is why we and the characters in Aiken's poems, seek love so persistently. Because we are evolutionary beings in an evolutionary universe, we all ardently desire the highest form of consciousness which is, in effect, the highest form of ourselves and to attain this highest form of consciousness, we must have love. As shown through the poems of *The Divine Pilgrim*, this obsessive pursuit of love in its various forms—romantic, erotic or narcissistic (*Rose, Senlin, Dust*) and evolutionary—(*Festus*) is one of the demands of our nature. We simply cannot live without love because without love, we are incomplete and less than our true selves. In an evolutionary universe, this is not a tolerable state of affairs.

The idea that love expands the horizons of the Self is a theme that receives its clearest and most powerful expression Aiken's later poetry, notably *Preludes for Memnon, Time in the Rock* and *A Letter from Li Po*. One of the clearest and most dramatic expressions of how love leads to synoptic consciousness is found in the quotation given below.

> Merciful God—
> This is the wondrous thing; that if she touch
> My fingernail with but her fingernail,—
> Or if she look at me, for but the time
> It takes a leaf to fall from leaf to leaf,
> I become music, chaos, light, and sound
> I am no longer I: I am a world.
> (*Preludes for Memnon*, XVI, 518; italics added)

Here we find a powerful expression of love's ability to expand the Self and broaden the base of consciousness. When touched by his lover, the protagonist loses his ordinary sense of identity—"I am no longer I" (ibid.)—and becomes "a world" (ibid.). We may understand this in two ways. First, it can mean that the Self has been expanded to the farthest possible limits of outward or eccentric consciousness in which the Self and the universe or world have become identical, or, second, it can mean that the concentric Self consciously realises that it is a microcosm already containing an entire world within it. In either case, Self and world are now united as one in Aiken's secular counterpart to the experiences reported by mystics who claim to have become one with the 'all', the universe, or and all-inclusive God. This union is precisely what constitutes synoptic consciousness, which, in the tradition of Canadian scholar Francis Maurice Bucke, might also be called "cosmic consciousness".

For Aiken, love is not merely a pleasant experience or entertainment but rather, an essential component in discovering the greatest, most expansive possibilities of our human consciousness and identities. It is an essential ingredient in our evolution, and, indeed, in the evolution of the cosmos itself insofar as human and cosmos become one. In short, appearances to the contrary, ordinary human love and the pursuit of love have cosmic significance and must not, therefore, be denigrated or unnecessarily hindered.

Through the power of love, the protagonist of *Preludes for Memnon* discovers his true identity.

> The thing itself—by God, the thing is music
> For when she touches me, or when she speaks—!

CONRAD AIKEN'S PHILOSOPHY OF CONSCIOUSNESS

> Then comes the little fly's wing of a flame:
> Then the brain lights and dizzies: then the body
> Grows light as brightness . . . And the thing is music.
> (*Preludes for Memnon*, XVI, 517)

Of note here is the allusion to two philosophers whose theories, according to Houston Peterson's *The Melody of Chaos*, had enormous influence on Aiken: Kant and Schopenhauer. Kant held that we can never know the noumenon or essence of a thing, that is, that we are forever ignorant of the thing-in-itself, because it is veiled from us by its phenomenal appearance to us. Since the phenomenal appearance of a thing is shaped by the brain's various processes, we perceive only our own, 'home-made' mental images of a thing and not the thing-in-itself as it really is. We are, in a sense, trapped in a world of images of our own making. Schopenhauer believed that he had a way out of this dilemma. Since everything, including us, is really a manifestation of the cosmic Will we can, in fact, actually know the thing-in-itself by becoming conscious of this cosmic Will *as it appears in ourselves*. The only way to become conscious of this cosmic Will in ourselves—and in everything else—is a decisive plunge into subjectivity, or concentric consciousness in which we see and experience the Will at work within us through our dreams and reveries. In other words, it is possible to know the thing-in-itself by recognising within ourselves the cosmic Will at work in all things. This recognition is best achieved by introspection, subjectivity or concentric consciousness because here the Will can work unimpeded by its own action in other things.

According to Schopenhauer, the closest analogue to the cosmic Will is music which is the art that most closely imitates the pure creativity for its own sake that characterises the workings of the cosmic Will. In that sense, the world is an example of 'art for art's sake' and has no further meaning than as a display of the creativity of the Will. Aiken seems to agree. This idea of observing the world process with detachment, of accepting the world as it is for its own sake is already prefigured in *The House of Dust*, where one participant in a debate about God and the meaning of the world asserts that he accepts the world simply as it appears to him and enjoys all phenomena without any need for a God to provide any additional meaning. He "takes all for granted" (*Dust*, III, 9, 163) and finds

> . . . . more varied pleasure
> In understanding, and so find beauty even
> In this strange dream of yours you call the truth.
> (*The House of Dust*, III, 9, 164)

In a more sober mood, while discussing the death of a friend, this character exemplifies a stoic acceptance of these events: "such things will happen" (*Dust*, III, 9, 164) he says, and endeavours to see "what things flow out of them" (ibid.). This is not much different than the detachment with which one may observe the development of a piece of music. He rejects any notion of providing further significance for these events by reference to the wishes and commandments of a personal God Who is aware of our individual existence. However, such detachment is rarely found in Aiken's work. To an overwhelming extent, his work manifests a passionate involvement in and enjoyment of the phenomena of the world for their own sake, and most especially of love which is able to unify us in sympathy with everything that exists. Such unification is the essence of synoptic consciousness.

Continuing our exploration of *Preludes for Memnon*, XVI, we cannot ignore the fact that the lady's touch also turns the Self not only into music but also into chaos: "I become music, chaos, light, and sound" (*Memnon*, XVI, 518). However, at this stage of consciousness, chaos is not so much a threat as a vast reservoir of potentials from which new worlds and selves may be created. Chaos, after all, for Aiken is not merely confusion and absolute disorder, but rather "our mother chaos" (*Memnon*, IX, 508), the source of our being which contains "music and beauty and the love of love / Music and love and beauty and all that" (ibid.). Since the experience of chaos is a necessary part of the growth process, chaos cannot be entirely negative. Only those who have "no love, to make the chaos bright" (*Memnon*, XXXVIII, 542) will be unable to overcome its dangers because they will waste their energies struggling to resist that which they should accept. Their struggles deprive them of the protection that love affords against chaos because love, after all, provides them with the positive attitude and the sympathy that allows the Self to grow into the chaos and accept its resources.

A further indication of the protection love provides against chaos is found in the following lines:

> In the beginning, chaos, and in the end
> Chaos; and the vast wonder come between,—
> Glory, bewilderment, all sense of brightness.
> Love, be that glory and that sense of brightness.
> You are what chaos yielded. Be my star.
>
> (*Preludes for Memnon*, XX, 520)

This passage implies that the character or nature of chaos is dramatically altered by love and synoptic consciousness which is described as a "vast wonder" (ibid.), a "glory," (ibid.), and a "sense of brightness" (ibid.). It is also described as a "bewilderment" (ibid.) because such an overwhelming experience is bound to upset our psychic equilibrium. This moment comes between the chaos prior to the first attainment of divisive consciousness, and the final chaos associated with synoptic consciousness, for which reason there is chaos at the beginning and "in the end" (ibid.). However, the qualities of the second chaos have been decisively altered by synoptic consciousness, since that chaos has given him the lady he loves. She is "what chaos yielded" (ibid.), but more than that, he wants to identify her with the "glory" (ibid.) of synoptic consciousness itself. "Love, be that glory" (ibid.) he tells her.

CONRAD AIKEN'S PHILOSOPHY OF CONSCIOUSNESS

The idea that love breaks down our ordinary identities and expands the Self is expressed in a more sexually explicit manner in the following quotation,

> And you who make love, you who attach yourselves
> to another mouth, who in the depth of night
> speak without speech, act without conscious action
> in all that lamentable struggle to be another,
> to make that other yourself, to find that other
> to make two one
>
> *who would be tree and earth*
> *cloud and ocean, movement and stillness,*
> *object and shadow*
>
> what can we learn from you
> pathetic ones, poor victims of the will,
> wingless angels who beat with violent arms
> what can we learn from your tragic effort
>   (*Time in the Rock*, XX, 684; italics added)

The connection between love and synoptic consciousness is clearly illustrated in these lines. Synoptic consciousness occurs when a unification of Self and world is achieved, as a result of love's natural tendency to impel a fusion between the Self and another. The assimilative aspect of this impulse is shown in the phrase "to make that other yourself" (ibid.); in short, the Self expands so that the other becomes part of it. When this happens, Self and other, subject and object, will be unified in a single 'entity' or state of consciousness just as "tree and earth / ocean and cloud, movement and stillness" (ibid.) will become one. These lines also suggest that the problems with most lovers is that their action is unconscious; they do what is required to attain synoptic consciousness, but without knowing the full significance of their actions. For this reason, they are truly "wingless angels" (ibid.) who achieve synoptic consciousness more by accident than by intention for which reason their efforts are described as "tragic" (ibid.). Despite this short-coming, they teach us that love is the key to attaining the highest form of consciousness available to humankind. To achieve this state, we need 'only' make the whole world the object of our love, our assimilative affections and not limit ourselves to one person or thing.

Section XX of *Time in the Rock* not only makes clear the correspondence between love-making and becoming one with the universe in synoptic consciousness, but also leaves us with a question about "what we can learn from [the lovers]" (ibid.). The first lesson to learn is "patience" (ibid.) in waiting for the full experience of synoptic consciousness to arrive: "O patience, let us be patient and discern / in this lost leaf all that be discerned" (*Time*, XX, 684). In other words, we must learn the skills of making the most of even the simplest experiences and perceptions. More, specifically, we must develop the patience and courage to learn all that be learned from the "sad violence" (ibid.) of the falling leaf because dying at one level of development to be reborn at another is an inevitable part of our evolutionary existence. We must sweep aside superficial objections and accept and even approve of this "sad violence" (ibid.) as both natural and good. Stated in the most general terms, this passage suggests that we must train ourselves to perceive and take full measure of the depths and complexities of ordinary things as well as of ourselves. In the face of the pressures exerted by ordinary, here-and-now day-time consciousness, this may be harder to achieve than we first expect as shown in the immediately following section, XXI:

> Deep violet, deep snow-cloud, deep despair
> deep root, deep pain, deep morning—must we say
> deepness in all things, find our lives in deepness?
> we are too deep? the breakfast salutation,
> that too is deep? Alas, poor Arabel,
> poor woman, poor deluded human, you
> who finick with a fork and eat an egg,
> are you as deep as thought of you is deep?
>
> (*Time in the Rock*, XXI, 685)

Perceiving the hidden depths of things is painful and perhaps even conducive to a "deep despair" (ibid.) because it means we must abandon the comfortable superficialities of ordinary life and face the fact that we live in a world made of things and people largely unknown to us. This unknown dimension of the ordinary gives rise to concern, and perhaps even fear of the unknown since it threatens us by drawing attention to the limits of our knowledge. The speaker in this stanza ends with a rhetorical question that plainly suggest she is indeed "as deep as thought of [her] is deep" (ibid.).

In the immediately following next stanza, the speaker begins by trying to deny what he has just asserted, but finds that at best he can put off or "defer the notion of the infinite" (ibid.) which is connected to his thoughts of her and the morning. In short, he backhandedly accepts the notion of the great inner depths of people and common things, but chooses not to deal with it at the moment. In the glaring light of every-day, common-sense, limited consciousness, the protagonist puts off any thoughts about "the infinite" (ibid.) we contain or can expand into just as he puts off any reflection on the present, past and future. For a few moments at least he prefers his complete engagement—or should we say, entrapment?—in the ordinary details of life.

Of course, as we have already seen, he need not defer his recognition of the depths of ordinary things if he is protected by love because love protects the Self from the threatening depths and chaos through which all seekers of higher consciousness must travel:

CONRAD AIKEN'S PHILOSOPHY OF CONSCIOUSNESS

> The thousand eyes, the Argus 'I's' of love,
> of these it was in verse, that Li Po wove
> the magic cloak for his last going forth
> into the gorge for his adventure north.
>
> (*A Letter from Li Po*, V, 908)

The "Gorge" (ibid.) in this passage symbolises the depths of things, the "magic cloak" (ibid.) symbolises love and the "adventure north" (ibid.) symbolises Li Po's struggle for a deeper and more inclusive consciousness. In this struggle—which requires recognising the depths in all things—we are protected by the special powers inherent in love.

Assimilative Love

The assimilative and expansive powers of love are, in fact, part of a larger theme which pervades Aiken's poetry from the beginning of his career, the theme of human consciousness as an assimilator of others and the world around them. To perceive is to take in or assimilate that which is around us, not in its substance but in its form insofar as the forms of things leave an impression on the mind. By means of an image, that which was external becomes internalised. While this is true of ordinary consciousness and perception, it is especially true of synoptic consciousness in which the individual and the world become unified. Consequently, this state of consciousness may certainly be seen as the expanding Self assimilating the world.

Throughout Aiken's work, the idea of assimilating the world is often presented in the image of eating which is often explicitly connected with love. This connection between love and devouring is, somewhat grotesquely, evident in the vampire theme which is especially prominent in *The Charnel Rose*, *The Jig of Forslin* (III, 4, 85), and *The House of Dust* (III, 11, 171). For example, the pursuer in *The Charnel Rose* describes himself as a "mouth for blood" (*Rose*, III, 2, 41) who devours "the leaves of autumn" (ibid.) and feels a "madness for red!" (ibid.) He becomes a beast as part of his pursuit of the mysterious woman haunting him. Fortunately, most of Aiken's other poems succeed in avoiding such lurid writing, but the theme of devouring remains. For example, as Festus prays for guidance to attain a new level of consciousness, he says,

> You who have been my guardian angel,
> Point before me once more to some new city,
> Yet more gorgeous kingdom of the east
> For me to feed my heart on like a beast!
>
> (*The Pilgrimage of Festus*, IV, 258)

In order to evolve his consciousness, he must take in or assimilate more experience and more knowledge, an idea that obviously equates perception with a kind of devouring.

This connection is made explicit in one of his last works, *A Letter from Li Po*, where we are told that "each morning we devour the unknown" (*Li Po* IV, 906) and that "we too have eaten of the word" (*Li Po* I, 904), that is, like Li Po, have studied and learned from the great sages of the past.

Aiken does not merely want us to accept that perception and love are a kind of devouring, he wants us to understand that it is a heroic trait because it enlarges man. This idea receives perhaps its most dramatic expression in one of his best and most mature works, *Time in the Rock*:

> And this digester, this digester of food,
> this killer and eater and digester of food,
> the one with teeth and tongue, insatiable belly
> him of the gut and appetite and murder
> . . . .
> this human, you or me—
>
>   look sharply at him
> and measure him, digesters! hear his speech
> woven deceit, colossal dream, so shaped
> of food and search for food—oh believe him
> whose hunger shapes itself as gods or rainbows
>
> is he not perfect, walks he not divinely
> with a light step among the stars his fathers
> with a quick thought among the seeds his sons
> is he not graceful, is he not gentle,
> this foul receiver and expeller of food,
> this channel of corruption,
>
>   Is he not
> the harbinger, the angel, the bright prophet
> who knows the right from wrong, whose thought is pure,
> dissects the angles, numbers pains and pleasures,
> dreams like an algebra among waste worlds—
> can we not trust him, sees he not the sure
> disposes time and space, condemns the evil-doer—
> in his digestion not an ample measure?
>
>   (*Time in the Rock*, XXVIII, 692-693)

This sometimes startling passage not only describes in detail our nature as eaters, digesters and "expellers" (ibid.) of food, but also praises this aspect of our existence and draws our attention to its metaphysical significance. These activities show that we are a part of the cosmic cycle of activities and materials, that we are so intimately linked to the universe that we can call the stars our "fathers" (ibid.). As a "channel of corruption" (ibid.) each of us participates in activities regarded as a 'low' and 'foul' while at the same time, each of us is part of the 'high' as well, an "angel" (ibid.) and "bright prophet" (ibid.). We "dissect" (ibid.) or take apart not only our food but also our perceptions and ideas in the quest for knowledge and discover and learn through assimilation or 'digestion'. Of course, the conclusion that the speaker reaches, namely that man ought to be trusted because he has true knowledge, is intended ironically. Precisely because he is "woven deceit" (ibid.) and "colossal dream" (ibid.) we must also be suspicious of him, and especially of any claims to final knowledge in a Heraclitean universe wherein nothing can ever be final.

A more moderately expressed parallel text can be found in *Preludes for Memnon*:

> All hail to selfhood, who is come refreshed
> From nightlong dark digestion of the things
> He trapped from chaos of the yesterday.
> And here is noon, and rest; and here is evening
> With all those golden flies which yet remain
> For conquest by the cunning. Self is strong:
> He shapes the world as should be. *He is wise:*
> *He understands the world as food.* He spins
> The broken rim anew and calls it good.
>
> (*Preludes for Memnon*, XII, 512; italics added)

Plainly, Aiken regards man's assimilative impulse in perception, love and synoptic consciousness as natural; love is perhaps only its most intense manifestation as two lovers become more and more like each other. As with the previous passage from *Time in the Rock*, here too it is important to note the undercurrent of irony. Humankind indeed possesses the admirable qualities attributed to it but we must never forget that the context is a Heraclitean universe in which everything is constantly changing—often into its opposite. Thus, we both have and do not have these qualities, a self-contradictory state of affairs that makes human existence inherently paradoxical.

It is worth noting that the association of perception, love and synoptic consciousness with assimilation or devouring is no mere intellectual idiosyncrasy on Aiken's part, but rather a logical consequence of his Kantian epistemological allegiances expressed in physiological terms. According to Kant, we assimilate raw data from the surrounding world, and, by means of the categories, 'digest', that is, reshape this data in our own way to produce an image of 'reality'. This image becomes a part of ourselves just as food becomes part of ourselves when we eat. Structurally speaking, the situations in perception and eating are identical.

Ontological Separation versus Isolation

One of the most important issues raised by Aiken's Kantian biases is that of ontological loneliness. This loneliness has two sources in Kant's philosophy. The first is the fact that the noumenal realm always retains its ontological integrity, that is, remains unaffected by any action in or from the phenomenal realm. In this sense, the noumenal is always isolated and alone—as is the phenomenal which can never break through to reach the noumenal. The second source of ontological loneliness lies in a solipsistic interpretation of Kant's philosophy, an interpretation asserting that only our own existence and nothing else can be certain for us. Since we only receive raw data from outside ourselves and then shape it into an image of the world, we are, in effect, trapped inside a 'bubble' of images that we project on whatever reality is. How can we know what the world outside our 'bubble' of home-made perceptions is really like? How can we know it is even there? Perhaps we are simply hallucinating the world. Even if we reject solipsism as too unlikely, we still face the problem of how we can truly 'meet' other beings from the world around us: they are separated from us by the image that we have made for them. How can we really know what they are like?

Until his later poems, the theme of ontological loneliness received relatively little, if any, direct attention in Aiken's work. It is indirectly present insofar as the majority of the protagonists in the poems of *The Divine Pilgrim* are alone with their own thoughts and imaginations and give the impression of being doomed to remain that way. Some images also suggest this theme. For example, in *The Pilgrimage of Festus*, Festus and the Old Man (a dream ego) discuss a pool inhabited by a crab whose very efforts to catch the star reflected in the pool distort and destroy the reflection. Because it is doomed to "lose the image of [its] desire" (*Festus*, V, 269), the crab is also doomed to remain alone, isolated from what it wants because the effort of reaching out will destroy what it wants. Both Festus and the Old Man seem to be aware that because of this we are inherently alone. We might also interpret some lines in Aiken's earlier poems as pre-figuring this theme. For example, one of Forslin's dream egos says it is possible that "all we know is lost, or only a dream, / That dreams are real and real things only dream" (*Forslin*, IV, 1, 89). This certainly shows some understanding of the possible solipsistic consequences of Kant's philosophy. If Kant's theories were true, we would all be ineluctably alone in our home-made dream worlds. However, the poem does not explore the personal, existential consequences of such a view.

In *Preludes for Memnon* we find the inherent loneliness of things emphasised in two particularly interesting passages. The first of these occurs in the context of a soliloquy on the necessity of using symbols in discourse. The speaker finds that the symbols he uses to talk about things

> Leave the silver core uneaten;
> The golden leaf unplucked; the bitter calyx
> Virginal; and the whirling You unknown.
>
> (*Preludes for Memnon*, V, 503)

CONRAD AIKEN'S PHILOSOPHY OF CONSCIOUSNESS

Despite the speaker's attempts to change this situation, that is, to actually 'make contact' with what he perceives or loves, there is no sign that he is successful. The "silver core" (ibid.), the "bitter calyx" (ibid.) and the "whirling You" (ibid.) all refer to the essence of thing whose integrity remains untouched by language in the same way that Kant's noumenon cannot be touched by any action in the phenomenal realm. This idea is somewhat reminiscent of the crab in the pool discussed by Festus and the Old Man; the star itself is completely unaffected by the actions of the crab and in that sense, the two remain inescapably isolated from one another. Both are inherently alone. The second passage in *Preludes for Memnon* emphasising the solitary nature of things is section X in which the lover and his lady are portrayed as Scylla and Carybdis: "it is ourselves who are these selfsame rocks (Memnon, X, 509). Neither this section, nor subsequent ones offer any hope of the two being joined, that is, overcoming their essential separation.

However, one of the curious consequences of Kant's philosophy is that although the noumenon is alone insofar as it remains unaffected by our thoughts and actions, it is not unconnected from the phenomenal of which it is the original source. In other words, 'connection' and 'ontological loneliness' are two different issues. For this reason the lover and his lady are ontologically lonely, that is, untouched in their noumenal integrity, but they are not unconnected because they are, in fact, connected by the very whirlpool that flows between them. Noting the numerous objects in the room between them, the speaker tells his lady, "All our communion [is] through them, and our speech / You there, I here, who half-perceive each other" (*Memnon*, IX, 508) The two are separated but not isolated, a somewhat paradoxical situation also found in Kant insofar as we are ontologically separated from the noumenon but still somehow connected to it by the phenomenal data we receive from it. As logically required by the Kantianism which informs so much of his work, Aiken uses the term "half-perceive" (ibid.) because the mind only does half the work: it is the noumenon that supplies the 'raw material' and shapes it into an image of the other. The mind and noumenon are partners in the venture of creating perceptions.

In *Time in the Rock*, Aiken explores one of the social consequences of our Kantian ontological situation. There, the "wounded one" (*Time*, VIII, 671) cannot really communicate his agony to the speaker, who only comes to his "own black heart again" (ibid.).

> And I thought with him, remembering with him, knowing
> nothing of his own words or world or wound,
> only my own wound that I could share,
> my own word that I could give
> (*Time in the Rock*, VIII, 672)

Just as the raw material supplied by the noumenon can only stimulate the creation of a phenomenological image, the 'other's' words seem capable only of evoking the speaker's own experiences by means of which he may analogously understand the 'other's' pain. Because we are inevitably separated, all understanding of another person is bound to be analogous and not an immediate reflection of how they actually are in themselves; in Aiken's view, such immediate knowledge of another's actual state-of-being is unattainable. The 'other's' experiences are forever unknowable to us. That is why the speaker uses the word "share" (ibid.) not so much in the sense of 'several making use of one thing' as in the sense of 'each making his own contribution' to a common activity. Each person can only experience his or her own pain and assume that the 'other's' feelings are similar. Our separation or ontological loneliness is beyond remedy. Despite all our efforts at communication, we are destined to remain mysterious to each other. This idea is reinforced by section XXII of *Time in the Rock* where change is portrayed as another reason for our ontological loneliness or separation. Since human beings, like Heraclitus' river, never remain the same, how can we hope to know them as they are, let alone join them in some essential way?

However, our ontological loneliness is not merely a capricious aspect of human existence. Indeed, it fulfils the extremely important function of guaranteeing our personal integrity and independence. This consequence receives perhaps its clearest expression in *A Letter from Li Po*:

> Sole pride and loneliness: it is the state
> the kingdom rather of all things: . . .
> . . . .
> Here is the divine loneliness in which
> we greet, only to doubt, a voice, a word
> the smoke of sweet fern after frost, a face
> touched and loved, but still unknown, and then
> a body, still mysterious in embrace.
>
> (*A Letter from Li Po*, III, 905)

Even in the most intimate physical contact, the other person remains mysterious. Yet this is not a reason to despair. Rather, we should take comfort in this situation because our ontological loneliness is also a "kingdom" (ibid.) and a "divine loneliness" (ibid.) providing us with the independence and integrity usually ascribed to God. We have no reason for fear despite all of the changes to which we are inevitably subjected in a Heraclitean universe. Furthermore, this independence underwrites our freedom since that which is beyond reach cannot be diminished by others.

Section IV of *A Letter from Li Po* explores some of the personal implications of this situation.

> Exiled we are. Were exiles born. The 'far away',
> language of desert, language of ocean, language of sky,
> as of the unfathomable worlds that lie
> between the apple and the eye,
> these are the only words we learn to say.
> Each morning we devour the unknown. Each day

> we find, and take, and spill, or spend, or lose,
> a sunflower splendor of which none knows the source.
> This cornucopia of air! This very heaven
> of a simple day! We do not know, can never know
> the alphabet to find us entrance there.
> So, in the street, we stand and stare
> to greet a friend, and shake his hand,
> yet know him beyond knowledge, like ourselves;
> ocean unknowable by unknowable sand.
>
> (*A Letter from Li Po*, IV, 906)

This passage clearly affirms the ultimate mysteriousness of others and the world from which we are apparently "exiled" (ibid.). The reason for this mysteriousness is clear: perception is Kantian in nature and, therefore, others must remain essentially unknown since they cannot be experienced in their essential selves. All we have in our life is our image or experience of them because we cannot transcend the limits of Self. The same is true of the world: we can never find "entrance" (ibid.) to the noumenal source of our phenomenal experiences. All that we really do know are the "unfathomable worlds" (ibid.) of experience that lie between the "[objective] apple and the [subjective] eye" (ibid.). However, as already noted before in the situation of the lover and his lady, the "apple and the eye" (ibid.), while separate, are not unconnected because they are joined by the "unfathomable worlds" (ibid.) that lie between them.

The ontological loneliness of things raises a problem for synoptic consciousness: how can there be a unifying relationship and assimilation of things that are noumenally separate? Here, too, the answer lies in Kant's philosophy in which the phrase 'the world' really means 'the phenomenal world of my experience'. Consequently, what we refer to as 'the other person', is really 'the other person as I experience her or him in the world that I have constructed.' After all, other things are always the objects of my experience. This means that the other and Self are always related to us *in our phenomenal consciousness* but, at the same time, are also, noumenally essentially inaccessible to us, shielded, paradoxically, by the very consciousness that joins them! Our consciousness which creates the phenomenal world from the materials supplied by the noumenon both separates and joins. From this we may conclude that Aiken sees human consciousness as marked by an inherent paradox of being separate yet one with things, distinct and yet unified with them.

The only way to resolve this paradoxical unity and separation of Self and world is to recall that all actions and encounters take place within consciousness itself. When we clearly and fully realise this, we attain synoptic consciousness at which level we recognise that

> The landscape and the language are the same.
> And we ourselves are language and are land,

> together grew with Sheepfold Hill, rock, and hand,
> and mind, all taking substance in a thought
> wrought out of mystery: bird flight and air
> predestined from the first to be a pair:
>
> (*A Letter from Li Po*, XI, 913)

"Language and landscape" (ibid.) can be "the same" (ibid.) because, in a Kantian sense, we 'make' the landscape by processing the data from the noumenal realm into what we call 'the landscape'. We also shape the landscape with the concepts and words we use to describe it, or, as Aiken says, "with the name / [we] bestow an essence and a meaning too" (*Li Po*, X, 913) Furthermore, the "language and the land" (ibid.) are the same because both are made of the same energy that constitutes the Self. In terms of our previous discussion of Schopenhauer's theories, we would say that language, land, landscape and Self are all made of and constituted by music is "the thing itself" (*Memnon*, XVI, 517). Being made of the same metaphysical 'stuff' makes all things the same, and, in a sense, unifies them or, at least, provides a basis for unity. This is the reason why we "grew with Sheepfold Hill" (*Li Po*, XI, 913); as our consciousness evolved, so did our perception of the world in which we live. Indeed, synoptic consciousness is the fully conscious realisation that the Self and the world are, in the last analysis, one and the same. Hence, the development of one is the development of the other.

The "bird flight and air / Predestined from the first to be a pair" (ibid.) expresses this idea by means of a concrete image. The "bird flight and air" (ibid.), symbolise the subject and object, the consciousness and world, the noumenal and phenomenal realms which are necessary for there to be a world for us to perceive. They are distinct, and thus ontologically lonely, but not absolutely separate; furthermore, they are made of the same metaphysical 'stuff', be it thought of as 'energy' or 'music'.

Like the theme of ontological loneliness, the notion that Self and the world are an essential pair made of the same 'substance' is a late development in Aiken's philosophy of consciousness. It is one of those blank spots on his intellectual or philosophical map that he filled in later as is own understanding of his philosophy deepened. For this reason, there are few if any suggestions of these ideas in his early works and we must wait until *Preludes for Memnon* for this theme to emerge. Here the lover realizes that "the 'I' changes, and with it the 'you' "(*Memnon*, XXIII, 526), that he and his beloved, like the "bird flight and air" (*Li Po*, XI, 913) are a pair, of inseparable correlates. He also finds that there are made of the same 'substance': "Is this my hand or yours? ah, no such thing. / It is the fog which curtsies to the fog" (*Memnon*, XXIII, 527). The two are formally different but substantially the same. Further on, the lover also realizes that since he and his beloved are essentially one, he cannot harm her without harming himself:

> Strike her till she be dead: and it is you
> Who will lie dead with the world's ruin about you.
>
> (*Preludes for Memnon*, XXX, 536)

CONRAD AIKEN'S PHILOSOPHY OF CONSCIOUSNESS

Aiken's philosophical beliefs mandate this conclusion for two reasons. In the first place, it follows from the belief, adopted from Schopenhauer, that all things are made of the same metaphysical 'stuff', namely, the Will (or music) that makes up the noumenon of all things (See *Memnon*, XVI, 517). It also follows logically from Aiken's Kantian premises. If the 'other' is really the 'other' as constituted by my experience, then to slay the 'other' is to slay the Self because the 'other' and 'my experience' are, ultimately, identical. The same idea of unity is expressed in the line "The 'I' changes, and with it the 'you'" (*Memnon*, XXIII, 526) because if the Self that constitutes the 'other' changes, the 'other' must change as well. In this connection we should also recall the statement in *A Letter from Li Po* that our ancestors live through us, that is, both through our consciousness of them and through the substantial unity we share with them as being made of the same metaphysical 'stuff'. Thus we "become new eyes / with which they see" (*Li Po*, X, 913). The same idea is found in *The Crystal*, one of the last poems Aiken wrote. The speaker greets Pythagoras

> Separate in time,
> and yet not separate. Making oblation
> in a single moment of consciousness
> to the endless forever-together.
>
> (*The Crystal*, V, 954)

In Aiken's view, all things are involved separately in this "forever-together" (ibid.) in which things are both independent and connected.

At this point it has become clear that for Aiken, consciousness is essentially dual in nature; it has two poles, namely the Self and 'other', regardless of whether that 'other' is human or not. Both Self and 'other' are contained within a single experience or moment of consciousness and are thus part of a comprehensive unity that embraces them both. Moreover, it is clear that in Aiken's view, consciousness does not destroy the distinctions between things, but rather enriches them by making them part of a wider, more inclusive unity just as the chemicals that make up our food are not destroyed but integrated into a new network of relations and thus fulfill additional functions. For example, iron in the blood does not lose its essential nature, yet carries out new functions and actualizes new potentials as a result of being part of the body.

The extremely radical nature of Aiken's theory of consciousness is also apparent at this point. If all things are contents of *my* consciousness, it means that, in a sense, they are mine. My experience of the 'other' is still *my* experience, or, put another way, *the 'other' is my experience.* As far as consciousness and experience are concerned, the 'other' and Self are one. When this line of reasoning is applied to all things, it soon becomes clear that startling as it may be, *I am the world!* After all, how can I be separated from my experiences and my consciousness? And since the 'other,' the world, is part of my consciousness if follows that the two must be one in some sense. In the plainest possible terms, this is the philosophical nature of synoptic consciousness, a state in which these realisations are experienced—not merely thought—with a clarity not given to words. In short, the difference between subject and object, which is essential in divisive consciousness is now entirely overcome.

The Thing Itself: Synoptic Consciousness

Synoptic consciousness occurs when the Self consciously realises that it is literally one with the world. This statement, however, is deceptively simple and requires explanation. It means, in the first place, that the Self knows, experientially and intellectually, that the 'other,' the world and cosmos—the only world and cosmos it can ever know—are possessed by the Self in its consciousness of them. After all, the Self constitutes them. When the Self understands fully that it *is* its experience and consciousness, the full force of this realisation strikes home: if I am my consciousness and the 'other,' the world is 'in' my consciousness, then I and the world must be one. Obviously the subject-object dichotomy no longer exists. Moreover, since the Self is conscious, the 'other,' the world itself, must also be conscious in some way. From this it follows that the Self is the consciousness of the world. We shall deal with this in more detail below.

This unification, however, leaves Aiken's philosophy of consciousness with a serious problem. While the Self may be experientially unified with an 'other,' has it become one with the 'essential' or 'noumenal' 'other'? Are they actually or ontologically one or only experienced *as if* they were one? Aiken's answer is that they are actually one, an answer that he derives as a logical consequence of his philosophical commitments to both Kant and Schopenhauer. In Kant's philosophy both the phenomenal experience which is created by the psyche from external data, and the noumenon which provides the external data are real, each in its own way. Since we can never pierce through and go beyond our experience to see what things are 'really' like noumenally, we have to accept our phenomenal experience as fully real. Where else but to our own experience can we turn for knowledge? From Kant's point of view, the psychological and the ontological cannot be distinguished simply because we cannot transcend our experience to compare it with anything else. Whatever we experience must, therefore, be accepted as fully real and there is no logical choice but to affirm as real Aiken's experiential unity of Self and 'other.' This conclusion is re-enforced by Aiken's commitment to Schopenhauer, according to whom we can experience the noumenal reality of all things because the noumenal reality of all things, including ourselves, is Will. When the powers and processes of Self have been fully experienced, the Self realises that the processes occurring within itself occur in the other as well. In fact, they occur in everything else at all times and in all places. Stated in plainest philosophical terms, this means that according to

CONRAD AIKEN'S PHILOSOPHY OF CONSCIOUSNESS

Aiken's philosophy, in synoptic consciousness the isolation and integrity of Kant's noumenon is overcome by the ubiquity of Schopenhauer's Will. While earlier forms of consciousness show their Kantian nature by recognising the noumenal integrity and "sole pride" (*Li Po*, III, 905) of all things, synoptic consciousness turns towards Schopenhauer. Kant's noumenal isolation is overcome because all things are made of and, therefore, connected by the Will. By turning inward to our own subjective experience of this Will, we can, in fact, achieve genuine unity with the entire cosmos. Synoptic consciousness makes us aware of this unity.

Aiken's theory of synoptic consciousness rests entirely on a three levelled pun on the word 'sum'. At the first level of meaning, 'sum' refers to the numerical 'sum total' of things while at the second level, it is Latin for 'I am', and shows consciousness of one's existence. At the third level, 'sum' refers to a 'summarisation' in the sense of an 'encapsulation' or condensation, as for example, in the traditional doctrine of humankind being the microcosm or a succinct 'encapsulation' of the macrocosm. With sufficiently subtle reading, we can often find all three meanings used simultaneously, as, for example, in the following quotation:

> And with each part we play
> we add to cosmic *Sum* and cosmic sum.
> (*A Letter from Li Po*, V, 908; Aiken's italics)

In every role we play—and Aiken sees life as role-playing—we add to the number of roles that have been enacted in the universe. This is 'sum' in the first, numerical or accumulative sense. We then come to the second, Latin sense of 'sum' as 'I am'. Because the universe and we are essentially one, our self-consciousness is also shared by the universe, which is, therefore, self-conscious through us. We are the self-consciousness of the entire universe. Finally, because each role we play and each moment of synoptic consciousness sums up, succinctly encapsulates or condenses the cosmic process to that very moment, each role also summarizes the universe. Here we have 'sum' in its third sense. In all of Aiken's descriptions of synoptic consciousness, the last two meanings, 'sum' as 'I am' and as an encapsulation are always present, though sometimes hints of the first meaning are also detectable.

The following quotation helps provide a clearer idea of 'sum' in the Latin, 'I am" sense.

> Ah here you have
> Poor wretch, poor wretch, *the essence of it all*:
> Catch here in agony the golden fragment:
> Be conscious, *for* a fraction of the world:
> (*Preludes for Memnon*, XL, II, 545; italics added)

In their condensed philosophical intensity, these lines are vintage Aiken. In the moment of synoptic consciousness we have "the essence of it all" (ibid.), that is, we have, in microcosmic form the essence of the cosmos because in such moments we are one with the Will that makes up all things. In these moments we have caught "the golden fragment" (ibid.), that is, the portion that summarises, or encapsulates the whole and is for that reason special, or "golden" (ibid.). We achieve this moment "in agony" (ibid.) because of the enormous sacrifices the Self must make to attain it. The pun in the last line makes it clear that human beings should be conscious not only during ('for') a brief moment, but should also be conscious on behalf of ('for') the world. In synoptic consciousness, we are to be the world's consciousness even if only for a moment or "fraction' (ibid.). When we achieve synoptic consciousness, the world itself becomes conscious.

The following quotation from *Landscape West of Eden* also exhibits the various meanings of 'sum'. Speaking to the protagonist, the angel says,

> what of the kidneys, the liver, the heart, the stomach?
> Your speech is these: it is the sum also of these:
> you are the sum of worlds within and worlds without.
> (*Landscape West of Eden*, XX, 647)

Our speech is the sum of our organs insofar as it is a succinct and total encapsulation of *all* the processes that constitute our existence, that is, of the "worlds within and worlds without" (ibid.). Because it is the final encapsulation of all, it is also the sum total of all things, the last number that defines totality. Finally, these lines state that we are the 'I am', or self-consciousness of the universe itself.

A further example of this vital pun is found in *Time in the Rock* where the protagonist asks,

> But who will sum the world? what god will add
> digit to digit, sand grain to sand grain,
> amuse himself, on the last wall of knowledge,
> laugh there, be boisterous, sum all things up
> in one vast thunderclap of synthesis—
> speak his own sentence, and be dead?
> (*Time in the Rock*, XXVI, 691)

The numerical meaning of 'sum' is immediately evident here in the reference to adding "digit to digit" (ibid.) until we have come to the last thing to add and stand "on the last wall of knowledge" (ibid.). There we are to be happy and "sum all things up / in one vast thunderclap of synthesis" (ibid.), that is, we are to summarise or encapsulate the entire universe in one moment of synoptic consciousness. However, in summing up the universe in this way, we will "speak [our] own sentence" (ibid.), that is, also summarise ourselves since in synoptic consciousness, Self and universe are one. In speaking our own sentence (note the pun on the judicial meaning of 'sentence') we die, we come to the end in our current identity and prepare to struggle for a new one.

In the next stanza, the protagonist re-enforces and elaborates these ideas, telling his beloved that in every moment there is enough time for

> new sentences, each wider than the last,
> new knowledges, new visions and revisions,
> that we ourselves are like that god; each moment
> is the last wall from which our laughter rings;
> the world summed up and there a new world found,
> vaster and richer, a new synthesis
>
> (*Time in the Rock*, XXVI, 691)

As we attain successive states of synoptic consciousness—and with them, new identities—we find that our lives grow more inclusive or "wider" (ibid.), "vaster and richer" (ibid.). We also discover that we are like God insofar as this process involves the continual re-creation of the universe as we re-create ourselves at successively higher stages of evolution. Finally, in each case, the attainment of synoptic consciousness requires us to sum up, that is, calculate the sum total of the world, to encapsulate its essence and to be the consciousness of the world itself.

It will have been noted that there is a close connection between synoptic consciousness and death. The connection is that the attainment of synoptic consciousness marks the furthest possible development of one identity and, therefore, its end, or death and the consequent beginning of the struggle for a new one. In a sense the old Self and the world become 'nothing' at this supreme moment when the "world is lost" (*Memnon*, XIII, 503):

> But if
> Miraculous vision gives us all at once,
> The universe of birds and boughs and all
> The trees and birds from which their time has come
> The world is lost . . .
>
> (*Preludes for Memnon*, XIII, 513)

The "miraculous vision" (ibid.) of synoptic consciousness summarizes the world, that is, gives it to us "all at once" (ibid.); however, at the same moment, this world dies for us as we embark on a new quest for still wider and richer visions. As a result, the protagonist in *Preludes for Memnon* says he has come "From a vast everything whose sum is nothing" (*Memnon*, LIII, 560). He has just emerged from synoptic consciousness, the "vast everything" (ibid.), which ironically is "nothing" (ibid.) because it means he must start his quest for identity and synoptic consciousness all over again. He has, indeed, achieved nothing but nothing at a 'higher' more advanced level than before.

In a similar vein, the protagonist of *Time in the Rock* advises his lady that

> For at one stroke—no matter whence it come—
> lightening or ice or blood—inward and outward
> will singularly cease and be the same.
> Then history will give to both a name;
> and so at last those things so bravely done
> will be at peace with what was merely known.
>
> (*Time in the Rock*, X, 673)

Here, too, we observe the close connection between synoptic consciousness when "inward and outward / will singularly cease and be the same" (ibid.) and death, the passage into history. In synoptic consciousness, the barriers that divide the world into inner and outer disappear, and consequently, the entire world becomes one. When this happens, the world is finished and passes into history, thereby requiring the creation of a new world. That is why the protagonist later tells the lady that "the sum of all your notes is nothing . . . / Make a rich note of this—and start again" (*Time*, XLVII, 712). Moreover, in the attainment of synoptic consciousness, the two, usually distinct, philosophical categories of 'doing' and 'knowing' will be unified: "those things so bravely *done*" (ibid.; italics added), will be reconciled with our intellectual knowledge of them, that is, with the "merely *known*" (ibid.; italics added). Thus, once again, we see synoptic consciousness portrayed as a unifier of differences.

It is also important to note the close relationship between language and synoptic consciousness. This connection has already been noted when the protagonist of *Time in the Rock*, used a rhetorical question to suggest that his lady "sum all things up / in one vast thunderclap of synthesis / speak [her] own sentence, and be dead . . . (*Time*, XXVI, 691). The final summarising action of synoptic consciousness is embodied in language. Aiken conveys a similar idea when he says that each syllable "sums all, means all, states the vast end / and vast beginning" (*Time*, XXIII, 687). At this point one might recall the incident in *Landscape West of Eden* where the one sage has a language "'in which the meaning is so concentrated, so terrible, so godlike!—/ that one quick syllable is a thousand years.'" (*Eden* X, 634). As a result of speaking this syllable, the characters suddenly "were changed" (ibid.), that is, summed up and ready to begin the next phase in the evolution of their consciousness. Obviously this sage has spoken the final summarising word, which puts an end to one world and begins the creative process of seeking another.

From the foregoing discussion, it has become clear that not only does language allow us to summarise, complete and, thereby, end one world but also that language allows us to rebuild the world anew. For this reason we may say that language is also associated with freedom: it frees us from the strictures of the old and permits us to re-create the world according to our choices. Moreover, language is also associated with death insofar as it helps sum up, complete and end the existence of things in one phase in order to begin another. This makes it clear that in an evolutionary universe in which change is ubiquitous, there must be a connection between freedom and death since the freedom to re-create requires the death of the old. We shall explore this aspect of Aiken's philosophy later.

If we ask ourselves what is achieved by the attainment of synoptic consciousness, the first answer is that in synoptic consciousness, the Self takes possession of the world which it discovers to be its own. What we call 'the world' is actually the world of the Self's experience. This idea of becoming one with the world is so important to Aiken that it finds its way even into one of his weakest and least readable long poems, *John Deth*. Here Juliana Goatibed is Aiken's symbol of consciousness. At her moment of triumph "she and the world became but one" (*John Deth*, IV, 441) whereupon the world turned into a "stone" (ibid.) and she "lay like stone" (ibid.). Obviously, the world's development has stopped in this petrified state; it has been summed up if only for a moment before Juliana begins the creative process again by "carve[ing] the rock beneath her head" (ibid.).

In synoptic consciousness, the Self also comes into full possession of itself. To understand what this means, it is necessary to recall that in the subject-object relationship, 'object' *actually* means 'object of the subject's experience'. When this relationship is seen as a real dichotomy, the subject Self is obviously alienated from a part of its own experience; Self thinks the object is separate and different from itself. Synoptic consciousness cancels this error, and reunites the Self with the 'other half' of its own experience, and in that sense 'heals' it of an unnatural division. The advance to synoptic consciousness is an advance towards health because it is an advance toward a wholeness or complete self-possession in which Self overcomes its alienated condition. The fact that synoptic consciousness provides total self-possession helps us to understand why Aiken frequently associates it with angels, the miraculous, and divinity. Only a divine being is totally self-possessed and possess complete self-sufficiency.

Finally, synoptic consciousness permits the Self to know the usually mysterious other beings in the world from the 'inside', that is, to know them essentially as beings like itself, that is, as manifestations of the cosmic Will and as parts of the entire cosmic process. Once this truth is fully realised there is no reason why the cosmos should not be utterly clear to the Self. This is undoubtedly why Aiken associates the attainment of synoptic consciousness with light and frequently with music.

However, the dynamic nature of consciousness and of the universe itself forbids the achievement of any permanent rest or stasis, even at the highest level. Inevitably, the Self must re-enter chaos and begin the struggle to reach synoptic consciousness at a still higher and more inclusive level; it is a process that leads us from "from God to chaos, and chaos to God again" (*Time*, XXVI, 691). This seems to be the only enduring pattern in the life of the Self. We must not, however, confuse this repetition with a 'circular' motion that goes nowhere; we must remember that the synoptic consciousness attained at the end of each round is higher than its predecessor. The implication is that the Self is not only involved in a 'circular' motion, but in a 'forward' motion as well. This forward motion is the subject of our next chapter on the evolution of consciousness.

CHAPTER NINE

The Evolution of Consciousness.

The best way to begin understanding Aiken's theory of the evolution of consciousness is to imagine the wheel of a car: the wheel not only circles its own centre but also moves forward towards a particular destination on the ground. Employing this metaphor, we may say that in the foregoing chapters we have focused attention on what is involved in the circular motion of the wheel. In this chapter, we shall focus on the path the wheel is following to its goal.

In order to understand Aiken's philosophy of the evolution of consciousness accurately, it is necessary to clarify what he means by the term 'evolution'. One of the best ways to discover what he means by this term is to analyse the images he uses to portray it. Not surprisingly, the most common of these images are stairs, journeys and sailing expeditions, all of which convey the idea of movement from one place to another.

Stair imagery plays an important role in Aiken's poetry, especially in the earlier works. We first encounter such images in *The Charnel Rose* where we find several references to the "eternal mistress" (*Rose*, V, 6, 46) to whose apartment a lover is climbing:

> The eternal mistress lifts her hand,
> To rearrange her hair,
> For the deathless lover who climbs and climbs the stair.
> (*The Charnel Rose*, V, 6, 46)

Almost identical images can be found in *The Jig of Forslin, Senlin: A Biography, The Pilgrimage of Festus* and among Aiken's later works, in *Blues for Ruby Matrix*. Forslin, for example, mutters that he has "climbed stairs with a candle between [his] palms / To seek the eternal secret behind the door" (*Forslin*, V, 1, 102) and that "Once in the darkness I heard her [the secret] singing" (ibid.). Senlin finds himself in a similar position, and at one point the lady even reaches down to him! The image of the stair-climbers is less frequently encountered in the work of Aiken's middle period. However, both *Time in the Rock* and *Landscape West of Eden* present easily recognised variations. In the latter poem, we find a reference to "angelic salmon" (*Eden*, VII, 630) that "reascend /

up the long cataract of God" (ibid.). The speaker in *Time in the Rock* describes a series of stepping stones over which man may cross (*Time*, XV, 679).

Aiken also portrays the evolution of consciousness as a journey. This idea is already implicit in the very title *The Divine Pilgrim*. However, the notion of man as a traveller is especially stressed in *Preludes for Memnon*, in which there are numerous references to a westward journey, often identified with the quest for the Northwest Passage, as well as a journey to the Poles. The image of the evolution of consciousness as a sea journey plays an important role in *Landscape West of Eden*, as it does in *The Crystal* where the protagonist, Pythagoras, sails "the westward pour of the worlds and the westward pour of the mind" (*The Crystal*, IV, 953). Toward the end of *Time in the Rock*, LXXXIX there is a long section devoted to the journey of consciousness. We should note that William Blackstone, the protagonist of *The Kid*, Aiken's only historically based symbol of the evolution of consciousness, is a traveller who journeys across the entire United States from east to west. Finally, we must recall that Li Po is a traveller, a "Rover of chaos" (*Li Po*, IV, 906) heading northward to the "Gorge" of chaos (*Li Po*, X, 912).

Death and Change

Like the evolution of consciousness, journeys involve change, and change is inevitably associated with death in Aiken's work because in all change some place, thing, person or condition is necessarily left behind. Relative to our new place or condition, they 'die' to us; they are no longer available to us as future possibilities for which reason we may say that all change involves dying in some way or another. In a Heraclitean universe in which everything evolves, this means that are "dedicated to death" (*Memnon*, I, 499), and that all things know death "and seek it gladly" (*Time*, XCIII, 754). The same idea is involved in the statement that "each moment [we] must die" (*Li Po*, II, 904). Among his early poems, Aiken's concern with death and evolution is most clearly evident in *The Pilgrimage of Festus* where Festus observes

> How the hunted stars together choiring climb
> From cloud to cloud, like pilgrims,
> Dreamily, slowly ascending the long blue *stairs* of fate,—
> Patient and pale, like those who, unresisting
> Go forth to death and close their eyes and wait,—
> (*The Pilgrimage of Festus*,I,6, 231; italics added)

Because the stars evolve, they must die to an old condition to enter a new one. These lines even suggest that in some way, they understand this because they do not resist their fate but sing as they climb the stairs to a higher level of being. Indeed, the use of the word "pilgrims" (ibid.) casts a religious light on their actions. Later in this poem, Aiken provides a far more startling image connecting death, evolution and creation—namely, the "orchestra of butchers" (*Festus*, V, 273) who are gathered for a holiday and make beautiful music: "The hands that held the cleaver draw the bow"(ibid.). Their music, which his dream ego, the Old Man, first hears as a "scream of pain" (ibid.) is really the music of evolution and growth, of the "cry of the finite for the infinite" (ibid.) as each things seeks to become more than it currently is. The fact that butchers play this music serves to emphasise the connection between evolution and death in Aiken's philosophy: death and destruction are preludes to creation and those who serve one, inevitably serve the other. Naturally, the death sought by life is not that of permanent extinction, but of additional and new life, which it shall achieve if it undergoes a "fruitful death" (*Memnon*, XLIII, 549). In *Blues for Ruby Matrix*, the protagonist tells Ruby that "Your hand that murdered men or drew the morning / out of the seventh vial . . . destroyed / the indestructible to create the new" (*Ruby Matrix*, VI, 619-20). Here, too, we observe the intimate connection between creation and destruction, as we do in the following lines from *A Letter from Li Po*:

> The locust tree spills sequins of pale gold
> in spiral nebulae, borne on the Invisible
> earthward and deathward, but in change to find
> the cycles of new birth, new life.
>
> *A Letter from Li Po*, V, 907)

Although Aiken does not emphasise it in his work, death also has a role as a preserver; the past is not simply obliterated by the present and future but also sustained by them albeit in a new form. Aiken's awareness of this preservative function of death is indicated in the following lines:

> The pages of our lives are blurred palimpsest:
> New lines are wreathed on old lines half-erased,
> And those on older still, and so forever.
> The old shines through the new, and colors it.
> What's new? What's old? All things have double meanings,—
>
> (*The House of Dust*, IV,3,185)

In other words, the past is not entirely lost in evolutionary change but rather reconstructed in a new form. For this reason, things are ambiguous, they have "double meanings"(ibid.) because they point to the old as well as the new.

The Art of Dying

In view of the ubiquity of death and change, and their inestimable role in the life process, the Self has essentially no choice but to "yield its depths to the silent flow of change" (*The Charnel Rose*, II, 1, 67). Every action, and even inaction and silence involve a "tacit acceptance of death" (*The Crystal*, II, 948) because they, too, are affected by change. Therefore, the least we can do is to whole-heartedly accept death, but—and this will lead us to one of the central themes of Aiken's work—we can do more: dying can be made into an art, into a consciously controlled 'technique' to be used in the growth of the Self and the evolution of consciousness.

To make the inevitability of death into a consciously applied 'technique', the Self's attitude to death and change must become active. "Learn first to wither!" (*Eden*, XI, 635) says the angel to the speaker in *Landscape West of Eden*, a sentiment echoed by the protagonist of *Preludes for Memnon* who says that we should become "like wise men ghosts before our time" (*Memnon*, LXV, 564). In other words, we should learn to die before we are forced to do so by the exigencies of time. Only in this way will we avoid being the unwilling and helpless victim of death and become, as we should, the masters of death. We must, in other words, consciously make death into what it really is: a servant of life because such co-operation with death is natural and serves growth. Unlike the speaker in *Time in the Rock* who calls on Christ and Confucius to explain why "the mind delights before its death to die / embracing nothing as a lover might" (*Time*, LII, 715) the perceptive reader of Aiken's work already knows the answer: without death there can be no growth or change. Later, the speaker informs the lady that flowers and birds, indeed, all things

> . . . already know death, in the mere adventure
> in the mere going forth they know and seek it gladly,
> they embrace it tightly . . .
>
> (*Time in the Rock*, XCIII, 754)

He sums up his speech by saying "Your ode to death is in the lifting / of a single eyelash. Lift it and see" (*Time*, XCIII, 755).

If death is the means by which change and life are maintained in nature, then the fact that Aiken wants us to become its master technicians has an unusual consequence. Consciousness, as seen previously, is freedom. Therefore, the idea that we should consciously obey the natural laws of the world by mastering death, to which we are subject in any case, means that freedom lies in conscious obedience to nature! Consciousness permits us to use nature, to 'intensify' it and to aid ourselves by a willing rather than a forced obedience. In stricter philosophical terms, the contradiction between freedom and 'determinism' has been dissolved and rendered meaningless for those who have mastered "the alphabet of change" (*Memnon*, LVIII, 567) because there is no longer a difference between our will and the necessity of death. Furthermore, at this point it is evident that consciousness does not alter life in the sense of affecting its flow, or laws but does make a profound difference in the quality of our obedience to the 'law of change' which, in turn, will affect the way we live. Our co-operation can be willing and conscious, or enforced, or even unconscious. The evolution of consciousness is, therefore, a 'qualitative' evolution that does not necessarily alter the actual course of events, but does alter the way these events are perceived, and consequently, the role they play in our lives.

Once the Self has consented to dying as the essence of its life process, it must decide how to go about making itself a conscious part of evolution. In Aiken's view, there are only two choices, both of which must, at one time or another, be invoked: murder and suicide. Naturally, these options are not intended literally; rather they refer to the idea of 'killing' as putting an end to an old, out-dated phase of existence either in oneself or in another. Without death, growth is simply impossible. Destruction is a prelude to creation. What makes 'suicide' and 'murder' so attractive to Aiken is that they show willing, conscious co-operation with death and not simply passive acquiesance to it.

Murder

The first major poem in which Aiken concentrates on the use of murder in the evolution of consciousness is *The Pilgrimage of Festus* in which the protagonist is characterised as a conqueror who has "sacked in imagination many cities" (*Festus*, I, 222). The connection between murder and conquest is self-evident. In view of Aiken's association of cities with states of consciousness (See the program notes, *Collected Poems*, 1021), we may interpret the success of Festus to mean that he is well advanced in the evolution of consciousness, although when he is introduced in the poem, his advance has been momentarily halted. The challenge facing him is to re-start his campaigns and in doing so, he will relearn many of the lessons he learned at lower levels of development.

In what way, we may well ask, does 'murder' represent a strategy in the evolution of consciousness? To answer this, we must lay aside our own personal feelings of revulsion at the thought and try to reflect on 'murder' philosophically. All perception is 'murderous' in nature because we 'take in' the 'other' and assimilate him into our own existence just as a murderer takes full possession of another's life, and makes it his own to dispose of as he wills. In effect, as already noted in a previous discussion, perception does the same: the 'other' becomes a part of us and remains at our disposal. (For this reason, the murder motif in Aiken is related to the motif of eating.) In short, he or she is ours in the same way that a murder victim 'belongs' to the murderer. Furthermore, the evolution of consciousness requires us to change, and, as we have already seen, changing ourselves changes the 'other' as well; at this point, the connection between murder and evolution is clear since change inevitably involves death. In seeking change, we die (kill ourselves in fact) but in so doing, we also kill the 'other' as he or she has been for us.

'Murder' is an important strategy in the evolution of consciousness in yet another way: all too often we allow the image of the 'other' to stand in our way as something that overawes, frightens or even paralyses us. It is all too easy to see the 'other' as a superior whose achievements and status we could never attain and, consequently, feel even too discouraged to undertake any efforts for our own development. From this point of view, it is perfectly correct to say that the 'perfect' 'other' is 'killing' us by hindering our development and, therefore, our 'murder' of the 'other' is justified as self-defence. In order to get ourselves moving again, it is necessary to 'murder' the 'other,' to change, to downgrade, depreciate or 'kill' him or her by revealing imperfections that he or she may share with us. Once we see that the 'other' is really like us, 'one' with us and no superior we will be free of the paralysing image of the other in order to resume our own evolution.

Once 'murder' has been understood philosophically, its relevance to the evolution of consciousness is immediately clear. We cannot evolve without 'getting rid of' the 'other.' It also becomes clear why Festus must vivisect a princess, that is, the image of someone seen as superior, and why it must be done so cruelly. This cruelty simply reflects the hatred we naturally feel (consciously or unconsciously) for those whom we perceive as superior and whose superiority impedes out our evolution and is, thereby, slowly 'killing' us. First appearances to the contrary, the cruelty of Aiken's vivisection scenes is not gratuitous and not merely a lascivious gratification of imaginary sadism. In fact, the vivisection has a clear purpose: Festus wants to see if the "passion we call life" (*Festus*, II, 3, 239) is the same in a princess as in anyone else. He wants to see if she is really so superior: "Is this the golden eyebrow we have loved? / Let us discover if its roots are gold" (*Festus*, II, 3, 240). The object of this exercise is revealed by the question he asks about exploring her brain's "enchanted forest" (ibid.): "Shall we explore it to its secret source, / To some black smoking pool?" (ibid.). In other words, he wants to find that in her depths, she is really no different than he is, and that, therefore, she cannot stop his evolutionary development. A similar scene occurs in *Senlin: A Biography* where the archaeologist exhuming the tomb of an Egyptian princess is grievously disappointed to find only her skull and withered brains. In dismay, he cries out "Princess, is this all / Something there was we asked that is not answered" (*Senlin*, I, 6, 202) and getting no answer, he "march[es] away" (ibid.), that is, carries on with his own life once again.

Festus, however discovers that 'murder' alone is not a viable strategy in the evolution of consciousness. There are limits to what conquest of others can achieve and has yet to learn the importance of 'suicide', or conquering himself. He does not relish this prospect which is why he is so dismayed when he asks "the grim sphinx" (*Festus*, II, 1, 234),

> Will you demand yet more of me?
> Desolate and heartless woman
> ....
> Is the anguish of my heart not enough for you?
> Is the sorrow of my flesh not sufficient?
> Must I destroy yet more of you,—
> Even, at last, myself?
>
> (*The Pilgrimage of Festus*, II, 1,235)

The last question indicates clearly that Festus has already glimpsed the hard truth that the next stage of his evolution involves 'suicide'. Rather than engage in self-slaying, Festus engages in self-deification, imagining that he is already the king of conquered cities, that all is done; he claims that "bloodshed bores" (*Festus*, II, 3, 239) him but, of course, his actions show that it does not. Such self-deification is the greatest single danger to those actively seeking to evolve consciousness because it causes the Self to remain stuck at one level of development. Thinking that he has reached the acme of his evolution, Festus, like others in his situation, misleads himself into thinking he is complete and perfect, divine. Therefore, he rejects suicide, that is, changing himself, as unnecessary.

This line of exploration leads to an alternative interpretation of the vivisection scene, one that also reveals important aspects of the evolution of consciousness. From this point of view, rather than commit 'creative suicide,' Festus chooses to murder the princess all for the sake of knowledge; "to explore this passion men call life . . . / . . . to tear aside / Curtain on steamy curtain of red fibre / In hot pursuit of—what but life or death?" (*Festus*, II, 3, 239). He even desires to dissect "the cry of pain itself" (*Festus*, II, 3 240). However, he soon discovers the futility of his actions; they yield no knowledge. This is not unexpected since the essential knowledge of death and life which he seeks can only be gained by the direct, personal experience of dying found in 'suicide'. Consequently, he finds his power "futile" (*Festus*, II, 3 242) and almost seems to understand that he should have turned these powers on himself, that murder was only a dodge motivated by fear. This is because all self-deification involves fear. The Self makes itself in its current condition like the gods, that is, static, permanent and, thereby, invulnerable because it is afraid to change. In this case, at least, murder is both cowardly and unimaginative. Its unimaginative nature is indicated in that what Festus performs is a grotesque parody of science and the method of objective knowledge.

In *Preludes for Memnon* the protagonist raises the subject of murder. He tells his lady to

> Hold out your hand, and stare
> At fingers, palm and fingernails, the wrist
> Supple and strong, and wonder whence it comes,
> And what purpose it is.
>
>   Its aim is murder:
> Murder in fact, in effigy, or both.
> Kill what you hate: hate what you will: love
> Only what you would kill. And if you love,
> Kill slowly, subtly; O invoke the power
> Of Shakespeare, nimblest murderer, for your art.
> He was a 'man of wax'—moulded and melted
> The things he loved and hated, lest he melt
> His own heart's tallow . . .

> Yet, despite his skill,
> Perished, in the fierce furnace of his will.
> Emulate Shakespeare, then, in all but this;
> Prorogue your murder, and protract your bliss.
> (*Preludes for Memnon*, XLIX, 556-557)

He tells the lady that the purpose of her hands is to murder symbolically, "in effigy" (ibid.) or actually, "in fact" (ibid.). The latter is not, of course, what he recommends in what follows, yet—as Aiken knew from the murder-suicide of his parents—it is always a real possibility that cannot be denied. He then tells her to hate whatever she wants and to kill what she hates. In other words, no matter who or what stands in the way of our evolution, we must 'kill' or overcome so that our growth may continue. Moreover, the speaker advises us to kill "only what [we] would love" (ibid.), the reason being that only those things or persons we love possess enough power over us to block our evolutionary development. (These lines also point to the hidden connection between hate and love: both involve intense concern for another person, one positive, the other negative. That is why much that is true of one is true of the other.) We are advised to "kill slowly, subtly" (ibid.) because the kind of 'killing' he means is 'killing' by personal growth and transformation, not gross bodily slaughter. We can 'kill' someone by helping him or her change which eliminates an 'old' personality and creates space for a new one.

The reference to Shakespeare, of course, confirms that the speaker is discussing murder in a metaphorical sense. Shakespeare is the "nimblest murderer" (ibid.) because he was able to take the ordinary people he knew and transform them into the noble or ignoble characters we encounter in his plays; he also transformed, 'murdered' characters from the stories he read. Yet, like Festus, Shakespeare 'murdered' others because he did not want to turn his powers upon himself "lest he melt / His own heart's tallow . . ." (ibid.). Moreover, like Festus, Shakespeare discovers the avoidance of growth and personal transformation is a futile endeavour; "despite his skill" (ibid.) at avoiding conscious evolution, he, nonetheless, transformed himself from an obscure actor into one of the greatest playwrights of all time. For this reason, the speaker wants us to emulate Shakespeare "in all but this" (Ibid.), that is, in everything except his refusal to voluntarily and consciously turn his powers upon himself in the quest for personal evolution. We are advised to "prorogue [our] murder" (ibid.), that is, we are told to take this technique as far as it will go, and then to discontinue it. When its limits are reached, we are required to begin a new phase of personal evolution—conscious creative suicide—and if we take advantage of this opportunity we shall "protract our bliss" (ibid.). In other words, through self-transformation or 'creative suicide' we shall find happiness. This theme shall be explored further in subsequent sections.

As we shall see in a subsequent discussion, 'Creative suicide' will bring us to happiness because it avoids the errors made by Festus and Shakespeare. By following this path, we shall not, unlike Festus, indulge in the paralysis of self-deification; nor shall we make the mistake of trying to learn about life through others instead of by direct personal experience. Furthermore, we will avoid Shakespeare's error of transforming others while trying to side-step the necessity of voluntary, consciously chosen self-transformation. As the protagonist points out, such change will happen in any case as it did with Shakespeare who "perished, in the fierce furnace of his will" (ibid.) and changed despite himself.

Regressive Murder

In *Time in the Rock*, Aiken also warns readers about the pitfalls of 'murder' as a strategy in the evolution of consciousness. Section XXXVIII, which tells a story with obvious affinities to the Biblical tale of Isaac and Abraham, shows that murder must not be used in an effort to return to a previous condition or level of consciousness. The slaying, the "dread exchange" (*Time*, XXXVIII, 703) results in the older man apparently achieving innocence: "the world-stained hand grew fairer and younger" (ibid.), while the child, the "holy innocence became unholy / the younger hand grew stronger and older" (ibid.). Because this murder is regressive, that is, is dedicated to regaining a past state of consciousness, the murderer seeks to "hide shameful eyes" (ibid.). Why should he do this if the transformation were genuine? After all, real innocence has nothing to hide. However, we know this transformation is not genuine because near the outset of this section the old man describes himself as "the guilty one alas who tried to learn / new innocence by giving back my shame" (*Time*, XXXVIII, 702). Instead of accepting and transforming his shame, the speaker tries to give it back, that is, deny it by regression, by returning to an earlier state of consciousness symbolised by the child. This is not the proper way to attain the "new innocence" (ibid.) that he desires, a fact emphasised again later in the poem, where the speaker rhetorically asks a child, "can we undo the done / unknow the known / unshape the shaped?" (*Time*, LIV, 717) He then answers his own question stating that it is not only disastrous to think of doing so, but impossible:

> It is disaster that we should think of this
> our death that we should think of this
> already we have turned back and returned
> who only thought of turning
> but we do not die
> for already returning from the past we have hoisted sail
> already our ship creates new islands
> where again we shall land and fail.
>
> (*Time in the Rock*, LIV, 717)

In the last analysis, this is the same mistake made by Shakespeare who, according to Aiken, also tried to avoid self-acceptance and subsequent self-transformation. Sooner or later we must accept the fact that we are going to transform ourselves, that is, create "new islands" (ibid.) whether we want to or not. Our inclinations to the opposite notwithstanding, the cosmos is progressive; the only real choices are between making progress unconscious and accidental, or conscious and intentional.

Progressive Murder

Despite its dangers, 'murder' for Aiken need not necessarily be regressive; there can also be 'progressive murder' as found in the following example:

> Where without speech the angel walked I went
> and strove as silently as he to move
> seeking in his deep kindness my content
> and in his grace my love
>
> walked without a word and held my arms as wings
> from stone to stone as gently stepped as he
> observed humility with humble things
> as I himself might be:
>
> till he it was at last who stood and spoke—
> Be man, if man you be! Or be ashamed.
> And turned and strode away. And on that stroke,
> (as if now I were named)
>
> in my own heart I looked, and saw the plan
> for murder unadmitted. Then I knew
> how mean the angel is who apes the man,
> or man to man untrue
>
> if he enact the angel. In that hour,
> I did the murder I had planned; and then
> sought out that fellow, my own dream of power,
> and mimicked him again.
>
> (*Time in the Rock*, XLIV, 709)

The murder in this section is progressive because its object is not re-entry into a past condition, but the achievement of a new one. The angel whom he 'murders' is his "own dream of power" (ibid.), that is, his 'better self', his more advanced state of consciousness. Therefore, by 'murdering' or assimilating him, the protagonist demonstrates that he is the angel's equal in power and courage, and is ready to advance in the evolutionary scale. In doing so, he is "to man untrue" (ibid.) insofar as being "untrue" (ibid.) to man requires disloyalty to a static condition achieved in the past; he must betray his current human condition for the sake of evolving into something better. By contrast, the angel would merely be aping man if he tried to be like us because to him we are an inferior form of consciousness. From this we may conclude that in Aiken's philosophy of consciousness, 'murder' is progressive if it is the 'murder' of a superior, that is, one's own next higher potential as symbolised in someone else. If we ask why this 'other' needs to be 'murdered', we must remind ourselves that 'murder' is Aiken's symbol of assimilating the 'other' by perceiving and / or understanding him; it is also a symbol for overcoming the 'other' as an overweening symbol of perfection that paralyses our own evolutionary endeavours.

The positive nature of hating and 'murdering' superiors is also emphasised in the following passage:

> Envy is holy. Let us envy those
> bright angels whose bright wings are stronger far
> than the bare arms we lift toward the star.
> And hate them too; until our hate has grown
> to wings more powerful than angel wings;
> when with a vaulting step, from the bare mountain,
> we'll breathe the empyrean; and so wheel
> gladly to earth again.
>
> (*Time in the Rock*, III, 667)

Here, too, we see the envy and hatred properly directed upwards, towards superiors who embody our own superior possibilities, or overawe us and, thereby, discourage further personal evolution. Such properly directed hatred (and, by implication, 'murder') turns us into superior beings with "wings more powerful than angel wings" (ibid.), that is, into actualizations of our highest possible selves. With these new powers we will "breathe the empyrean" (ibid.) of a higher, more advanced state of being and even return "*gladly* to earth" (ibid.; italics added) because after achieving this higher state of being, this return to our origins is not stained by regression, defeat and shame.

However, even in this higher "empyrean" (ibid.)

> there too burn higher angels, whose wide wings
> outspan us, shadow us hugely, and outsoar us;
> rainbows of such magnificent height
> as hide the stars; and under these we'll cower
> envious and hateful; and we will envy,
> till once again, with contumacious wings,
> ourselves will mount to a new terror
>
> (*Time in the Rock*, III, 667-8)

Here too a superior state of consciousness is always possible and the processes of envy and hatred will begin again and so on *ad infinitum*. In Aiken's philosophy, there is no inherent end to the progressive evolution of consciousness.

However, 'progressive murder' has a severe limitation, namely, that it is, intentionally or not, directed outward against an 'other.' Even if the 'other' is really a dream ego, it is still an 'other' in intention insofar as the Self treats it as a separate and external entity. Focusing on the 'murder' of an 'other' allows the Self to avoid facing the necessity of embarking upon voluntary and consciously undertaken self-transformation and as long as it does this, it has not fully appreciated the need to overcome itself. This Self-overcoming can only be pursued by a policy of 'creative suicide', that is, a conscious acceptance of the importance of intentionally leaving behind old, familiar and comfortable states of consciousness in order to attain a higher level of development.

Creative Suicide by Self-Devouring

Having pointed out the limitations of outward 'murder' as a strategy in the evolution of consciousness, Aiken's protagonists have no choice but to turn their evolutionary efforts on themselves. Obvious as it appears in retrospect, Aiken himself does not seem to have reached this conclusion until *Preludes for Memnon*, since there is little if any sign of the theme of 'creative suicide' in any of his earlier works. The motif of devouring and eating is certainly plentiful throughout *The Charnel Rose*—and, as already noted previously, clearly related to the concept of assimilation in perception and 'murder'—but the theme of self-devouring does not occur until later, when it appears in the rather startling quotation that follows:

> Then is it that the moment falls between us,
> Wide as the spangled nothingness that hangs
> Between Canopus and Aldebaran.
>
> Woman, and I am lost without you, I go
> Downward and inward to such coils of light,
> Such speed, such fierceness, and such glooms of filth,
> Such labyrinths of change, such laboratories
> Of obscene shape incessant in the mind,
> As never woman knew. There, like the worm,
> Coiling amidst the coils, I make my home;
> Eat of the filth, am blessed; *digest my name;*
> *Spawn; am spawned; exult; and am spewed forth;*
> And so come back again, to you, and time—
> (*Preludes for Memnon*, XXXIV, 539; italics added)

In this special, timeless moment of insight that "falls between" (ibid.) the protagonist and his lady, he plunges inward where he finds all of the negative aspects of himself. There "like the worm" (ibid.) among the coils of the intestines, he eats and digests himself, breeds and then, in what is surely one of the most grotesque images in English literature, excretes himself back "to you [the lady] and time" (ibid.). We must, however, set aside the grotesque nature of this image and understand it in terms of Aiken's philosophy. In this passage, the protagonist has accepted himself and especially his negative characteristics; rather than deny them, he has chosen to embrace them and use them as the building material for a new Self. He has made himself the object of his own imaginative processes (digestion), and in doing so, he is not only renewed but also becomes his own ancestor. This self-creation makes him 'divine' insofar as God, too, can have no ancestors but Himself and must be the source of his own being.

Later in *Preludes for Memnon*, the protagonist points out the option of suicide in another, more religious context.

> But if you search in vain the book of words,
> And Christ and all his prophets beat their wings
> Vainly before you—if the word of words
> Set down in gold by fiery seraphim
> Means nothing, less than nothing, to your heart—
> Then take your heart out and devour it mortal,
> Eat out its shreds of bitterness, and taste
> The god you were before dishonour hid you.
> Jesus is not the spokesman of the Lord:
> Confucius neither, nor Nietzsche, no, nor Blake;
> But you yourself.
>
> (*Preludes for Memnon*, XLIX 556-557)

In this passage, self-devouring is offered as a strategy of consolation to those who can no longer find comfort in the religious wisdom of the past. If such is our spiritual situation, the protagonist advises us to take out our disappointed heart and "eat it mortal" (ibid.). In other words, we are to accept ourselves and our spiritual condition and make them the materials from which we will build a new Self. Doing so will reveal to us our own strength, "the god [we] were" (ibid.) before our despair at our seeming lack of faith made us feel worthless and dishonourable; our power and potential for divine self-creation will become clear to us and we will realise that we, not any of the great religious figures of the past are "spokesman of the Lord" (ibid.).

The theme of self-devouring is also found in *Time in the Rock* when the protagonist asks the "comfortless child" (*Time*, LIV, 716), "Did you bring with you a heart to eat / shall we sit now upon these rocks and eat our hearts [?]" (*Time*, LIV, 717). The heart, of course, symbolises the inmost essence of a human being and eating our heart becomes, therefore, a symbol of changing ourselves by assimilating all that we are and using it to create a new identity and reach a higher state of consciousness. Because in self-devouring, the Self is recognised as both subject and object, both the 'doer' and the 'done-to' of our evolutionary endeavours, self-devouring, like all forms of creative suicide, is related to, though not the same as, synoptic consciousness. Both are associated with divinity since both share a conscious unity of perceiver and the perceived object, but they differ in regards to intention or goal. In synoptic consciousness, the goal is to experience and realise the essential unity of *all* being whereas in creative suicide the intention is to evolve a new Self. Logic suggests that 'creative suicide' and self-devouring cannot take place until synoptic consciousness and its realisation of unity has been attained.

Self-Carving

Another form of 'creative suicide' in Aiken's philosophy is self-carving, which must be understood as a symbol of shaping, changing, developing oneself. As soon as we do this, we are inevitably involved in 'killing' ourselves as we pass judgement on and reject old versions of the Self in favour of new ones. Self-carving and the 'creative suicide' are also closely related because each involves a conscious and wilful act of self-reference, of making the Self the object of its own actions which is, of course, an implicit assertion of the Self's existence. That is why 'creative suicide' is not an absolute negation of Self. Indeed, it is quite the opposite. The creative suicide is perfectly safe despite the paradoxical nature of this strategy, since the Self, while being annihilated in one form is actually in no danger of real annihilation.

If we recognise that the essence of the concept of self-carving is consciously undertaken self-shaping, or self-transformation, it becomes clear that the idea of self-carving, though not necessarily the image per se, has a long, though not always obvious, history in Aiken's work. Indeed, we already see this idea as early as Aiken's first major long poem, *The Charnel Rose*, where the protagonist realises that

> To shape this world of leaderless ghostly passions—
> Or else be mobbed by it—there was the question:
> (*The Charnel Rose*, I, 5, 32)

These lines (repeated in *Rose*, II, 8, 38 and III, 1, 48) show the protagonist's clear realisation that he must become the object of his own transformative actions and that unless he is able to shape himself, he will never be the master of his own life. Implicit in the idea of shaping himself, is the necessity of seeing and acting on himself as if he were his own material, that is, as if he were the object of his own actions. Forslin indirectly faces the same issue when as asks, "Am I one, or a million, men?" (*Forslin*, IV, 4, 93). He, too, feels his inner multiplicity and the need to shape it into a singular, coherent identity. The first unambiguous indication of the self-carving theme in Aiken's work occurs when Festus sees himself as "[i]mmense and dark on a pinnacle of the world, / Lying in starlight, hugely carved in stone" (*Festus*, I, 6, 232). Since Festus is, at this moment, in the concentric, or inward turned phase of consciousness, he is the only one who could have carved this statue of himself, and, by implication, his own inner psychic process are the winds and sands that blow against the statue and gradually change it. The first unambiguous reference to self-carving in Aiken's work occurs in *John Deth*. If we remember that Juliana, Millicent and John Deth are all symbols for different aspects of the evolving Self, then the last section of the poem features a clear instance of self-carving. Juliana sits

> Carving the rock beneath her head,
> Carved it vast with hammering thought
> Out of terrific vision wrought.
> It was the world. Nought else there was.
>
> (*John Deth*, V, 441)

The world she creates is, of course, the Self since in Aiken's philosophy, Self and world are so closely correlated that they are, for all intents and purposes, one. Any change in the Self is bound to change the world and vice versa. Thus, Juliana symbolises the Self carving itself, and, beginning thereby, a new phase in the endless self-creative project. The connection between the world and the Self is made perfectly clear in *Preludes for Memnon* where the protagonist realises the necessity of "[r]eshaping the dark earth which is ourselves" (*Memnon*, XXVII, 532). Here, too, we observe the clear connection between the world and the Self and that a change in one is automatically a change in the other.

Aiken's clearest statement about self-carving is found in *Time in the Rock* where the protagonist announces categorically, "Who would carve words must carve himself / first carve himself" (*Time*, XLII, 707) and even repeats this advice later. The most obvious meaning of this statement is that those who would be artists, must transform themselves before they can do the same for the world and others. To use the language of the preceding discussions, suicide must precede murder. There is, however, a deeper level of understanding available if we bear in mind that in Aiken's philosophy, we are all artists continually re-creating ourselves through an endless diversity of forms. Like any sculptor, we carve our Self-images, that is, our identities which are made of the words we use to describe ourselves and to think about ourselves—but these words cannot be changed unless we change first: the way in which these words are shaped depends on the kind of person shaping them.

The theme of self-carving also appears in one of Aiken's last long poems, *The Crystal* in which the soul or Self is described as a "self-shaping crystal" (*The Crystal*, III, 951), and humankind as "the godhead designing the god" (ibid.). The "self-shaping crystal" (ibid.) symbolises the evolving Self, which Aiken identifies with divinity. The reason for this identification is easy to discern: the power of self-creation, in effect, the power of being one's own ancestor, is a self-sufficiency that most theological systems grant only to God. The Self is also the "godhead" (ibid.) insofar as it is the creative power by which the Self shapes itself and the concomitant world. The Self designs "the god" (ibid.), that is, it projects the image of a superior goal which it strives to attain.

The self-carving motif clearly shows that in Aiken's philosophy of consciousness, the Self is to be made into a work of art. This observation might be rephrased to say that the evolution of Self and consciousness is essentially an imaginative artistic process of self-transformation. From this it follows that the artist—or, at least the properly enlightened artist—is the model to whom all others should look for guidance in their lives. Indeed, all should strive to be artists creating their lives as their major work.

Suicide by God

Evolution, of course, requires more than mere change, it requires progressive change leading to new and / or enhanced abilities to continue the evolutionary struggle. For this to happen, something must be pushing or attracting the Self into a particular direction, a function that in Aiken's theory of consciousness is taken over by God. Before continuing to explore this theme, we must remind ourselves that for Aiken, God is certainly not the supreme deity envisaged as a superior personality Who creates and controls the material world. Nor is He the ground of being on Whom everything depends. Rather for Aiken, as for the German philosopher Schleiermacher, God is simply the projected image of our highest possibilities towards which we struggle in our evolutionary endeavours. In that sense, we create God, and He in turn, creates us by 'luring' us upward and onward to a new, more inclusive and more insightful level of evolutionary consciousness. Once we have 'killed' our old, inadequate Self, and become the God we strive to attain we are 'divine'—at least for a moment—until we realise that we inevitably face new possibilities embodied in yet a new God Who lures us on still further. The idea of God thus functions like the proverbial carrot on a stick and we, in Aiken's view, 'kill ourselves' to get it.

One of the clearest expositions of Aiken's ideas on this issue is found in *Time in the Rock*.

> On that wild verge in the late light he stood,
> the last one, who was alone, the naked one,
> wingless unhappy one who had climbed there,
> bruised foot and bruised hand,
> first beholder of the indecipherable land,
>
> the nameless land, the selfless land,
> stood and beheld it from the granite cliff
> the far beneath, the far beyond, the far above,

> water and wind, the cry of the alone
> his own the valley, his own the unthinking stone
>
> and said—as I with labor have shaped this,
> out of a cloud this world of rock and water,
> as I have wrought with thought, or unthinking wrought,
> so that a dream is brought
> in agony and joy to such a realm as this
>
> let now some god take also me and mould me
> some vast and dreadful or divine dream hold me
> and shape me suddenly beyond my purpose
> beyond my power
> to a new wilderness of hour
>
> that I may be to him as this to me,
> out of a cloud made shore and sea,
> instant agony and then the splendid shape
> in which is his escape,
> myself at last only a well-made dream to be—
>
> and as he spoke, his own divine dream took
> sudden kingdom of the wide world, and broke
> the orders into rainbows, the numbers down,
> all things to nothing; and he himself became
> a cloud, in which the lightning dreamed a name.
>
>   (*Time in the Rock*, XXXIX, 703-704)

In this section, the Self stands at the "wild verge" (ibid.) of its own mind, meaning that self-development has come as far as it can go without some radical change in the technique of making progress. The Self, the "wingless unhappy one" (ibid.) who has not yet attained divinity, has reached a "nameless land" (ibid.), a "selfless land" (ibid.). This situation symbolises that the Self has caught sight of a realm in which its present, limited personality is not to be found, and into which it cannot proceed without some radical change. However, this landscape, this "valley" (ibid.) and "unthinking stone" (ibid.) is "his own" (ibid.) insofar as it is his future or destiny that he is shaping consciously or unconsciously for himself so that he can bring his "dream" (ibid.) there. His dream, of course, is his God, his future possibilities or Self that transcends his present limitations. The protagonist wants this God to take the Self and "mould" (ibid.) it, to make it part of something greater than itself; he wants "some vast and dreadful or divine dream [to] hold me / and shape me suddenly beyond my purpose

/beyond my power" (ibid.). In short, the protagonist wishes to be remade as a new being transcending his former Self. Then he, in turn, wants to be for the God what the God has been for him and make a new world—in effect, a new Self since world and self are correlates in Aiken's philosophy—in which it is the protagonist's turn to be the "well-made dream to be" (ibid.). As the protagonist speaks these words, "his own divine dream" (ibid.), that is, the God he strives to be, breaks down the protagonist's world, or Self and "all things to nothing" (ibid.); he becomes "a cloud" (ibid.) which has the potential for becoming a new Self or a "name" (ibid.). In this dialectical process of mutual change, the destruction of the world by the "divine dream" (ibid.) symbolises the creative suicide that the protagonist must undergo in order to make progress in the evolution of consciousness.

The purpose of the 'suicide' is clear: by becoming part of a greater dream, the Self is able to transcend its own former limits, since it will be shaped "beyond [its] purpose" (ibid.) and "beyond [its] power" (ibid.). The Self has willed itself to become the 'material' from which something greater can be created; alternatively, we might say that the Self has willed to become a stepping stone along which its superior future Self may pass. The Self is, therefore, to be the "escape" (ibid.) route for God, the future Self, just as the land which the Self imagined is its escape route out of the limited condition of a former personality. In joining itself to something greater, the Self is dissolved, but at the same time gives birth to a god, and enlarges its own powers!

Our reading of this passage is confirmed later in *Time in the Rock*:

> The great one who collects the sea shells I beheld
> he was like the fog with long fingers he was like a cloud
> stooping over the mean fields and the salt beaches
> brushing the sad trees with kind shoulders
> but again he had no shape, his shape was my imagination
> and I beneath his foot like a dry pebble.
>
> The fog went above me with long hands and a soft face
> above the ships with a cold breath above the sails
> what he loved he took and kept well, beyond death,
> but I noticed that especially he loved little things
> the seaweed, the starflower, the mussel, the bones of a small fish
> on the sand
>
> I separate from him, but not separate, because I loved him
> thinking of him among the marshes, the wet woodpaths, the grasses,
> thinking of him who was myself but who was more loving than myself
> alas that the pebble cannot move or be moved
> nevertheless I imagined him, he was my creation

CONRAD AIKEN'S PHILOSOPHY OF CONSCIOUSNESS

> O god of my imagination, god of my creation,
> whom thus I impersonate, my father, my mother,
>
> whom I create out of the visible world, as you created me
> out of the invisible, let me be the one
> who loves the seaweed, the starflower, the mussel, the
>   bones of small fish on the beach
> and I among them like a smooth pebble.
> <div align="right">(<i>Time in the Rock</i>, LXXVII, 737-8)</div>

In this section we observe that God, who is described as a "fog" or "cloud", has a shape that is strictly the product of the Self's imagination: "I imagined him, he was my creation" (ibid.). Nevertheless, this imaginary God is "the great one" (ibid.) because he is what the protagonist aspires to be, the future form of the Self which the protagonist recognises as superior to him. This God is gathering souvenirs on the beach, among them the "smooth pebble" the protagonist identifies with himself. The symbolic nature of this action is self-evident: the Self is being gathered up by the future Self or God in order to become united with this god in some way. In effect, the Self is committing 'suicide' by allowing itself to be incorporated into something greater than itself which is, of course, its own more advanced future state. Becoming part of something greater requires the end of one's old, more restricted being.

The protagonist describes the God whom he creates as his father and mother because his new identity, his new Self and higher state of consciousness, will grow out of this imagined God. This means in effect, that by imagining this God, the Self has created itself, that is, become its own ancestor, or, in philosophical terms, is *causa sui*, its own cause. Moreover, we note that while the Self creates its god-parents from the materials of the visible world—where else could the imagination get its material?—the parents have created the Self from the "invisible" (ibid.) world, that is, these imaginary or "invisible" (ibid.) god-parents make Self or personality possible by providing an ideal or model to imitate. For this reason the protagonist says, "God of my creation / whom thus I impersonate" (ibid.) Without ideals to model oneself after no person can gain a real, that is, a coherent Self or personality, since these provide the orientation that is required to develop and grow. In this sense, the ideals may well be regarded as parents, albeit self-created ones.

However, for the strategy of 'suicide by God' to work, we must beware of one devastating mistake, namely, self-deification, the notion that the new Self towards which we evolve is only a mirror image of what we currently are. Aiken warns us against this in the following passage:

> But having seen the shape, having heard
> the voice, do not relate the phantom image
> too nearly to yourself, leave the bright margin

> between the text and page, a little room
> for the unimagined. What's here, beneath your hand,
> is less and more than what you see or feel;
> deeper than air or water; deeper than thought
> can dive, whether between stars or between gods;
> deeper that the sound of your heart. Walk right or left
> it is no matter, whether in room or field,
> under a tree, beside a road, the shape
> will be deciphered only to elude you.
> Is the fog only the shape of yourself, idiot?
> And the fog an idiot too? Is the god
> your own vast fog of folly projected?
> Think better of your love than this!
>
> (*Time in the Rock*, LXXVIII, 738)

These lines remind us to recognise a difference, a space, "a bright margin" (ibid.) between ourselves and the "phantom image" (ibid.) of the God whom we strive to emulate. In other words, we must not identify our current Self too closely with the ideal for which we struggle because if we do, we will not only fail to grow into something new and different but will also end by deifying ourselves in our current state. Doing so would, in essence, be falling into a static condition in which we have attained a perfection that does not need changing. In Aiken's Heraclitean universe, however, this is impossible, and any attempt to do so leads to enormous difficulties: we must always remember that the Self is divine not as it is in any particular condition but only insofar as it manifests the ever-changing creative processes in the universe.

Furthermore, these lines reveal one of the most important differences between the process of becoming consciousness and the process of evolving consciousness. In our becoming conscious, narcissism is necessary, since without it, there would be no way to become conscious of oneself; on the other hand, in the process of evolving consciousness, narcissism is fatal because there would be no real progress if the God towards whom we strive is merely an image of our current selves. The worship or deification of a limited specific Self can lead only to vanity and evolutionary paralysis. To prevent the evolutionary struggle from becoming mere self-deification, it is vital that 'god-as-goal' be differentiated from the specific Self we are.

(It may be objected that Aiken's identification of man and God encourages self-deification but this is to misunderstand Aiken's concept of God. As we have seen before, for Aiken, God is not the supreme creator and lord of the universe but rather the next stage in our personal evolution; He is a goal to be overtaken and not a static entity to be worshipped. In addition, we must bear in mind that man and Aiken's God are identical not as specific individual entities, but *as processes* because in Aiken's philosophy, God is also evolving towards a still higher God.)

CONRAD AIKEN'S PHILOSOPHY OF CONSCIOUSNESS

The theme of the margin is one way of helping us remember the vital difference between ourselves and God.

> God
> is such a margin as thus lies between
> the poem and the page's edge, a space
> between the known and the imagined, between
> the reported and the real.
>
> *Time in the Rock*, LXXVIII, 739)

The space between "the known and the imagined" (ibid.) ensures that there is room for the unknown, the surprising, or what Whitehead called "novelty", that is, room for real growth and change so that the new Self will not merely be a repetition of the old. In that way, we will always be transcending ourselves and avoiding stasis at one stage of development. Aiken emphasises this idea in the following stanza.

> Now the poem is perfect,
> now it says everything. You rise and turn
> proud of your handwork, and walk beside
> the margin of the sea . . . .
> . . . .
> you see
> the wilderness; and in the face of this
> your poem becomes the perfect shape it is:
> the sea left out!
> And thus, you know the world.
> Thus, with a phrase exclude the absolute.
>
> (*Time in the Rock*, LXXXII, 742)

Our notions of perfection are obviously ridiculous when we compare our so-called 'perfect' work to what has been left out. The fact that perfection whether in poetry, or in a state of consciousness can only be achieved by leaving out almost everything makes it clear that our evolutionary task is never finished, and that we must always strive to include more. In short, we must never deify ourselves and thereby succumb to stasis. The margin is there to remind us that we always have more growing to do.

Self-Deification versus Real Growth

The dangers of self-deification or personal aggrandisement in the evolution of consciousness pre-occupied Aiken virtually from the outset of his career. He seems to have realised quite early that self-deification, that is, self-satisfaction with and devotion to one's current condition, would stagnate the evolution of consciousness. Nowhere among his early works is this realised more clearly than in *The Pilgrimage of Festus* where Festus "struggles in the net of himself" (*Festus*, IV, 258) and calls three times upon his guardian angel, "the Old Man of the Rain" (ibid.), to point him to "some new god" (ibid.). He obviously wants to keep evolving but to do so, he needs a god who is greater than himself. He cries out "I will not have a God who is myself!" (*Festus*, IV, 1, 258) showing, thereby, that he understands the need to avoid self-deification. Indeed, he wants "the ancient god whose secret is creation" (*Festus*, IV, 1, 259), that is, the God who knows the evolutionary necessity of dying in order to be reborn as something greater. Festus knows that to identify the Self completely with the God of one's creation can only result in a condition of self-satisfied stupor because there is no longer anything to strive for; there is no longer anything greater in which the Self can be dissolved, and through which it can be reborn with intensified powers.

Despite his clarity on this point, it seems that Festus never achieves a clear and complete understanding of how God can be used in the evolution of consciousness. He certainly seems to know that his essential nature is to be nothing—"only in nothingness / we have our being" (*Festus*, II, 2, 207)—that is, he knows we are 'no thing' but rather a process. His bitter speech to the sphinx demonstrates that he knows the need for sacrifice. Nevertheless, his vision of the orchestra of butchers reveals only the murderous aspect of the cosmos and avoids the whole issue of 'creative suicide'. Either Aiken is not aware of it at all or he is not yet ready to use it. In either case, at the end of the poem he sets out as a conqueror, as murderer of others rather than as a conscious self-slayer.

The most obvious example of self-deification in Aiken's writing is found in *Punch: The Immortal Liar*. Punch pursues a false strategy of self-deification or self-aggrandisement by means of lies as he tries to expand, or add to, his current personality rather than strive for true inner transformation. By means of his outrageous lies, he glorifies and celebrates the person he is without ever making any fundamental changes in his character which consequently remains stable throughout the entire poem. He claims that something drives him "on to seek for change" (*Punch*, I, 316) but his claim is not convincing because the nature of his lies never changes. They always involve Punch overcoming others and not himself. Indeed, the root of his problem is that he seeks a God or ideal too much like himself and, thereby, 'deifies' himself at one stage of development by wanting that particular version of Self to endure. He wants an alteration in lovers and in scenery. The Self is to be glorified:

> Well, then, if others lied, he too would lie . . .
> These faces of the smiling men he knew,
> Baker and constable and mayor and hangman,
> What did they mean? Were they, as they pretended,
> Such gloating misers of illegal riches?
>
> (*Punch: The Immortal Liar*, II, 2, 339)

Punch's plan to become a liar like the others shows no recognition of man's changeful nature, nor of the courage and humility required to pursue genuine and perpetual self-renewal.

However, we must recognise that Punch's endeavours are heroic, although he is not a hero. In seeking to transcend his limited, and inherited Self, symbolised by the humpback with which he born, Punch correctly turns to his imaginative powers for aid. He also dramatises himself in dreams and in this way, gains vital self-experience of his own potentials. Finally, he correctly perceives that the secret of growth is self-shaping, or carving, that is, forming the Self as if it were a work of art. By these means he hopes to transform his limited Self into something divine. The fact that he pursues a proper end, and uses means that are, at least partially correct is sensed by almost all who know him. Even Polly, who claims to think of him only as a fool, admits "there was about him / when he was young, as then he was, some presence / some swagger of the flesh . . ." (*Punch*, I, 2, 332). Others agree that there is something extra-ordinary about him: "The man we knew as Punch was no mere mortal" (*Punch*, I, 2, 302) says one speaker, who proceeds explicitly to link him to Satan. The narrator says,

> Yes, there was something noble about the man.
> He was half mad, no doubt, a sneak, a villain:
> And yet, somehow, the world seemed greater for him:
> And smaller when he died.
>
> (*Punch: The Immortal Liar*, I, 1, 301)

Punch's virtues notwithstanding, we must recognise that he lacks the humility to embark on a strategy of real inner change. In the last analysis, like Festus, he cuts a somewhat foolish figure because of his self-deification and is, therefore, unsuitable as a model for development.

The Advance into The Unknown

We might also view self-deification as a rejection of the advance into the unknown. However, in Aiken's view, it is imperative that we develop the courage to leave behind the familiar no matter how attractive it is. As the protagonist of *Preludes for Memnon* says,

> Deluded sentimentalist, will you stay
> In this one room forever, and hold only
> One withered flower in your withered hand?
> This is the ship that goes to No Man's Land.
>
> (*Preludes for Memnon*, XLVI, 553)

By definition, "No Man's Land" (ibid.) must be unknown, since no one could tell us about it; it must also be unreachable, like Aiken's ever-receding God whose image draws us ever onward. In *Time in the Rock* the narrator encourages the lady to join him on his journey "into that nameless space" (*Time*, LXXXIX, 3, 751) and experience "this serene bewilderment, this leaving / of the half-known for the half known" (ibid.). Such movement is the essence of evolution of consciousness. In *The Kid*, Aiken embodies our innate evolutionary drive in the historical character of William Blackstone who always felt an irresistible need to move into new territory. Blackstone chooses to live on the margin of civilisation and moves further west into unknown lands whenever settlements get too close. The Kid's westward journey, of course, symbolises his inner self-exploration:

> What thoughts? what hymns? what prayers? what altar?
> Words out of tempest, and footsteps falter.
> The sea-dark sounded, the dread descent
> to fathom's meaning, a depth unmeant:
> eyes to the self's black sea-heart turned,
> the fouled line followed, the labyrinth learned.
>
> (*The Kid*, VIII, 861)

This journey into the unknown within himself is endless as he finds "mask under mask, face behind face" (ibid.) as he seeks ever new worlds and changes himself in a process in which the soul or Self is "shot down" (*The Kid*, VIII, 862) and then "resurrected again" (ibid.). Probably Aiken's most direct statement on the issue of living for the unknown frontier is the final verse of "Evil Is The Palindrome":

> Live for the frontier of the daily unknown, of terror,
> for the darkness hidden in the thinking mind
> the darkness under the valve of the beating heart:
> live for the borderland, the daybreak, whence we start
> to live and love . . .
>
> (*Evil Is the Palindrome*, 870)

These lines suggest that in Aiken's view, humankind is by nature restless, a threshold being always living on the threshold to somewhere else, a "*homo viator*" (a traveler) as Gabriel Marcel calls us, forever in transit and forever living on "the borderland" (ibid.).

At this point it is possible to define the concept of the 'evolution of consciousness' more precisely than before. The unknown towards which humankind is to advance may be identified with the margin, which, in turn, has been identified with God or the cosmic process. In other words, the evolution of consciousness is an advance towards divinity, a struggle to identify itself with the cosmic process which constitutes all things both mental and physical. However, because the development of consciousness means that consciousness is widened, this evolution may also be defined in the following way: the evolution of consciousness is a struggle for an ever more adequate awareness and experience of the Self as cosmic process. The Self and consciousness are to become increasingly more inclusive. This is the only way in which the self can retain its divine nature. As we have already pointed out, this widening and changing process is the Self's only true identity. In summary, by consciously, wilfully, engaging in the evolution of consciousness, the Self attains its only real identity and becomes increasingly God-like.

Love and the "Eternal Feminine"

Though we have defined the evolution of consciousness, it is still necessary to find a motive for engaging in this often frightening project. What power can draw the Self forward, convince it to engage in a continuous cycle of suicide? According to Aiken, the answer is 'love', more precisely love for the "Eternal Feminine" (Goethe, *Faust*, II) as embodied in a particular women. This term, of course, is a reference to the song of the "*Chorus Mysticus*" which, at the end of Goethe's dramatic epic, sings that in this world in which everything is a transitory symbol of the eternal process, it is the "Eternal Feminine" that draws us onward to ever new heights of development. It bears noting at this point that Aiken probably became familiar with this concept as one of George Santayana's special students who studied the professor's influential literary classic, *Three Philosophical Poets* which focuses on Lucretius' *Rerum Natura*, Dante's *Divine Comedy* and Goethe's *Faust* as the three greatest philosophical poems in western literature. According to Goethe, the "Eternal Feminine" is that cosmic principle which incites love in both genders and which is more adequately represented in women than in men. She is, as "*Chorus Mysticus*" says, the Holy Virgin, the Mother, the Queen and the goddess. Whether or not we agree with Goethe or think these ideas out-moded is obviously irrelevant because what matters here is that Aiken accepted and modified them.

The presence of the "Eternal Feminine" can be traced through most of Aiken's writing although she manifests herself in a wide variety of forms. In *The Charnel Rose*, for example, she is a "woman of fire, a woman of earth / Dreamed of in every birth (*The Charnel Rose*, II 3, 39) whom the young nympholeptic lover pursues. To Senlin she frequently appears as the "harlot-queen of time" (*Senlin*, I, 8, 217) to whom he climbs "the golden-laddered stair" (ibid.) through the "void" (ibid.). She is, of course, the woman to whom all the various men in the 'stair-images' are going. To Punch, the "Eternal Feminine" appears as Sheba, and in *Landscape West of Eden* she makes her appearance as Lillith who helps the speaker gain the consciousness of evil he will require in order to continue his development. Ruby Matrix is also a symbol of the Eternal Feminine. The lovelorn speaker addresses her in lines reminiscent of Goethe's description of the "Eternal Feminine" as Virgin. Mother, Queen and goddess: "matrix, mother, mistress menstrual moon / wafer of scarlet in the virgin void" (*Ruby Matrix* VIII, 621). These are the many roles she plays in his life. In *The Coming Forth by Day of*

Osiris Jones she appears as "The Face" which Jones identifies with "sweet food, sweet softness, incalculable depth / unassailable but protective height" (*Osiris*, 592) and which addresses him as "Divinest of divine and love of loves" (*Osiris*, 606). She also appear in *Preludes for Memnon* and in *Time in the Rock* as the lady listening and occasionally interjecting in the protagonist's extended monologue.

Naturally we must not interpret every woman in Aiken's poetry as an example of the "Eternal Feminine", because the "Eternal Feminine" or a woman acting in that capacity has one outstanding attribute: she is always beyond grasp, ineffable, inaccessible, impossible to define or pin down. Were she to discontinue withdrawing from the suitor's advances, his progress would end and the evolution of consciousness would cease. *The Charnel Rose,* Aiken's earliest major long poem, already makes her inaccessibility plain.

> Now you no longer escape me—I have you!
> This is you, this light in my fingers,
> This air of my palm!
>
> (*The Charnel Rose*, II, 2, 237)

For his part, the protagonist of *Preludes for Memnon* finds her slipping through his attempted descriptions of her. "This is not you? These phrases are not you?" (*Memnon*, VI, 504) he asks desperately, and concludes, after several attempts, with the statement: "And there I find you written down between / Arcturus and a primrose and the sea." (*Memnon*, VI, 505). Even if the protagonist were thinking of a particular woman at the beginning of his speech, this is clearly no longer the case when he decides she is between "Arcturus and a primrose and the sea". Since no individual woman could be found in such a location, she has obviously slipped away from him and assumed mythical attributes. The "Eternal Feminine's" withdrawing or receding function is most clearly expressed in section of *The Coming Forth by Day of Osiris Jones* entitled "The Face" (*Osiris*, 592).

> and then the face withdrawn, farther withdrawn,
> into the sunset red behind the lighthouse,
> beyond the river's mouth, beyond the marsh,
> far out at sea, or stars between two clouds,
> farther and farther, till it lives again
> only in nearer things—and it is now
>
> all stirred and stirring in a wind from somewhere
> far off and half remembered—from that sky,
> that ceiling, that bewildering light, that shawl
> of stars from which the voice of voices came;
> then lost once more, and half seen farther on,
> glimpsed in the lightning, heard in a peal of thunder—

> diffused, and more diffused, till music speaks
> under a hundred lights, with violins,
> ....
>
> and it is life, but it is also death,
> it is the whisper of the always lost
> but always known, it is the first and last
> of heaven's light, the end and the beginning,
> follows the moving memory like a shadow,
> and only rests, at last, when that too comes to rest.
>
> (*The Coming Forth by Day of Osiris Jones*, 593-594)

The face's motherly nature is indicated by its association with "sweet food, sweet softness, incalculable depth" (*Osiris*, 592) and the opening image of a mother bending over a crib. To the child, the mother naturally appears as a tower, like "Igdrasil" (*Osiris*, 593), the Nordic world-tree, on which its life depends. Of interest, too, is that the mysterious face may manifest its powers not only through "nearer things" (ibid.), that is, through ordinary things such as "violins" (ibid.) but also through "life" (ibid.) and "death" (ibid.). Furthermore, the final verse suggests that the Eternal Feminine itself is never actually found, though always glimpsed and pursued. It also makes clear the connection between the "Eternal Feminine" and music is also apparent there indicating her close association with the world process.

Because the "Eternal Feminine" is inaccessible, she also remains completely mysterious. We may see her manifested in her physical form in a particular woman, but the pursuit of that woman will always lead us beyond the ordinary physical reality of an individual person into unknown and mysterious realms. The protagonist in *Preludes for Memnon* affirms as much when he says that in touching the lady's face, he knew "[b]eyond all knowledge of the hands or senses / The truth that only one such face can tell" (*Memnon*, XXV, 529). A similar point is made in *Blues for Ruby Matrix* where the protagonist addresses her as "O undiscoverable and unpursuable one" (*Ruby Matrix*, I, 612) and says that he knew

> ... those curves of hers that curve beyond
> geometry of hand or eye or mind
> into the bloodstream and above again,
> westward under the sea with setting suns.
>
> *Blues for Ruby Matrix*, IV, 616)

In other words, proximity to Ruby takes him beyond this world to somewhere mysterious and unknown. Indeed, the narrator's attempt to discover more about her results, by his own admission, in "geometric frostbite in his brain" (*Ruby Matrix*, IV, 617). *Time in the Rock* also makes a point of emphasising the "Eternal Feminine's" mysterious and frustratingly unpredictable nature when manifested in a particular woman. The lady he describes is mysterious because she is an incomprehensible mixture of earthly and unearthly qualities, much like the "woman of fire, [ ] woman of earth" (*The Charnel Rose*. II, 3, 39) already encountered in Aiken's earliest works. Not only is she a mixture of contradictory qualities but also, at times, she seems to disappear from him.

> She is of quicksilver. You might as well
> pillow your head on a cloud, as on her breast,
> or strive to sleep with a meteor: when you wake
> she is gone, your own hand is under your cheek,
>   (*Time in the Rock*, LXXXIV, 743-4)

The idea of the lady's receding, disappearing and ultimately mysterious nature is also conveyed in the humorous image of comparing her to a tree who "picks up her roots and goes / out of your world, and into secret darkness" (ibid.).

The "Eternal Feminine" and her manifestations in individual women play an important role as partners in the evolution of consciousness. More specifically, as we have already seen, they are important in attaining synoptic consciousness

> Beloved, there is time,
> between this morning's instant and that wall,
> for such infinitudes of delight and grief,
> such patient addings and subtractions, such
> new sentences, each wider than the last,
> new knowledge, new visions, and revisions,
> that we ourselves are like that god; each moment
> is the last wall from which our laughter rings;
> the world summed up; and then a new world found,
> vaster and richer; a new synthesis,
> under the sand grain, and above the star.
> Come, let us read the book, look up each word,
> say dark or bright, be frightened, pick our way
> through the fierce multitude of thoughts and things—
> from god to chaos, and chaos to god again—
> in the unending glossary of the world.
> Was that a bell that struck? A moment gone?
> A voice that spoke, a bird that flew?
> They were the shadows of a speech to come.
>   (*Time in the Rock*, XXVI, 691)

In these lines, the protagonist begins by describing the process of attaining synoptic consciousness: the world—or its correlate, the state of consciousness—widens to include "new sentences, each wider than the last" (ibid.) as well as "new knowledge" (ibid.) and "new visions" (ibid.). This finally ends at "the last wall" (ibid.) when one world or state of consciousness reaches its maximum development at which point we have "the world summed up; and then a new world found / vaster and richer, a new synthesis" (ibid.). The protagonist invites the lady to explore this world, to "read the book" (ibid.) and engage in the dialectic process of going from "chaos" (ibid.) that is, from a fragmented and confused world or state of consciousness, to the ideal of a new "god" (ibid.), that is, to a new, more advanced and inclusive unity and then begin the process again at a higher level with a plunge into new chaos. The lady is a necessary partner in this project because without her love, the protagonist would lack the incentive to continue this arduous process. It is precisely the pursuit of the feminine, which begins with but does not end with biological attraction, that draws him on to seek new and possibly higher levels of consciousness. Thus, man's physical attraction to woman has an ontological dimension.

The woman has this effect on the protagonist because her touch produces both chaos and synoptic consciousness:

> For when she touches me, or when she speaks—!
> Then comes the little fly's wing of a flame:
> Then the brain lights and dizzies: then the body
> Grows light as brightness . . . And the thing is music.
> It is the sound of many instruments—
> Brass melting into silver, silver smoothly
> Dissolving into gold; and then the harsh
> And thickening discord: as if chaos yawned
> Suddenly and magnificently for a forest
> Swallowed its tangle of too gorgeous bloom;
> Devoured its beauty, derisively, and clashed
> A brassy gloating after . . . Is it this?
> Yes; and the chaos then—the chaos, then—
> Ah, what a heaven of sweetness of pure sound
> It yields to God! A clear voice, like a star
> And farther off another,—then another,—
> Each, like an angel, taking his own station;
> As if a thousand tapers, one by one,
> Were lighted all the way from Here to Nothing.
> *(Preludes for Memnon,* XVI, 517-518)

The woman's touch has miraculous effects. At first, her touch launches an episode of synoptic consciousness in which "the body / [g]rows light as brightness" (ibid.) and he experiences the cosmos as a complex and beautiful music in which all elements harmonise. However, this soon changes because every attainment of synoptic consciousness is succeeded by a fall into chaos, a "harsh and thickening discord" (ibid.), from which, of course, a new synoptic consciousness will eventually arise. Aiken expresses this by saying that chaos "yields to god" (ibid.) a "heaven of sweetness of pure sound" (ibid.). As indicated by the image of an endless line of stars and angels "all the way from Here to Nothing" (ibid.), this is an endless process.

Readers should bear in mind that in different passages about this process, Aiken focuses on different aspects of the experience. For example, in *Preludes for Memnon*, XXV, he pays special attention to the horrors of the disintegration into chaos. The terrors notwithstanding, the passage still ends on a positive note with a moment of synoptic consciousness: "And in a sudden glory he was lost" (*Memnon*, XXV, 530). Indeed, we might note at this point that even the negative aspects of the "Eternal Feminine" play a positive role in the evolution of consciousness. In a section that begins with advice to avoid the obvious, the protagonist describes how the "king is murdered in his counting house" (*Memnon*, XLVIII, 555) by his "light of love" (ibid.). Rather than draw self-evident conclusions, the protagonist then says she did this "all that he might know / Why something new" (ibid.) which would happen in a new state of consciousness. Then he offers an alternative scenario in which the king "stops his heart / on the loud note of doubt" (ibid.) because of the powerful presence of his lady "dressed like a playing card" (ibid.). Again, we see how a world or state of consciousness has been crushed by the Queen, a manifestation of the "Eternal Feminine", described as a "mincing queen" (ibid.) and associated with "witchery" (ibid.). She displays her "false nature in a mask" (ibid.). Notwithstanding the negativity of such descriptions, the king is advised to "make love to her; / Praise her false beauty which is richly true" (*Memnon*, XLVIII, 556), and even to "kiss that mask / Whose poison kills the subject it inflames" (ibid.). In effect, the king is being asked to acquiesce in his own death, making it a suicide. Why should he do this? The protagonist's answer is clear: so that the king may "propound / The subtle theory of pure consciousness" (ibid.), that is, experientially know and consequently be able to explain the concept of synoptic consciousness which marks the end of one world and the beginning of another.

An analogous course of events can be observed in *Time in the Rock* when the lover and his lady out on a walk, observe "the flight of bones to the stars, the voyage of dead men" (*Time*, XXXVII, 701). Such a journey is an apt metaphor for the evolution of consciousness since it involves dying to our old identities at various stages of our development. Standing there with her "in the bright instant between two instant deaths" (ibid.), they kiss, and he praises her power, despite some of its seemingly negative effects:

> but what delight that was, O wave who broke
> out of the long dark nothing against my breast,
> you who have lifted me violently so that we rose together,
> what delight that was, in that clear instant.

> even as we shone thus, the first, the last,
> to see the flight of bones, the everlasting,
> the noiseless unhurrying flight
> of the cold and shoreless ones, the ones who no more
> answer to any names, whose voyage in space
> does not remember the earth or stars
> nor is recalled by any spider, by any flower,
> the joyless and deathless dancers—
>
> speak once, speak twice
> before we join them lady, and speak no more.
> (*Time in the Rock*, XXXVII, 702)

As we examine this, a familiar pattern emerges: the lady's touch leads to an extraordinary "clear instant" (ibid.) in which they both shine as "the first, the last" (ibid.) and see "the flight of bones" (ibid.) making its way through space. They can now see the other dead because they are dead too, dead insofar as their moment of synoptic consciousness has put an end to one identity, Self or state of consciousness in preparation for the development of another. To the extent that we are all involved in the evolution of consciousness, we are all part of that "flight of bones" (ibid.), something the protagonist seems to realise when he invites the lady to "join them" (ibid.) in their journey.

It should be clear, of course, that we have in essence returned to the discussion in the previous chapter where synoptic consciousness is followed by chaos, from which the entire process of the 'cycle of consciousness' begins again. In other words, the chaos through which the Self advances in the evolution of consciousness, and the chaos it attains in the 'cycle of consciousness' are the same. However, each episode of chaos is an 'enrichment' of the last, since it contains all previous achievements and experiences as raw material from which to create, and, therefore, represents 'progress'. Thus, we can see that the struggle to attain full consciousness and the evolution of consciousness are closely related, the first being a pre-condition of the second. However, they are not identical. They are different insofar as the struggle to attain full consciousness involves the discovery that Self and the world are so closely correlated as to be virtually one, whereas in the evolution of consciousness, the Self discovers its identity with the world *as a process*.

The Benefits of the Evolution Of Consciousness

Aiken sees a wide variety of benefits accruing to us from the evolution of consciousness. The first of these is that the Self's powers of speech and, thereby, creation including self-creation will be increased.

> What without speech we knew and could not say
> what without thought we did and could not change

> violence of the hand which the mind thought strange
> let us take these things into another world
> another dream
>
> *(Time in the Rock,* XLVI, 710)

In this stanza he invites the lady to join him in taking their shortcomings and deficiencies—what they knew "and could not say" (ibid.)—into a higher stage of development, or, as he puts it, into "another dream" (ibid.). The result of doing so is made clear in the last stanza of this section:

> what without speech we know we then shall say
> and all our violence there will be gay
> what without thought we do will be but play
> and we shall live
>
> *(Time in the Rock,* XLVI, 711)

By making even our shortcomings and deficiencies part of the evolution of consciousness, we will be able to put our deeds and thoughts into language and, thereby, attain mastery over them because we can talk about them in a relatively detached or objective fashion. They will become part of a game we "play" (ibid.), that is, a source of pleasure as we experience the growth of our powers. Even our violence will be "gay" (ibid.) since we know that it is part of a process of growth and not an irrevocable act that serves absolutely no purpose. The end result will be life: "we shall live" (ibid.) says the protagonist for the good reason that this process is life itself.

An increase in our linguistic powers also means an increase in our powers of imaginative expression, that is, an increase in our imaginative powers. This increased imaginative activity—especially in the inward, concentric phase of consciousness—adds to the self-experience needed to become conscious. The process of imaginative self-experience also helps us achieve an increasingly explicit identification of ourselves with the cosmic process. Furthermore, it is clear that the evolution of language involves perpetual self-creation in the evolutionary process since language and Self are so closely related. Finally, since God plays an essential role in the development of consciousness, we can also say that the evolution of consciousness is the evolution of God.

Another result of the evolution of consciousness, that is, the co-evolution of Self, world, God and language, is that the Self becomes increasingly 'healthy' in the sense of being whole by virtue of having accepted itself as it is. That is why he advises the lady that "Out of your sickness let your sickness speak—/ the bile must have his way" (*Time,* V, 668). When she asks why she should "keep / sad record of this filth" (ibid.), that is, put it into language, he replies that "this is health" (ibid.), and adds, "Let poison spit its blister from your tongue" (*Time,* V, 669) because "thus to the knowledge of your wings you come" (ibid.). "The knowledge of [her] wings" (ibid.) is, of course, her awareness of her essential nature as an evolutionary process and what this requires of her. The evolution of consciousness also heals the self's wounds by 'speaking' the wounds, that is, expressing his pain in language. "Where shall we go for healing?" (*Time*, VIII, 671) asks the protagonist and answers his own question later when he praises the "saltatory fool," (*Time*, XXVII, 692) the evolutionary 'clown' who will indulge any silliness or crime if it furthers the evolution of consciousness, by saying that "he [ ] of his bitterness makes the healing word" (ibid.). Because he does so, this "fool" (ibid.) is healed and "goes / by the bright path that only godhead knows" (ibid.), that is, he follows the evolution of consciousness.

Ethics of Evolution

By now it should be apparent to readers that the evolution of consciousness requires a radical revision—if not outright abandonment—of Judeo-Christian ethics. Indeed, it demands what Nietzsche, in *The Genealogy of Morals* calls the "transvaluation of values." This simply means that at certain levels of development in the evolution of consciousness, a value radically alters its character. Evil may become good, or, as Aiken puts it in a passage just quoted, "our violence will . . . be gay" (*Time*, XLVI, 711). The usual horror aroused by violence will be changed into joy because the meaning of the act will be altered by its new context. Another example of the transvaluation of values is found in the following lines:

> Envy is holy. Let us envy those
> bright angels whose bright wings are stronger far
> than the bare arms we lift toward the star.
> And hate them too; until our hate has grown
> to wings more powerful than angels' wings.
>
> (*Time in the Rock*, III, 667)

Envy and hatred, instead of being considered as evils, are, in this case, virtues. The reason is not hard to discern. Without envy of superiors the Self would not be motivated to advance on the evolutionary ladder; lacking hatred it would probably be unable to muster the energy needed to overcome the superior. In effect, two usually undesirable emotions have become essential to growth. This makes them good—under these specific circumstances. Yet another example of transvaluation may be found in *Landscape West of Eden*. The speaker points out that "faithlessness" (*Eden*, XIV, 638) of bees and butterflies ensures the fertility of flowers. Fidelity to one person or thing only, usually considered a virtue, is, from this point of view, a vice. A final example is the laudatory arrogance and self-righteousness of the beans in *The Pilgrimage of Festus*. Without the praise they lavish on themselves they would lack the self-confidence needed to continue growing.

It is often assumed that according to the doctrine of the transvaluation of values all values are relative. In the case of Aiken's philosophy, this is erroneous. The absolute values in Aiken's view are growth and progress in the evolution of consciousness and all other values are judged by the service they render this absolute. Values change their character in relationship to this absolute; whatever encourages growth is good, whatever hinders it is bad. 'Growth' is the key word in Aiken's ethical vocabulary.

The transvaluation of values is not the last word to be said about Aiken's ethics. Some of his other values are quite conventional, though they are applied in unconventional ways. An example of this is the tremendous value of humility in Aiken's ethic, a matter already considered in the discussion regarding the error of self-deification. This, as we have already seen in *The Pilgrimage of Festus* leads only to cruelty to others. A few other comments on this virtue are in order. Humility is obviously required for the Self to consciously, wilfully, obey the law of universal change. In this obedience there is an implicit judgement of the present limited Self as 'worthless' or needing to be overcome. Only the proud will attempt to preserve a small specific Self. Their pride is an attempt to go against nature and, of course, they are doomed to fail. Aiken's heroes, on the other hand, are engaged in the *imitatio natura*, they obey the cosmic command to change, and make it their own will. Consequently, they prosper. Those who willingly change, i.e. master death, become, thereby, the freest of men. They attain this freedom through obedience! They understand, as the speaker in *Landscape West of Eden* says, "wisdom will be change and faith in change" (*Eden*, XV, 640). All other commitments may be abandoned, except this faith in and commitment to change, growth or evolution.

Other, more or less conventional, attitudes in Aiken's ethic are the stress on self-reliance, the importance of forgiveness, and the need for faith. The issue of self-reliance has already been discussed in Chapter Two. The importance of forgiveness is stressed because without forgiveness we cannot advance beyond an old identity into a new one. We remain 'stuck' where we are and once we understand this we will learn "in wisdom, not in kindness to forgive" (*Time*, II, 666). What is meant here is that we should forgive not out of 'good feeling' but out of a desire to facilitate change. Failing to let go of the past simply arrests change and growth.

As indicated by his belief that wisdom is "faith in change" (*Eden*, XV, 640), faith also plays an important part in Aiken's evolutionary ethic. This can also be seen in the fact that the advance towards consciousness is undertaken for "no reason" (*Eden*, II, 624) except for the desire to evolve: this undertaking must be begun for its own sake and with faith in its value. Faith is required, as well, in the effort to evolve consciousness, in the "leaving / of the half-known for the half-known / before there is conceiving or believing / or with self-knowledge the eyes are done" (*Time*, LXXXIX, 3, 751). The Self must simply go forward, although it may feel that it requires more preparation. Faith and courage are, of course, closely related insofar as courage requires a certain amount of faith in oneself and the rightness of one's actions. A further manifestation of faith is the optimistic belief that the world process is essentially benevolent and that all ends well in the evolutionary process. The speaker in *Landscape West of Eden* sees "the world ending in a laughter of pure delight" (*Eden*, XIV, 639), while the 'mad-song' in *Time in the Rock* XIV is a humorous expression of faith our powers of endurance as we experience the pains of evolutionary development. The same faith in endurance is found in *Preludes for Memnon*, where the speaker reveals his faith in immortality by saying that "The heart says heart will never cease." (Memnon, XXVIII, 534).

Finally, Aiken's work shows his belief in the power of love. This has already been noted and requires only a few additional comments. The focal point of this love is the Self, which should learn how to love itself properly. This means that it must submit to change so that its true nature will emerge, and so that it can grow. The love for the Eternal Feminine is part of this proper self-love, since only those prepared to change and advance through chaos will be able to love her. Proper self-love also requires the Self to make itself a 'project', a work of art that reflects, with ever increasing adequacy, the Self's nature as cosmic process. The various forms of creative suicide (suicide by God, and self-carving) are the major ways of achieving this end. The ethic of self-creation naturally requires an acceptance of spiritual violence and pain as part of the process.

Chapter Ten

Summary and Conclusion

Throughout his writing career, Conrad Aiken has been consistently concerned with three main themes, consciousness, identity and the evolution of consciousness in a Heraclitean universe in which everything is subject to constant change. For Aiken, consciousness is primarily self-consciousness for which reason the quest for consciousness and identity are closely related. We cannot be fully conscious without true knowledge of who (and what) we are. However, the Self of self-consciousness is a far more complex entity than we might think not only because it exemplifies the processes at work throughout the entire cosmos but also because it potentially includes the whole universe within itself. Depending on which state of consciousness dominates at a particular moment, the Self can be either the microcosm or the macrocosm.

Aiken's theories are radically subjective insofar as according to them the only way to know other human beings and the universe is by means of a thorough exploration of ourselves. The reasons for these beliefs are to be found in his allegiance to the idealistic philosophies of Immanuel Kant and Arthur Schopenhauer. According to Kant, all knowledge is a product of the human mind, which receives raw data from the external world and processes it until we have an image of what we suppose is the 'external world'. However, we can know nothing about this 'external world' because it is our mental processing that adds such qualities as color, shape, size, cause and effect and even time. Our knowledge—including scientific knowledge—is limited to the 'phenomenal world' of our own making; ultimately, we can know nothing about the 'external' or 'noumenal world' beyond that it exists as a source of data. All knowledge is, therefore, inescapably subjective—though not entirely random since human beings as a whole tend to process the data in similar ways. Because we are locked into a world of our own perceptions and images, science and metaphysical beliefs do no more than tell us about the workings of the human mind. What we call facts and 'things' are simply ideas we have, that is, interpretations of data from the noumenal realm.

From a Kantian point of view, our situation looks solipsistic. However, Schopenhauer found a solution that Aiken adopted. By going into ourselves, by pursuing a course of radical subjectivity, we can, in fact, through ourselves, know all things because all other things and beings are exactly what we are—expressions of the universal Will in perpetual creative process. Subjectivity leads not only to self-discovery but discovery of the cosmos as well. For this reason, almost all of Aiken's long poems are dominated by characters who seek themselves and consciousness by means of concentric consciousness, inward turned reveries and dreams, or by long, highly subjective soliloquies that are really self-explorations conducted aloud.

However, the fact that we live in a constantly changing universe complicates the quest for identity and consciousness. If everything is in perpetual state of flux, it is simply impossible to achieve a stable identity and if that is the case, it is impossible to reach any final conclusion about who or what we are. Without any stability or consistency that endures through time, the whole concept of 'identity' becomes meaningless. This puts us into a seemingly untenable situation: we desire to know who (and what) we are, but we live in a universe that, by virtue of its ever-changing nature, frustrates the discovery of such knowledge. Without this stable identity and the self-knowledge it provides, we can never attain genuine consciousness, and, consequently, can never evolve our consciousness. Thus, we seem doomed to life-long frustration. On one hand we experience an imperative to know our identity while on the other, the cosmos seems designed to prevent us from acquiring such knowledge.

Aiken's adopts a radical solution to the problem. According to him, our most basic identity is as the being who seeks his identity. More than anything else, we *are* the quest for identity, we *are* the very process in which we seem trapped. This leads to the paradoxical conclusion that as long as we pursue identity and consciousness as though we did not have them, we actually do have them, whereas, if we delude ourselves into thinking that we have achieved a stable identity and consciousness, we have, in fact, lost them. The process *is* our identity and this process will never end, not even with the seeming termination of physical death; all that changes is our form insofar as we live on through our effects in the lives of others. The effects we initiate become causes in the lives of others and there is no conceivable end to such a causal chain.

According to Aiken, human beings have basically two modes of consciousness, inward turned concentric consciousness and outward turned eccentric consciousness. The Self oscillates between these two states of consciousness. In the former it is wholly absorbed in its inward life, whereas in the latter it focuses on the outer world in which it lives and on its outer, more public identity. In the eccentric state of consciousness, the Self is more 'objective' and aware of how others might see it. Complicating all this is Aiken's belief that just as the dream egos of concentric consciousness are projections of the dreaming Self, the eccentric Self as seen in the world is no more than an inward-turned projection of the universe itself. In effect, Aiken's universe is like a set of Russian dolls or Chinese boxes with an infinity of levels and worlds. Indeed, we have many identities in many worlds. The quest for a single identity is utterly futile and, for both good and evil, we must accept our multiplicity.

As already indicated, the concentric consciousness predominates in Aiken's major long poems. In this phase of consciousness, the protagonist explores himself by means of dreams and reveries in which a variety of dream egos—projections of himself—act out all kinds of dramas and fantasies. Having such imaginative, vicarious experiences is essential because no single human life can live out all of his or her potential lives. Yet, these imaginative experiences too are an essential part of our identities and must be included if we really wish complete knowledge of who we are. Thus, imagination plays a vital role in discovering our identities and attaining consciousness. We cannot rely on memory in the quest for identity and consciousness because there is no reliable way to distinguish a remembered fact from an imagined episode since both are simply ideas we have. Other challenges the Self experiences in its pursuit of identity and consciousness are alienation from various unacknowledged and unwanted dream egos, the unreliability of the mind itself as a source of knowledge, solipsism, narcissism and the discovery that a perpetually changing Self is ultimately a 'zero', a nothing or 'no thing'. Furthermore, the Self discovers that it must make a world for itself because it cannot simply inherit a ready-made world of concepts and beliefs without betraying its innermost nature.

In Aiken's thought, consciousness has a history, that is, stages of development through which it must pass in its evolution. The first stage in the development of consciousness is *divisive consciousness* in which the Self distinguishes between itself and the surrounding world and believes that these distinctions are real. There is a division between me and not-me, between the perceiving subject and the perceived object. This stage of consciousness originates in the experience of terror from which the Self must not recoil, but rather, learn to use. At this point language emerges as a correlate of consciousness as the Self learns to say 'I' to distinguish itself from its environment. Language is one of the tools by means of which the Self shapes itself and the world. Indeed, as Aiken's work later makes clear, there is no essential difference between language and the world, all of nature being a language as well.

The second stage in the development of consciousness is *narcissistic consciousness* symbolised most dramatically by the man cutting faces for himself in the mirror or, in a mental equivalent, imagining how he must appear to others. In this higher stage of evolution, the subject / object dichotomy remains but it is no longer a distinction between me and not-me. In other words, the Self is actor as well as the audience and critic. However ludicrous the Self may appear in this stage, it has, nonetheless, taken a step forward because, even thought the subject / object division still exists, we no longer have a division between me and not-me. In this stage, the Self also discovers its god-like nature.

The third stage in the development of consciousness is *synoptic consciousness* in which the Self experientially overcomes the subject / object division between itself and the world and recognises that it and others are, ultimately, one. By clever word play on the word "sum"—which means 'I am' in Latin—Aiken conveys the idea that the Self realises its identity as the consciousness, the sense of 'I am', of the entire universe. It becomes aware that although it is ontologically distinct from the world, it is not necessarily isolated from the since love, a key factor in this drama, dissolves the Self's usual boundaries and opening the Self to the rest of creation. In synoptic consciousness, the Self comes into full possession of its highest possible development at that point in its history by realising its oneness with the processes that make up the cosmos. However, we must understand that the three stages of consciousness may occur at higher or lower levels, that, for example, the moment of synoptic consciousness for a child is less inclusive than such a moment for an adult who has dedicated his or her life to the evolution of consciousness.

Even moments of synoptic consciousness are temporary because the Self's development is never complete. As soon as one instant of supreme consciousness has been reached, the quest for a still more advanced, more inclusive form begins. This forward motion towards ever more sophisticated forms of consciousness is the evolution of consciousness. To evolve, the Self must realise that all progress depends on accepting the fact that old, former identities must not only be abandoned, but also actively killed in what we have called 'creative suicide.' We must learn how to practice 'the art of dying'. Murder—metaphorically, of course—also plays a role. If the self wants to evolve it must be able to overcome (mentally speaking) all others who, for whatever reasons, block its development. Aiken has several images of 'creative suicide', the most interesting being what we have called 'suicide by God'. For Aiken, God is the ideal Self which we struggle to achieve; once we have reached it and 'become' god ourselves, we must immediately start again struggling to reach a greater God yet. In other words, for Aiken, the idea of God is a lure that entices us onward in the evolution of consciousness. The other lure is love, symbolised by Aiken as the "Eternal Feminine" who calls us to an endless pursuit.

How, then, are eccentric and concentric consciousness, the three stages of consciousness and the evolution of consciousness related? The answer is relatively simple. The Self begins in the eccentric, outward state of consciousness which is also divisive consciousness since it makes an absolute distinction between itself and the world. In the quest for identity, this state of consciousness is inadequate. The Self thus turns inward to concentric consciousness, which is first correlated with narcissistic consciousness and then with synoptic consciousness. We have, therefore, the following progression: *eccentric / divisive consciousness* leads to *concentric / narcissistic consciousness* and then to *concentric / synoptic consciousness*. Once concentric / synoptic consciousness has been reached, the whole process begins again at a higher, that is, more consciously inclusive level. This, broadly speaking, is Aiken's philosophy of consciousness.

This study has richly confirmed the truth of Stephen Tabachnick's claim that Conrad Aiken's work possesses "a characteristic that much contemporary poetry and fiction lacks: a real coherence, a staggering thematic and symbolic unity, a philosophical argument, that stretches forty years" (Tabachnick, "*The Great Circle Voyage of Conrad Aiken's Mr. Arcularis*"). On the basis of these criteria—coherence and "thematic and symbolic unity" (ibid.)—there is little doubt that Aiken's work rivals the achievement of Ezra Pound's *Cantos* which also developed a philosophic argument through nearly a thousand pages composed over several decades.

It is precisely on this point that a possible reason for Aiken's neglect becomes clear. Whereas Pound deals with history, politics, culture and financial issues whose relevance is readily apparent, Aiken deals with epistemology and metaphysics, subjects whose relevance to daily life and public concerns is not so easily seen. Furthermore, the knowledge needed to at least begin making sense of Pound is more wide-spread among readers of serious literature than detailed considerations of abstract epistemological and metaphysical questions and how we might experience them in our daily lives. Pound requires new readers with a certain general knowledge about the Odyssey and Greek mythology, the Renaissance and American history, and, at its most far-flung, Chinese history and Confucius. On the other hand, Aiken demands readers and critics come intellectually equipped with a good understanding of the theories of Heraclitus, Kant, Hegel, Schopenhauer, Nietzsche and Freud to mention only the most prominent.

Given the difficulty of approaching Aiken's work, the question becomes, Is it worth the effort? Does it provide rewards that justify the struggles involved? Perhaps he has been neglected because he demands too much for too little. In my view, there are at least three reasons why the exertion required to comprehend Aiken's work are worthwhile. The first—and this alone should make Aiken of great interest to all philosophers and philosophically inclined readers—is that Aiken's work is a detailed exploration of how various philosophical positions are actually *experienced* in ordinary life. What are the every-day ramifications of Heraclitus' views about flux for our sense of identity, for our moral standards, for our yearning for stability, for our love affairs and even the simplicities of having breakfast? What is the *personal meaning* of saying that we create our phenomenal world from data from an ever unknowable noumenal realm? What happens to words like 'truthfulness', 'loyalty', 'love', 'I', 'you', 'good', 'evil' and 'God' if Kant is correct? Aiken thought he was and explored the ramifications of this view through the course of everyday life. For this reason alone, Aiken's poetic works are invaluable to everyone interested in philosophy as a relevant activity not just for a few academics but for all thoughtful human beings. In short, Aiken's work is an original and outstanding contribution to the 'Great Dialogue' among the philosophers.

The second reason why the effort to understand Aiken is worthwhile is the aesthetic values of his poetry. Indeed, this is what has kept his work alive even among those who do not fully understand the intellectual sophistication underlying the beauty. This study has not paid too much attention to this aspect of Aiken's poetry because there was enough challenge in explicating his 'system', yet, if nothing else, Aiken has written some of the most exquisite love poetry in modern times. It is hard to imagine love poetry more touching than "Music I heard with you was more than music / And bread I broke with you was more than bread" (*Collected Poems*, 18) or

> Beloved, let us once more praise the rain.
> Let us discover some new alphabet,
> For this, the often-praised and be ourselves
> The rain, the chickweed, and the burdock leaf,
> The green-white privet flower, the spotted stone,
> And all that welcomes rain; the sparrow, too,—

CONRAD AIKEN'S PHILOSOPHY OF CONSCIOUSNESS

> Who watches with a hard eye, from seclusion,
> Beneath the elm-tree bough, till rain is done.
> *(Preludes for Memnon*, VII, 505)

However, this is not to confine his finest work to the sub-genre of love poetry. He demonstrates an amazing capacity to use startling and beautiful images to express philosophical ideas, as in "Precious chameleon of the human soul" (*Time*, XC, 752). Those familiar with his philosophy of change will find this image even more effective than those who appreciate it simply for its beauty. In addition to the beauties of imagery, Aiken's work exemplifies an unusual gift for crafting memorable lines:

> The language and the landscape are the same,
> And we ourselves are language and the land
> (*A Letter from Li Po*, XI, 913)

or, from his earlier work,

> We hold them all, they walk our dreams forever,
> Nothing perishes in that haunted air,
> Nothing but is immortal there,
> And we ourselves, dying with all our worlds,
> Will only pass the ghostly portal
> Into another's dream; and so live on
> Through dream to dream, immortal.
> (*The Jig of Forslin*, V, 8, 115)

A consideration of Aiken's use of images and symbols as well as the craftsmanship of his lines, is, of course, another study. At this point we shall have to confine ourselves to drawing attention to the high aesthetic values of Aiken's work and trust that interested readers will explore them for themselves.

In addition to the aesthetics and philosophical sophistication, Aiken's poetry has at least one other attribute that make them appealing though to a somewhat narrower audience. This is his wide-ranging humour, from the obscene and lewd, the lurid, the morbid and black, the metaphysical and literary to the mad. His clever use of parody and puns is highly reminiscent of Joyce's *Ulysses*, a book that had a tremendous impact on him. Aiken's skill with in these areas mark him as one of the twentieth century's great literary humorists.

These three great attributes will, I believe, ensure that Aiken's work survives until the development of a larger audience willing to take the time and effort needed to enjoy the virtues of his poetry. When that might be is anyone's guess, though I hope that the present work and its companions will make a viable contribution to that end.

SELECT BIBLIOGRAPHY

Aiken, Conrad. *Collected Criticism.* New York: Oxford University Press, 1968.
Collected Poems. Second Edition. New York: Oxford University Press, 1970.
Ushant. New York: Oxford University Press, 1971.
Copleston, Frederick. *A History of Philosophy,* Vol. 7, Part II. New York: Image Books, 1965.
Cowley, Malcolm. "*Conrad Aiken: From Savannah to Emerson*" in *The Southern Review.* XI, No/ 2. Spring, 1975.
Emerson, Ralph Waldo. *The Works of Ralph Waldo Emerson.* New York: The Caxton Society, n.d.
Hart, James. D. ed. *The Oxford Companion to American Literature.* Fourth Edition. New York: Oxford University press, 1980.
Hegel, G.W.F. *The Phenomenology of Mind.* Trans. by J.B. Baillie. New York: Harper Torchbooks, 1967.
Hoffmann, Frederick. *Conrad Aiken.* New York: Twayne Publishers, 1962.
Kant. Immanuel. *Critique of Pure Reason.* Trans. by Norman. K. Smith. New York: Macmillan and Co. 1964.
Critique of Pure Judgement. Trans. J.H. Bernard. New York: Hafner Publishing Co., 1968.
Locke, John. *An Essay Concerning Human Understanding.* http://arts.cuhk.edu.hk/Philosophy/Locke/echu/
Marten, Harry. *The Art of Knowing.* Columbia: University of Missouri Press, 1988.
Martin, Jay. *Conrad Aiken: A Life of His Art.* Princeton: Princeton University Press, 1962.
Peterson, Houston. *The Melody of Chaos.* New York: Longmans, Green and Co., 1931.
Schopenhauer, Arthur. *The World as Will and Representation.* Trans. by E.F. Payne. New York: Dover Publications, 1968.
Spivey, Ted R. and Waterman, Arthur ed. *Conrad Aiken: A Priest of Consciousness.* New York: AMS press, 1990.
Tabachnick, Stephen, E. "*The Great Circle Voyage of Conrad Aiken's "Mr. Arcularis",* American Literature. Vol. XLV, No. 4. January, 1974.
Waterman, Arthur. "*The Evolution of Consciousness: Conrad Aiken's Novels and Ushant*", *Critique: Studies in Modern Fiction.* XV, No. 2. 1973.
Wilbur, Richard. *Conrad Aiken: An Interview ".* The Paris Review,Vol.11, No.42. Winter-Spring, 1968.